DICKOTOMY

TM

DICKOTOMY [dik-kot-uh-mee]
1. a division or contrast in a man that determines if he is either a Rick or a Dick at any given time.

A DICKLESS MEMOIR
by Petra Weiser

DICKOTOMY: A DICKLESS MEMOIR

by Petra Weiser

Published by Petra Weiser LLC

www.petraweiser.com

© 2020 Petra Weiser LLC

Cover by Petra Weiser.

Paperback ISBN: 978-1-7344038-1-7

First Edition

Petra Weiser LLC has applied for trademark protection for:
The DICKLESS logo and word
The CROSSED-LEG WOMAN logo

LEGAL DISCLAIMER

This is a memoir. I have tried to recreate events, locales, and conversations from my memories of them. I recognize that other people's memories of the events described in this book may be different than my own. All characters in this book are fine, decent, and hard-working people.

Moreover, I did not intend to be offensive toward anyone who reads this book. If anything written can be perceived as hurtful to any community or person, I apologize, but that was not the purpose of my writing it.

I regret any unintentional harm resulting from the publishing and marketing of DICKOTOMY: A Dickless Memoir.

Fuer meine Schwester!

INTENTION

The purpose of this book is to increase awareness: AWARENESS of the world around us, our circumstances, who we are dealing with, and how we react and why. This memoir is my perception of my life with all its feelings with the hope that you, the reader, will see how I became more aware with age and experience to make better decisions.

You may come across a character or two who seem familiar as we journey down the road to my awareness. Keep in mind that meeting either a Rick or a Dick does not draw any conclusions on who is good or evil. Understand that YOU are responsible for how you feel, no matter what anyone does to you or WHO this person is. It is your perception at times that will lead to judgment, so it is important to always step back to consider what or who you are facing.

Every one of us has value. We each have goals, fears, past experiences, insecurities, and ambitions that play into everything we do. Acknowledge your feelings. Be honest. Don't run away from them. Realize the value that others bring to you.

Awareness knows no gender. I would love for men to read this book in order to gain a better understanding of some of the struggles women go through.

But most importantly, I would love for women to start being more aware so that they can step up and reject the status quo.

Dickless is making a positive out of a negative.
Being a woman is great. Just as great as being a man.

TABLE OF CONTENTS

DADDY DEAREST

I t seems unfair and difficult to have to start out with the most complex man-woman relationship there is. Doesn't every girl want to live up to her father's expectations and strive to gain approval by that authoritarian figure? Maybe, in one way, to apologize for having been born a female when it seems so ingrained in human nature to be prouder if born a male to continue the name and lineage.

Describing my father will make him sound like a tyrant. Growing up that's what it felt like. I know and understand him better now. I can see who he wanted to be, but despite himself, failed at times, because of his inner *Schweinehund[1]*. Those were the exact words my dad used in his only letter to me which I read on the airplane during my flight from Germany to the United States to start my new life with an alcoholic husband.

There are many stages in everyone's life, and I believe that we progress to these stages based on experiences, learnings, and willingness to change. It has been encouraging to see the positive progression in my dad, and it shows that you can teach an old Schweinehund new tricks. But, for the sake of not dicking around any longer, let me begin with my dad as I remember him from my childhood:

Dad worked rotating shifts as a printer for a major German newspaper and the most frequented term in our house was, "Be quiet, Dad is sleeping". It was amazing to me that someone so non-present could make us obey his rules. It must have been difficult for my mom trying to control two girls into quietness for most of their childhood, while those girls also shared their room under the roof above their parents' quarters. There could only be hushed conversations and tippy-toed steps; no running, jumping, laughing, or horse playing.

Dad was, and still is, a man of few words. At the dinner table, he forbade any conversation or verbal sounds other than his own, asking for a second helping (which my mom would promptly serve). Mealtime was for eating, not for chatting. Every task was one of purpose and efficiency not to be wasted with pointless inadequacies. There was no shuffling of food items, no noisy chewing, no slurping, and by God, that plate better be empty. If there was something you did not like, you would not dare to get up until that something was chewed up and on its way down into your stomach.

I was about eleven, my sister thirteen, when one particular carrot salad almost broke my spirit:

Seated around the kitchen table, we were eating lunch together as a family. This was customary on days when Dad's shift schedule allowed for it.

"What's the matter?" Dad asked, pointing to the bowl next to my lunch plate. The bowl was filled with an extremely thinly grated, creamy carrot salad.

"She does not like my carrot salad," Mom responded on my behalf.

Indeed, I despised this orange butchered mess in front of me. Strangely enough, I loved carrots, but there was just something about the mushy consistency of this salad that was appalling to me. I had eaten everything on my plate, but I could not bring myself to face what was still left in my salad bowl.

Dad got up, giving Mom the signal to clear off his dishes. She started stacking her plate on his, grabbed their empty salad bowls, and then also took my empty plate. Then, she got up from the table and carried the load over to the kitchen sink. My sister followed suit with her dishes.

"You know you can't get up until you've finished your carrot salad!" Dad made sure I understood the rule.

Typically, Mom would not carry my dishes over to the sink, which had to be washed and dried by hand by my sister and me.

Today was different, because I was not allowed to get up from my seat at the table; and that included carrying my dishes over to the other side of the room. Even that disruption to the clean-up-after-yourself-rule ended in punishment that day.

Everyone was done. My parents had exited the kitchen, leaving me and my sister behind. She started to run hot water into the sink, added dish soap, and proceeded to clean the empty plates. I would have to dry the dishes once I was done with my salad. She avoided looking at me, which wasn't hard because her back was to me focused on her chore. I could hear intentional clatter in the sudsy water as she kept ignoring me.

The kitchen door was closed. The message was clear. I had no way out of this other than by finishing the task at hand.

There I sat at the table, staring at a single bowl of cruelty placed in front of me.

In our household, food was divided up proportionally by importance. Dad got the most and was served first. My sister and I were next, getting equal servings of everything. Mom always put herself last. It wasn't her fault that my serving looked so huge. I sighed. There was no way around it. I had to do it. Throwing the salad into the trash was not an available option. They would find out. The trash bin was so small, it would have had a hard time hiding a piece of gum.

I lowered my fork into the bowl and picked up the largest heaping of carrot salad that it could hold without collapse. The salad was dense, and it kept together as I moved the fork closer to my mouth. Once inside, I had to face the toughest challenge. Chewing and swallowing. As soon as I started to chew, I realized my mistake. It was just too much at once. It felt as if the salad was expanding exponentially. The large clump of tiny carrot pieces sucked the saliva right out of my mouth. I wondered where the cream had disappeared to which surely had been mixed in earlier. My throat started constricting, and I fought to suppress the intensifying panic which had embedded itself into the carrot ball lodged in my mouth. I gasped for air, but since the salad was grated so finely, carrot particles were sucked right into my airways. I couldn't hold it in any longer; the desire to survive became more important than the need to finish the mission. Bending my head forward, I opened my mouth, and the ugly orange mess dispensed back into the bowl.

I sat at the table in disbelief. This was daunting. Minutes passed. They seemed like hours. My sister, done with the dishes, threw one sad look my way before she left the room, softly closing the door behind her. The clock was mocking me with every tick.

I reloaded my fork. This time with less volume. Once in my mouth, I held my nose. Maybe I could fake out my brain if it did not smell like carrot salad? I chewed once, twice, and then swallowed. Realizing that, due to the baby food consistency, there actually was no need to chew, I turned into a carrot-salad-swallowing-machine. Until it was gone without regurgitation.

Rules ruled our lives:

No talking during meals as explained above, alongside no slurping, smacking, or burping.

No slouching at or elbows on the table.

No napkins. Utensils must be used properly. Only babies needed bibs.

No sleepovers; neither at our house nor our friends'. We all had perfectly good beds at home, and they weren't meant to be shared with others.

No candy or begging for candy at the grocery check-out line. There would be no embarrassment or scene in public.

No cereal for breakfast. The options were: German bread with jam or Nutella for something sweet or German bread with cold cuts and/or cheese for something savory. Cereal was relatively new to the German breakfast table in the early eighties and considered contraband in our household. Cereal was an American thing and my dad despised anything American, which I wasn't aware of until the age of seventeen. His dislike came from growing up in an American-occupied Germany after World War II. He had observed American troops wasting food very publicly (to demean the German losers). They were unwilling to share, simply driving the point home that Americans were better because they had more. Americans had established a pattern of arrogance and ignorance with my dad.

Breakfast to this date has proven difficult for me, because I could and still can not eat first thing in the morning. My body and mind need at least two hours to be open for food intake. By the time I sat down at the kitchen table each morning as a child, only about thirty minutes had elapsed from when I had first gotten up. I dreaded breakfast. Every morning, I forced half a slice of bread down my throat. Then, I left the house to arrive hungry at Kindergarten or school.

One year, on Saint Nicholas Day[2], St. Nick paid us a visit. I must have been around five or six. In past years, my basket with chocolaty St. Nicks would wait for me outside my room on the morning of December 6. I had heard of other children being visited in person by St. Nick, but he had never shown up at my house when I had been awake. Good kids got chocolate and praise, bad kids got a whipping, coals, and reprimand. So, that year, instead of going to bed in anticipation of chocolates the next morning, my sister and I were informed that old St. Nick wanted to see us in person. He would visit that evening.

He arrived in his red outfit with a wooden whip attached to his belt and a sack on his back. My sister and I expected to be whipped before being handed our coals. We assumed there had to be a reason for his physical presence; we had to have done something bad not deserving of automatic chocolates left by our bedroom door as in previous years.

St. Nick, now seated on a chair in our living room, looked straight at us. We stood at attention facing him. His white beard did not distract from his piercing eyes – they went right into our souls. We braced for the unknown.

In a big voice and with a serious look, he asked, "Petra, have you been naughty or nice?"

"Nice," I said innocently while trying to avoid direct eye contact.

"Have you now," he bellowed, "what about that candy bar you snuck into Kindergarten."

It was a statement, not a question. I had been caught. I blushed with guilt and shame.

"Have your parents told you that breakfast is the most important meal of the day?" he asked.

"Yes," I squeaked.

"So why don't you eat more for breakfast? That half a sliver of bread isn't enough if you want to grow tall and strong," he said. "Obviously it's not enough breakfast, or you would not be sneaking candy. Candy of all things! Candy has no nutritional value. It's all sugar. You should not keep any secrets from your parents. You know *I* will always know if you have been naughty or nice."

I nodded my head. *It was true, how else could he have known about my secret?* It had been so long ago, I had forgotten all about the Snickers bar.

It was my grandmother who had given me the Snickers. She knew I loved chocolate, and she was aware that sweets were hard to come by in our household. She had winked at me as she had handed me the candy bar. "Our little secret," she had said. I had stuffed the bar into the waistband of my pants and hidden it in my jacket's side pocket when I had gone back upstairs for dinner. The next morning, wearing my jacket to Kindergarten, I had taken the Snickers out of the side pocket. Everyone had to hang up their jackets in the lobby at Kindergarten, and I had known that I would not have access to the candy bar until it was time to head back home, unless I could come up with another hiding place. So, on the short walk there, I had forced myself to eat almost half of it to be able to stuff the rest in one of my small front pant pockets for later consumption. When my stomach had noisily announced its emptiness shortly after my arrival, I had pried the remaining Snickers from its secret spot. It had gotten soft and squishy; it had been a messy delight.

Unlike this very moment.

St. Nick did see and remember everything. I looked down at the floor; I was too ashamed to face my parents, who sat beside St. Nick.

My sister was next. I didn't pay any attention to her as I kept reliving the memory of my own—now public—bad deed. I wished St. Nick would leave soon. When I dared to look up again, I searched for my sister's eyes, hoping to find comfort there. She was frowning, her face a deep crimson, her eyebrows crumpled; her face showing pure agony. I instantly felt better knowing that she had not fared better than me.

Before St. Nick headed back out to torture the other children, he turned to us one more time and said, "Listen to your parents, you hear?" And with that, he handed us our chocolates.

I have to say they didn't taste as good that year.

Fortunately, St. Nick never came back for another visit.

Every time I eat a Snickers bar, I think about that moment. It has never kept me from enjoying it; quite the opposite. Snickers to this day reminds me of my first experience of public shaming and how it has helped me to define my defiance in the long run.

Now, back to the rules:

No bathroom use at night. This caused quite a dilemma for me and my sister as our bedtimes were relatively early. This made for some long nights.

Along with the no-bathroom rule, the no-noise rule became the most challenging for bedtime. It was a set-up for failure.

One late evening, when I was around five years old and my sister seven, we were in our bunkbeds. Our small room under the roof was immediately above the living room where our parents watched TV before going to bed. Depending on his shift schedule, Dad could be watching TV all night.

Unable to fall asleep, we started our typical quiet nighttime routine, which wasn't that entertaining, but more fun than counting sheep in our heads: from the lower bunk, using my left hand, I flung my crocheted Indian doll up to my sister's level. Once caught, my sister would drop the doll back down toward me on my right, down and along the wall. The doll was perfect. About six inches in height and filled with less than an inch of soft material, she made no noise. Therefore, we did not have to worry about the doll landing off target, or when it slid back down alongside the wall. Too much noise, and one of our parents would come upstairs, and there would be consequences, since it violated the no-fun, no-noise rule. Consequences could mean a firm warning, getting grounded, having toys or privileges taken away, all the way up to a wooden spoon to the behind.

"I have to go," I said quietly as I caught the doll with my right hand on one of its return trips down.

"You can't," my sister whispered.

"But I can't hold it all night!"

I flung the doll back up on my left. The slight movement only confirmed my predicament.

"I gotta go SOON."

There was a sigh above.

"Me too."

"We could go ask?"

With past toilet emergencies, one of us would venture downstairs to ask our parents for permission to use the bathroom. Granted, we would always receive the sought permission, but neither of us wanted the embarrassing task of having to make our way into the lion's den. No noise was supposed to come from our room, so whoever was chosen to go ask, had to do it very quietly and had to reach the lion's den before the lions went on the move to confront the prey.

"No!"

I sat up to peek at my sister's face hanging over the left side of her bunk, her hands holding the railing.

"What are we going to do?" I asked, looking to her for leadership as my older sibling. "I really have to go." I could feel the pressure on my bladder and felt panic at the thought of not being able to relieve myself soon.

She said, "Whatever we do, we have to keep it in this room. We can't make any noise."

We scanned our room for options. To our left, we faced a slanted ceiling with a window. At the bottom of the slanted ceiling was just enough straight-walled space for some cabinets with drawers. To our right and behind, walls. We looked toward the front of the room where our two desks framed the door on each side - occupying the remaining floor space right next to the walls.

"What do you think about that spot?" My sister looked toward the front of the room and pointed to an empty floor area between the bunkbed and the door.

"It's perfect," she whispered, "the carpet will soak it up. You first."

I left the safety of my bunk, tiptoed to the chosen spot, pulled down my pajamas, squatted, and started to pee. Carefully, of course, as not to alert my parents below with any sound. The floors could be squeaky with any activity. The carpet was dark brown and had a pattern. It quietly soaked up the liquid.

It felt wrong, but also good.

My sister climbed down from the top bunk and with careful foot placement, she took the position next to me. She looked down at the spot.

"I should probably go next to yours." And with that, she pulled down her pants, squatted, hovering a bit off-center from where I had just peed.

"Oh look! It darkened the carpet," she mumbled as she finished and pulled up her pants, "and it looks wet. We need to cover it up."

We had no experience or knowledge of what covered urine would do to a carpet in a room under a roof in summer without air conditioning. I trusted my sister with the fact that we had to conceal our newly created en-suite toilet. Naturally, we did not have many options to choose from given the late hour and noise restrictions. Whatever we used or whatever we were about to do – it had to come from our room and in the quietest manner possible.

"How about those comic books?" I pointed to the stash on top of the drawers.

"No, they will get wet and then look all wrinkly. Mom would pick them up in a second, because they would just be lying on the floor. That would look messy. We need something bigger that can stay there for a while."

We started opening some of the drawers, making small movements to avoid any noise. Tucked away in one of the bottom drawers, all the way in the back, we found multi-colored building blocks. We hadn't played with building blocks in a while. We looked at each other and nodded. This could work.

"You can give them to me, and I will put them over our spots," my sister instructed.

I started handing her the individual pieces, varying between green, red, and blue blocks.

"That's enough, no more." She was done.

I softly closed the drawer and turned to look. My sister had built a colorful circle on the floor over the wet area. It was a good size circle, at least a foot in diameter.

"Looks good," I said.

Relieved in more ways than one, we went back to bed.

In the morning, we asked Mom not to move the blocks. As the housewife with a strict cleaning regimen, this must have struck her as an odd request. While she did not come up to our room daily, she vacuumed the floors weekly. The arrangement of the building blocks in the middle of the room must have looked as fitting as a crop circle in a corn field.

We used our make-shift toilet a few more times. But, after a few days, our secret was uncovered. The blocks could not hide the less-than-fresh scent originating from our warm room.

There were no serious consequences other than a reprimand and a pissed-off mother, who had to deep-clean the carpet.

"I can't believe you two did that. Whatever possessed you to do that? Why would you not come and ask?" She looked exasperated. "Haven't we always given you permission to go to the bathroom? Of course, we are going to let you go to the bathroom. But like this? Using the floor as a toilet like a wild animal? You should be ashamed of yourselves. Both of you know better. I'm very disappointed in you."

Dad did not say one word. He did not have to: his sharp eyes and tight frown showed his disapproval.

To this day, I make sure to locate the bathroom right away when going somewhere. The thought of not knowing where the bathroom is, makes me anxious.

It goes to show that in its core value, we obeyed the no-bathroom rule, since we never physically went into the bathroom located across the hall from our room.

And that is how the bathroom rule was abolished.

Both, the bathroom and Snickers incident, forced me to consciously accept my *Don't Ask, Don't Tell*[3] policy; not despite its previous failures in getting caught, but because of them. *Don't Ask, Don't Tell* made sense early on: "No" was the standard answer when asking for anything. Watching my sister get bombarded with NO while trying to find the battle lines, also confirmed that some questions were just not meant to be asked.

The most important lesson I had learned was that if rules were to be ignored or modified by me, some premeditation was needed as not to get caught. If the risks could not be eliminated, then I had to accept and expect the potential consequences (as taught by the Snickers and bathroom episodes).

As part of this silent resistance movement, I would, on a few occasions, sneak out of the house at night to go to a community sponsored social meeting held in our town's civic center once a week. Only five minutes away from our house on foot, it ran from seven until ten. It was a safe place for teenagers to hang out and listen to the latest club music.

There were multiple challenges with sneaking out.

I knew all of them and was willing to face them that night one-by-one. I was on my own. My sister had turned eighteen that year and was working for a bank. As soon as she could afford it, she rented an apartment, grabbed her few belongings, and moved out. At sixteen, I had years left before gaining my own independence. Still, it was wonderful to have my own space; not having to share anymore.

Having gone to bed in what I hoped to be a cool outfit: tight jeans and a tank top with a fishnet layer, I waited for darkness. Dad was working the night shift and had left a few hours ago. Mom liked to watch TV in her bed when he was working. It was a good sign that she was in her bedroom already when I said good night before going up to my room. Mom had the habit of falling asleep while watching TV in bed, and I hoped tonight would be no exception. I had placed my multi-colored sneakers by the basement door earlier, when I had taken down the empty glass bottles to their respective crates. The beverage man would exchange the empties for full ones when he came back during the weekly delivery. We always got soda water, beer, and lemonade.

With my shoes waiting for me in the basement, I did not have to worry about carrying them all the way down several floors. Plus, most of our daily shoes were located in our pantry, which was straight across from my parents' bedroom. For the purpose of sneaking out, it was not feasible to pick up my shoes along the way. Fortunately, the entire second floor living quarters were separated from the stairway by walls. As was the first floor where my grandmother lived.

I waited patiently for a few hours until the night sky was visible through my slanted window and had turned completely dark. Then, I got out of bed and headed for the bedroom door. I was careful not to step onto the large area in front of the door. Sometime after the peeing incident, the wooden floors there had become even creakier. I held my breath as I moved the door handle down to open the bedroom door to the hallway. The handle needed greasing; it could make a high pitch squeak if moved too quickly. As the door opened silently into the bedroom, I could see the bathroom straight ahead. To my immediate left was the chimney covered with plaster and white wallpaper. The hallway, as it continued toward the left past the chimney, was lined to its right by closets. To the left was a large open area that had once been my parents party room and, most recently, had served as my sister's bedroom. A door opposite this area led to the wooden stairs that would guide me down to the second floor.

Instead of taking a step to my immediate left into the narrow hallway, I gently pushed myself off the chimney wall to take a large leap toward the open bathroom doorway. This approach was almost opposite of where I wanted to go, but that middle section of the hallway right outside of my bedroom was prone to groan when stepped on. It had to be avoided by any means. My legs were too short to cover the distance, so a slight push and gentle jump were needed to accomplish this. The first foot down had to be inside the bathroom doorway as it was lined with tiles which would absorb any sound. I prayed a silent prayer as I reached the bathroom doorway as quietly as possible.

My heart was racing.

I waited for about a minute to ensure I hadn't made too much noise and to calm my heart. There was no reaction from below. I continued my escape and took a step to my right into the hallway. I made it to the former party room and stood before the open door, which I had not closed earlier on my way up.

The toughest part was about to begin: The descent to the second floor, down thirteen wooden, noisy steps. Thanks to a window at the bottom of the stairs, there was enough moonlight to help guide my way.

Drawing in shallow breaths, I soldiered on. I placed my right foot onto the first step, keeping it close to the right. The steps were more solid near the baluster and less likely to creak. The wood was cooperative that night and made no sound as I journeyed downward. My breathing returned to normal until I approached the fourth step from the bottom. The dreaded fourth step always popped. The only safe way was to completely avoid it. I took a deep breath, held it, and prayed as I placed my feet between the thick columns of the baluster. The baluster ran alongside the entire length of the stairs. It was slanted to accommodate the flow of the steps down to the lower level and barely left any room to maneuver in between. I hoped beyond hope not to slip. I grabbed the top rail with white knuckled hands to help carry my weight past the fourth step. Once past, I put my aching feet on the third step, exhaled in relief, and took a minute to recuperate my shaking legs. Two more steps and I had made it to the next level.

Reaching the wooden landing was a major accomplishment. I dried my sweaty hands on my jeans, mentally preparing for the next hurdle. I had about ten feet of wooden floor in front of me that could not be walked on. Luckily, another baluster would offer safe passage. I stepped in between the metal rails while holding on to the top of the baluster with my hands.

It was a most fortunate design feature that houses built in the sixties had stairways completely isolated from the rest of any living spaces. It was like an apartment complex, each floor with its own apartment and different entry.

While I knew that I could easily reach the next set of thirteen stairs without much noise, I also knew that I was visually the most vulnerable at this point. The door that separated the stairway to our main living level was made of glass. My parents' bedroom was the first room to the right of the hallway once you passed through the glass door. Mom never closed the bedroom door when she was by herself. If Mom decided to leave her bed for any reason, she would see my shape hanging on to the metal railing that ran alongside the landing.

Another breath held. And another released as I reached the top step. This was pivotal. If Mom had not heard me and if she now remained in her room, I was home free. The next set of stairs was made of stone and would absorb any noise.

I wasn't too worried about making it past my grandmother's entry door, which was right across from the door to the basement and also made of glass. She, too, watched TV every night and would not go to bed until much later. Unlike my mom, she watched TV in her living room; the second room down the hallway. The first and second floors were identical in layout. Since she was hard of hearing, her TV's volume would cover any noise from here on out.

I opened the basement door and was immersed in darkness. The basement stairs were cement and cool to the touch. They were always cool no matter the time of year. I hated this part of the escape. Taking careful steps, I ventured into darkness. My right hand was guiding me downward, feeling the slight curvature of the wall. I tried not to think about the cellar spiders and hoped my hand would remain free of any unwanted creature encounters. Thirteen silent steps later, I reached the bottom of the stairs. The basement was built into the ground, and a few narrow windows were located near the ceiling. A window to my left allowed some moonlight through its small frame. At least now, I could see shapes in the darkness. If it would have been daylight, I could have seen the pavers that lined our side yard through the window.

The basement gave me the creeps. It had a winding hallway that led to many different rooms. I worried about bad things jumping out at me.

At the bottom of the steps, I faced the boiler room. I thought it was particularly scary because I did not like the contraption that housed oil, flames, and all kinds of weird noises coming from it. A lot of times I wondered what would happen if they ever blew up. The only good thing about the boiler room was that it was always warm. I liked being warm.

I turned to my left. I had reached the solid door; my final physical obstacle. Five more steps lay beyond, this time leading up to the ground level. I had made it. I looked down at my waiting shoes. I slipped my feet into them and tied the laces.

Unlocking the basement door with the key stuck on the inside, I stepped out into the night. The basement door would remain unlocked until I decided to return.

World, here I come.

Of course, I felt guilty about having to resort to this measure and to deceive Mom in the process. I was a good kid, never had given my parents any reason not to trust me. I had proven to be very obedient. Once I reached a certain level of maturity at age sixteen, it felt unfair to be treated with distrust. I deserved some fun after years of having to contain it!

Despite the rules, my childhood was awesome in many other areas. Early on, I spent hours hanging out at a small pig farm just two hundred yards from our home. Besides pigs, there were cats and dogs, and I loved them all. I had always been drawn to animals, feeling at ease in their presence. There must have been familiarity in their non-verbal way of communicating that I could relate to. But no matter what age, much of my time was spent outdoors. Children of various ages met and played in the community playground. My friends and I would ride our bicycles through town chasing the unknown, or each other, stopping only to buy candy and comic books at the kiosk[4]. We would use clothes pins to attach pieces of thin cardboard or playing cards between the spokes of our bikes, announcing our presence to everyone.

Another favorite pastime was climbing trees.

The tree by the cemetery was perfect for that. My sister and I often made plans to meet there after our lunch chores were completed. Just like one sunny day in mid-summer. All the trees had luscious green leaves, and the cornflowers were in full bloom, dotting the fields with blue flowers.

Since my sister had dishwashing duty, she got done first. I was drying the dishes and putting them away. By the time I was heading out the front door, she had already left the house. I knew I would not catch up to her, seeing that the tree was only three hundred yards from our house. Once out on the street, I turned to my right, continuing straight onto the tarmacked path that ran parallel to the back side of the cemetery. A row of thick evergreens on my right flanked the cemetery, preventing curious eyes from looking in. To the left of the path were a few hobby gardens. It wasn't uncommon for people to buy land at the edge of town to grow vegetables, especially if their homes were built on small lots.

As I approached the back gate of the cemetery, I could see a tree limb swaying up ahead on my left. The tree was located opposite the gate across the pathway. A small dumpster for flowers, plants, and soil stood next to the gate. The movement of the tree was subtle, but I knew that my sister had climbed the larger of the two trunks of our favorite tree. It offered the best viewpoint.

Nearing the tree, I heard my sister's alarmed, yet hushed voice, "Not now, someone's coming!"

I immediately stooped down, pretending to tie my shoelaces. I did not want anyone seeing me climb the tree. It stood on private property. Plus, the plan was to covertly watch people in the cemetery. The best spies go unnoticed.

An elderly woman walked through the gate. It was Mrs. Dick, who lived in our town. She held a bunch of faded and dried-up flowers in her wrinkly left hand and a small garden rake in her right.

"Good day!" I said politely, as was expected of me.

"Good day!" she responded with a frown and proceeded to throw the flowers into the small dumpster. She turned without giving me another look and headed back into the cemetery. She was probably on her way to

Petra Weiser

loosen up the soil on the gravesite to plant fresh flowers. In those days, and probably still to some extent today, the dead were buried in leased gravesites and then covered with real flowerbeds; ensuring that the remaining living would have to come back frequently to maintain an orderly and respectful gravesite.

"It's good now." My sister's voice was just loud enough for me to hear.

I was still crouched down as I looked around to verify that nobody would see me disappear into the bushy embankment. With no one in sight, I went to the left and down the bank that anchored a short line of trees at the bottom. The perfect climbing tree was the first one, and I looked up to see my sister perched on a limb that had grown out of the larger trunk. She was about fifteen feet up.

Straddling the smaller trunk, I climbed to where the trunk split into two branches, just three feet short of my sister's position. The larger branch stuck out a bit over the pathway below, and I rested my upper body on the strong limb. My feet, placed on the other branch, provided stability.

The leaves gave us just enough cover not to be seen, while breaks in foliage allowed us to fully take in the scenery in front of us. Once situated, I looked at the rows of graves. Most were covered with flowers and plants imbedded in soil contained by a marble or stone barrier. A few graves were completely covered with marble slabs. Those were for the lazy survivors; the ones that weren't into earthy maintenance on a regular basis. The gravesites with just a heaping of soil were the fresh ones. Those did not have headstones yet; they bore a small wooden cross with the deceased's name, birth, and death date.

"Look, Mrs. Dick and Mrs. Rick are exchanging gossip again!" My sister had spotted the commotion at the far right, in the older part of the cemetery.

I stretched my neck, trying to get a better view.

"Yup," I whispered back, "Mrs. Dick looks like she is going to gouge Mrs. Rick's eyes out with that hand rake." It was the old woman with the flowers. The rake, still in her hand, was all over the place as she gestured excitedly while talking to the other woman.

"Poor Mrs. Rick can't barely get a word in," my sister giggled, "I wonder why Mrs. Dick is so upset?"

"Maybe someone played Schellekloppe[5] with her?"

"I don't believe it; she probably wouldn't even hear the doorbell." Mrs. Dick did have horrible hearing. Another reason why poor Mrs. Rick didn't stand a chance to say much.

Mrs. Rick looked like she wanted to leave, her weight shifting from her left foot to her right and back while her eyes searched for an escape route. Mrs. Dick stood boldly in her way, the rake swooshing by with each arm gesture, preventing her departure.

We giggled in unison.

It is one of the few places where I felt closest to my sister.

Cemetery tree time was sacred.

Also sacred was the dairy farm that became my second home during my early teens. I would spend hours inside the barn watching the cows eat and poop. While I went to the same school with the farmer's son and we were friends, he wasn't always there when I came to the farm. His parents didn't seem to mind. There were cats, of course, cows, dogs, and even a horse; I would try to make friends with all. I had a favorite calf that I watched grow into a young bull. I would, at times, go into the fenced paddock and sit on his back. This does not strike me as a good idea now, but back then it seemed normal because I had established a bond; even if I was the only one convinced of it. It broke my heart when he was gone one day. Guess there's not much use for male cows on a dairy farm. Seems to be one of the very few occasions where being born a male comes with some disadvantages.

The point is that I had a lot of freedom when it came to decide what to do while playing outside, away from my home. I had no worries or fears, didn't have an inkling of an idea of the responsibilities that would surface with adulthood; and I realize now how lucky I was to be so free of burden and worry.

The time spent outside also got us out of our dad's hair and gave him more opportunity to catch up on sleep during his ever-changing shift schedules. It was a win/win.

Having that outdoor freedom was made possible by a hometown that was extremely safe. With around two thousand inhabitants spread out over two townships about a mile apart, it was an ideal place for families. We lived in the older part while the newer part was considered "the settlement"; a term I never understood, but thought it was because it was established later and residents there weren't necessarily locals. This seemed weird because I knew that my father's parents settled in my hometown in 1946 when they were expelled from theirs after World War II. They had lived in Mährisch Schönberg, which was the German name for Šumperk, now in the Czech Republic. So, they themselves hadn't been locals when they built the house in which I was raised.

Some people did not lock their doors. Everyone knew everyone. If you forgot to properly greet your elders as you passed them, your parents would hear about it. We would take a broom to the sidewalk on weekends and brush up the dirt. It seems idiotic to be cleaning dirt off a road or sidewalk; but the German mentality is not necessarily about logic, it's about being dedicated to a task that is expected of society.

German society and mentality can be difficult for anyone to understand. Germans themselves may not even be aware of the roots of their behaviors and views. But the influence of the American presence in Germany immediately after WWII cannot be underestimated. Post-war Germany lay in ruins. There wasn't much left of buildings, culture, economy, education – Germans started to rebuild everything from scratch. First though, there had to be a clean-up. Germans have always taken pride in their homes and their surroundings by keeping things neat, clean, and organized. Maybe brushing up the dirt reflected the clean-up after the war and meant that Germans were trying to normalize life; or it served as a constant reminder of a history not to be repeated.

The Potsdam Agreement[6] after German capitulation ensured that Germans had limited freedom: the new political, economic, and educational life could only be created with American permission.

About twelve million Germans were resettled from Eastern Europe to Germany in accordance with the Potsdam Agreement after the war. It is estimated that about half a million Germans died because of the expulsion. State governments used and encouraged force, but some Germans also died from imprisonment at the former death camps, forced labor, rape, abuse, etc. The long journey into a bombed-out Germany also proved fatal for many refugees due to malnutrition, hypothermia, and disease; conditions that persisted well after their arrival into Germany. Germany was not ready to support the survivors financially or with other resources, such as living quarters and food.

My dad was just a few months old in 1946 when his family was evicted from their home and forced to board freight trains to an unknown future.

While he was born after the war, his memories of his childhood are all a reflection of circumstances of that time. His parents (and him and his older sister) lived the consequences of other people's decisions. He grew up knowing the heartbreak of his parents having lost a home and all their possessions. He had lost the right of ownership of all that they had been forced to leave behind. He saw the hardship of his parents trying to rebuild their lives as refugees. He saw American military personnel act derogatory toward Germans; a constant reminder to him that he was not worthy in their eyes.

It may be easy to point toward the horrible atrocities that Germans committed during the dark period of WWII and that the consequences they had to live with were justifiable, but some thought and empathy should be given to the next generation of children who had no part in the war. After any conflict, how a dominant country and its people act toward the weaker counterpart in everyday life, can have a larger and longer lasting impact than its best intentions stated on paper. This is still true today anywhere in the world.

The official American occupation ended in 1955, but Americans stayed in Germany with a heavy military presence until the late nineties and a lighter military presence thereafter as part of the NATO alliance. Germany joined NATO[7] in 1954, after the U.S., France, and England agreed to end military occupation and to recognize Germany as a member of the western alliance against the Soviet Union.

Most all war survivors struggled financially and emotionally. If there was money, there was no splurging it on unnecessary things. I remember both my grandparents as financially stable people. Yet they would wear the same clothes for decades if not longer. Nothing got replaced until it broke for good. This was normal life for the generations after the war, and still, most Germans today think carefully about how and where they spend their money.

If I asked my grandparents for money, e.g. to go to the fair in town, I would get a very small spending allowance. I was more likely to be given chocolates from my grandparents than money. In hard times, food outvalued currency.

My parents were also frugal with their hard-earned money. I am thankful that they were, because it instilled the value that work provided financial freedom and stability. Financial stability is another German pride.

I barely asked for money throughout my entire life; money had more value if it was earned by me. Taking it from others—asking for money that is—was lazy and weak. Money was and still is a serious matter for Germans, and while it is a private matter, it does not mean that it is not discussed when the need arises. If money was borrowed within the family, terms were drawn up and timely repayment expected. Money meant leverage over others (=power).

The financial power structure in my family was clear: Dad was the money earner, and Mom had the supporting role. She worked part-time throughout my childhood so that we were able to go on vacations and have money saved for emergencies. Otherwise, the money allowed to Mom by Dad was barely enough to cover clothes, shoes, groceries, and other necessities.

"That man still gives me the same monthly amount he has over the last ten years. He doesn't have to buy any groceries, or clothes for growing children, or school supplies. He has no clue what things cost nowadays. Nothing's getting cheaper. I am not sure how I will manage with this little allowance," she would protest.

Yet Mom always found a way to provide with what she was given. I credit her with my now pit-bull mentality that no is never an answer when faced with a challenge.

As soon as I legally could, I took a job distributing weekly advertisements in my hometown. Once at trade school, I rode the bus, which allowed me to become a cashier at a supermarket, located on my way home from school. I wanted my own money; money that would eventually enable me to move out. A means toward my independence.

It was clear to me early on—maybe not on a conscious level—that I was not going to depend on a man to get me what I wanted and needed.

♀

THE PEDOPHILE

I am on my way home. I am walking on the right side of the paved road because there is no sidewalk. I am not supposed to walk on the road, but there is no choice. There is no traffic. My house, at the edge of town, has more tractors than cars passing by on any given day. There are farm fields to my left. It is warm. The sky is blue. I am happy. I can see the brown fence and a white sliver of the front of my house straight ahead on the right.

I am close, maybe one hundred yards to go.

I hear a sound behind me. It's a car, but I don't turn around.

I make sure I'm all the way over to the right, close to a metal fence lining the empty property. The car pulls up slowly on my left and then stops. I do too. The passenger window is down. The man behind the wheel is calling to me.

I don't know what to do. I'm supposed to be polite. But I'm not supposed to talk to strangers. I cannot make out what he is saying. I think he is lost and needs directions. I decide to get closer. He says something. Again, I don't understand. I realize that he is not speaking my language. He is not Turkish by the way he looks. The Turks I know have black thick hair, and I'm familiar with the way their language sounds. I don't know of other cultures other than the Turks. The man's hair is light brown and cut very short. He also looks very pale. He chuckles.

The car is close, I can touch it. I'm hesitant, but I partially lean my head into the passenger window. I see an open map on his lap. He is lost. I am relieved. Maybe I can help.

The man says something; a question maybe? He lifts the map. The man is not wearing pants. He laughs. He lets his eyes wander to his private area. He's letting me know to look – down there. I do. I don't know what I'm looking at, but I know that something does not feel right. I'm scared. I push myself away from the window, turn to my right, and make a run for the safety of my home as fast as I can. I can't tell if the car is following me. I hope that by calling out to my mom, he will know that

she is close. I know she's in the garden behind the house. I know I have to tell her.
I think I have just done a bad thing.

For me—as it is for most of us—it is difficult to recall many early childhood memories. This one though, from the age of six or seven, ranks right at the top. It was a memory locked away until adulthood, when I started to realize that the world was much bigger and not as nice as my innocent child-self had imagined.

I did not know what a sexual predator was until in my twenties. I had been sheltered. Nothing truly bad had ever happened growing up. I did not know that life ended at some point for all of us until, at the age of fourteen, a friend committed suicide. He was my sister's friend, who at age eighteen, along with his new girlfriend, decided to jump in front of a train.

The above "stranger-danger" incident remained dormant throughout my life, until more and more media coverage emerged about children being abused. That's when my brain kicked in, the memory surfaced, and I was able to process the what-if scenarios of that sunny day.

My parents had kept me in a bubble, disconnected from prejudice and evil for the longest time. And because our town and surrounding area were safe, the Internet did not exist, and my parents' priorities were focused on private matters, they cannot be solely blamed for my naivety. I am thankful that I could grow up in the moment, not aware of an outside world that came with all sorts of opinions, threats, and expectations. At the same time, our family did not talk about emotions and so a lot of subjects were never discussed. I wish someone would have explained life—in its entirety—to me as to prepare me for some of the emotional challenges in dealing with life.

Would that be realistic? At what age is one ready to learn about death and the ugliness of human behavior?

I wonder if there can be a balance of preparedness without fear versus waiting for life to throw its first ugly curveball and hope for the best? It must be a struggle for parents to decide how to keep their children safe while also keeping their minds open to the world in a good way.

I had too little fear/knowledge of the evil in the world, while too many children are burdened with too much.

To me it is scary to think that if I, living in such a sheltered spot, had made contact with a pedophile, how many other incidents were there in any given space and time? How many pedophiles may just be coming into their own; experimenting with different locations, strategies, excuses, disguises? Testing the waters? How many children are exposed to danger unknowingly? Lucky to be able to go home untouched – physically and mentally? Was I one of the few? Or hopefully one of the many?

It is easier to talk to your parents about a stranger. I cannot imagine being faced with a friend, a family member, or a public and authoritative figure as the perpetrator. I may have not said anything then, because I was a very trusting child who obeyed adult direction.

As to my pedophile; he was never seen again. After I ran home, I found Mom in the garden. She was upset after I told her what had just happened, even though she tried to hide it. We immediately went inside the house to phone the parents of my best friend, whose father worked for the police. Cellular phones did not exist. With the police informed and other parents warned about the potential danger, life returned to normal. Even for me. Soon thereafter, that memory was locked away.

Once it resurfaced, I wondered about the feeling of guilt that came with it. Had it been my fault that the stranger did that to me? My parents had taught me, "Don't talk to strangers. Don't take candy from strangers. Don't ever get into a car with strangers."

I concluded that I felt guilty about having talked to the stranger. I could have avoided this experience for everyone if I had just listened to their instructions.

The no-stranger rule had never been explained when first introduced to me. But there were a lot of rules in my life that just were. Sometimes they did not get an explanation.

Subconsciously, I never trusted a stranger from that day on.

♀

THE DICK PRETEND

"Kiss me," she said, and I giggled.

My cousin threw her head up, flinging her blonde hair backward with one smooth motion. She could be bossy, and she typically got her way.

"What are you waiting for?" she asked impatiently.

I giggled again, unsure of my next move.

We had set up "house" in my grandmother's hallway, isolating the other rooms with their individual doors away from our imaginary home. Noone could see us. I was the man this time. I was not accustomed to playing the husband in our play-pretend world. And since my cousin was bossy, she typically ended up being the man and making the decisions.

"First, let's get under the covers," I said, not wanting to give in to her demand. *She was the woman now, and she had to listen to me!* We scurried to the blanket, after having turned off the hallway light. Lights were always turned off when people went to bed, or when they snuggled. The hallway wasn't completely dark; some daylight filtered in through the glass from the living room and front entry doors. We got situated under the blanket, cross-legged and facing each other.

I puckered my lips and put them on hers.

"Ugh," she said, "you have to close your eyes when you do it."

"Sorry," I was embarrassed, I wasn't a good man. "What next?"

"I don't know, let's pretend to have sex."

We had no clue what that truly meant.

"You have to get on top of me," she said.

For as little as we knew, we knew men were always on top.

I moved to lie on top of her.

"Move around, and I will make some noise."

She was bossy, but she was more experienced at everything.

I rotated my hips over hers, and she made little moaning sounds. It was hot under the blanket. I rubbed my hand on her flat chest. I decided we were done and lay back next to her.

I finally said, "Okay, that's good. Let's go back to playing house."

And with that, we were back to the wife who was cooking dinner, and the husband who was coming home from work. We switched roles; I seemed to be a better follower than a leader. I had been a complete failure as a man.

Role play always followed the same script. There was a man and a woman. I enjoyed role play as preparation for my adult life. I never questioned it. Nobody ever said it could be different.

Role play is important in finding out where one's sexual preferences lie. A child, who role plays as the opposite gender, may have not had any previous thoughts about sexual preferences or gender identity. This subconscious experience is important in exploring one's deeper, potentially hidden, feelings. The opportunity for role play should be there for all children—with adult support and guidance—but without adult expectations, insecurities, or prejudices.

Society has the habit of hiding away sexual issues. *Don't Ask, Don't Tell.* Especially in America, the human body in its naked form is still confused with sex and considered taboo. It has improved over the years, but growing up in Germany, nudity was not shameful. The daily newspaper showed a semi-nude woman on the front page, there was nudity on TV, there were topless women at beaches, guys at work had centerfolds displayed all over. (In hindsight, I realize that most nude subjects were women, but let's stick to the main point that nudity was not hidden away in Germany). The message was more about the naturality of nudity – everybody had it.

And while I saw more nudity growing up in Germany than most Americans see in their lifetime (ok, in public life), I remained very conservative when it came to my own body and sexuality.

♀

THE STALKER

"Who is that boy?"

Mom looked at me with one of her eyebrows raised in a question mark. I was sitting on the couch in the living room reading a book. I was fourteen. She was standing by the glass door that led out onto the balcony. The door was open to welcome in the sunny rays while at the same time airing out the staleness of the room. The long, bright-white curtains swayed in the breeze.

"Is that someone you know?"

It sounded accusatory.

Mom knew all my friends. Even the few ones I had made at junior high, located in another town about four miles away.

I got up from the couch and hesitantly walked over to the balcony door. Pushing the curtains to the side a bit—it was hard to see through the thick pattern—I took a deep breath and held it.

The balcony, located at the side of the house, first faced our neighbors, an elderly couple, to the right. Their house was at the corner of our street, which ran alongside the cemetery. Separating its contents from the outside world, a row of large and bushy hedges stood tall and proud. There was no looking through it. A drainage pipe ran parallel between the cemetery and the road, covered by grass. A manhole in the grass section allowed town employees access into the underground sewer system, which was covered by wooden boards for protection. All around the wooden boards, thin metal rails posed as a fence to discourage anyone from walking over that area. The railing was about five feet tall.

It was a good meeting point for teenagers as it offered some space to sit. If you perched your behind on one of the four corners, it wasn't that uncomfortable. The spot was also perfect for hanging out because it offered relative privacy despite being in the open. With the cemetery to one side, wide open farm fields and a forest to the front, a few houses to the left, and the rest of the small town behind, nobody paid it much attention. Unless you hung out for hours; and nobody had any reason to just linger those days.

I let out my breath as I observed the scene from fifty yards away.

A bicycle leaned against the railing. A boy sat atop the leaning bike. He was short at about five feet and skinny, with blond hair that was mid-length and fell toward his face. He wore shorts and a T-shirt. He looked unsure of his position or his next move. The bicycle appeared to be tall and new.

I squinted, trying to focus in on him.

"I don't think I know him," I finally said.

"Well, he's been there for an hour," Mom said. "There's got to be a reason why he's hanging around."

I did not have an answer.

That spot was a convenient intersection to two bike trails leading in opposite directions. Maybe he was waiting on someone.

"He keeps looking over here."

I had noticed it too.

I wondered if he had seen the curtains move from his vantage point. *Did he know we were watching him?*

After a few more minutes, something clicked; something familiar in the way he had moved.

"It's Pee-Wee," I admitted.

"Who?" Mom asked.

"Pee-Wee is his name, but I don't know him," I scrambled. "Well, I know *of* him, but I have never talked *to* him, ever. He's not in my class. I'm in 8a. He goes to 8*b*."

"What does he want from you?" Another raised eyebrow.

I felt myself blush.

I shrugged, hating myself for blushing. Blushing was an admission of guilt. I hadn't the slightest clue what this boy was doing over there. But I knew it could not be because of me. I was short, hairy, and had big teeth. I wasn't a beauty.

My mind was racing for an explanation.

"He doesn't even live close to here," I said. "He lives over in Freecourt, and that's over four miles away."

It became clear that there had to be a reason for him being there – fifty yards from my house. Nobody ever showed up uninvited. I felt uncomfortable. Yet, it seemed logical. I was the only one in our town who knew this boy.

He had come because of me!

My mind was still racing, unknowing what to do next. I felt pressure to get rid of him so that Mom would leave me be. If I ignored him, she surely would remind me of his presence every five minutes.

She must have felt and seen my embarrassment.

She stepped out onto the balcony.

"Mom, please, don't!" I whispered.

Too late. She took another step on the balcony to shorten the shouting distance.

"CAN I HELP YOU?" she yelled toward Pee-Wee.

I had lost all visual as I was crouching on the floor in mortification.

"Is Petra home? Can I see her?"

I wanted to die. We did not know each other at all; had never spoken to one another. *What had I done to encourage this behavior?*

"SHE IS NOT HERE. YOU CAN GO HOME."

I couldn't believe Mom lied for me. *She never lies. We never lie.*

Mom came back inside where I had picked myself off the floor. Closing the balcony door, she said, "He's gone." And he was.

For a while anyway.

Pee-Wee returned to the corner of the street near my house for several weeks. There he would continue to spend hours throwing desperate glances my way from his bike. And I would continue to hide inside the house, feeling like a princess in a tower who did not want to let her hair down.

Pee-Wee and I never spoke during that time, even though we saw each other in school every day. I hoped that if I continued to ignore him, eventually, he would go away on his own. I was relieved when he did.

Many years later, I ran into him at a carnival festival in Germany while visiting my parents. Ironically, it was my mom who located Pee-Wee in the crowd and who made sure that we got to meet and talk in person. Poor Pee-Wee was embarrassed, but I still made sure not to linger too long in the conversation.

We had a good laugh about it.

Irony is when you are being stalked while you stalk someone else without realizing it. At about the same time, I developed a huge crush on a boy from the neighboring 8b class. I had never spoken to him, and he wasn't aware that I existed. He was a heart throb for sure. About six feet tall with dark brown hair, dreamy brown eyes, and a very sexy smile. His upper lip sported a slight peach fuzz, hoping to become a mustache at some point. He lived in the town where my junior high school was. I got to school by carpooling; Mom would drive us (me, my sister and two of our classmates) in the morning, and the classmate's mom would pick us up early afternoon as soon as school was out. This did not leave any time to meander into town, where I could innocently pass by his house multiple times in the hope that he was home and would just happen to step outside his front door. I thought about it a lot though. The only remaining option—since there was no Internet or social media, etc.—was to make a landline phone call, praying to get lucky with him answering. Calling I did, several times.

In my defense, I had sweaty hands and a nauseous stomach every time I dialed the number. His dad answered a few times, pulling the "No, he's not home right now" excuse. More than once, the phone just rang. Most households did not have caller ID or answering machines back then.

Of course, that wasn't stalking, that was admiring. Making repeated phone calls surely does not count as invasion of privacy. It's completely different than showing up and lingering.

I could not connect the dots when it came to my admirer and me admiring someone else. I only had empathy for myself.

♀

NOMANSLAND

I am not sure how my parents pulled it off: I went most of my childhood without the awareness of major prejudices. Maybe it was my sheltered upbringing and not talking about one's emotions; but I consider myself extremely fortunate.

Dad's decisions and opinions were based on his personal experiences. While he would impose his decisions on the rest of the family, he would never explain the reasoning - no matter how silly. For all my dad's opinions, he never volunteered any of them; especially when it came to other people. He was not concerned with other people and what they thought or said.

May it be that Dad did not care about other people, or the fact that he spoke very little in general, he taught me not to judge a book by its cover. He taught me the gift of observation.

While I could see, I was also blind:

Age? Just a number. I was taught to respect all ages. Maybe more respect toward the elders.

Gay, straight, bi? I had no clue why that would matter to anyone. I knew I liked boys. When I saw same sex couples, I did not skip a beat. Love was love.

Catholic, Lutheran, Islamic: We were born into religion; I assumed everyone had one; the format did not matter to me. I was raised Catholic, but I never believed that religion ruled my life.

Black, brown, white? It was all the same; I did not see.

Until, at age fifteen…

"Did you hear about Melanie?"

"No, what's going on?" I turned to face my sister for an explanation. We were doing the dishes.

"She's in big trouble with her parents," my sister said, "because of the guy she's seeing."

Our friend Melanie was dating an American soldier. I would often see his car parked by the cemetery when walking home from the bus stop after school. His car stood out: it was an older Buick with an American license plate. Germans did not drive Buicks. It was a brand seen mostly in American movies. There were no car dealerships around in the late eighties that sold American made cars. Germans liked German cars. Or, if it had to be a car from another country, Japan was next in line.

The Buick's windows were tinted so dark that one could barely see through them. I knew that Melanie and her boyfriend would occasionally make out in the car. Which would also explain why he parked three hundred yards down the road instead of in front of her house.

My sister continued, "Why do you think Melanie meets him down by the cemetery instead of her house?"

"Because they make out in it?" I questioned back.

"Well, that's one reason," my sister laughed. Then she got serious, "He's not allowed in the house, and Melanie does not want to tell her parents when she meets him. This way she can keep him a secret."

It made no sense to me. "Why's that?" I asked.

"Because he's black," she said.

"I know," I responded, "...and?" I waited.

My sister rolled her eyes in disbelief.

"Some people think that blacks are bad people. You know...," she was looking for words, "...they are not as good as white people."

"Why wouldn't they be? What's wrong with them?" I asked.

"Nothing. It's just what some people think. Same as with the Turks," my sister tried to explain.

"What's wrong with the Turks?" I asked, earning another eye roll from my sister.

"Boy," she said, "you really don't get out much, do you?"

She had a point. I had spent most of my early teens playing with two things: pigs and cows. And while I had a few close friends, my exposure to the outside world with its opinions had been very limited. Like my father, I hadn't been that concerned with other people up to that point.

My sister, however, with her new job at the bank and a much larger social network, knew of and had experienced many other viewpoints. Plus, she had two more years of life under her belt.

"Well, I think most Germans don't like the Turks, because they took advantage of the guest worker program[8]," she said. "First, the guest workers came to do the stuff Germans did not want to do, like trash collecting, cleaning, manual labor. Then they brought their entire families. People say they take advantage of our social programs. Plus, if you are a woman dating a Turkish man, then you don't have much to say, because you are a woman. And you have to walk behind the man, like, six feet...." she paused, "...at least, that's what I've heard others say. It's a different culture. And I think they have another religion, which does not get along with ours. It gets complicated, I guess," she ended.

She looked at me, started to say something, but stopped herself before any words came out. Then, she just shrugged her shoulders and left the kitchen. The dishes were done.

I stood in the kitchen for the longest time, the towel knotted in my hands, while trying to sort out this new information. I had never heard of such ridiculous thoughts.

To be judged by the color of the skin, or culture, or religion.

It's something I wish I could unlearn.

♀

I started dating boys at fifteen. After what seems like hundreds of ever-changing crushes and two super short-term boyfriends my own age, I turned my attention to the more experienced. I had had enough of boys who were simply too insecure. Inexperienced themselves, they didn't know anything about girls. Don't you just hate it when they slobber all over your mouth pretending to be experts at kissing?

THE LAZY OPPORTUNIST

Rich, at age twenty-three, was a good kisser. I deeply regretted that I only got to experience that once: December 31, 1987, seven days before my sixteenth birthday.

My parents were out of town for a week, including New Year's Eve. I had heard about the party from Dickie, who had told me to stop by any time; and I was thinking, *I should make an appearance.* I knew I would be the odd-one out at that party. They would all be adults in their early twenties. But it wasn't my concern what other people thought of my presence or age. All I could think of, was that I would have a chance to be close to Dickie. We had been flirting with each other for a while. Nothing serious had happened between us; it was all just sweet talk, light touches of the hands, and knowing looks between us when no one was paying attention. After all, Dickie had a girlfriend.

I did not mind that she would be with him at the party. There would also be other, single young men. Maybe I could fall in love with one of them to get my mind off Dickie.

Around 10 P.M. on New Year's Eve, I walked the familiar path to Dickie's parents' house. It took twenty minutes to get there, and as I neared the house, I could hear lively voices and music coming through the basement windows. The basement windows were similar to the ones in my house: they were small and located at the bottom of the house facade at foot level. The glass on the windows was thick and patterned and allowed for no visibility; in or out. I went to the rear of the house to the basement door, which would lead me to the party. Unsure of what or whom to expect, I stepped into the basement and went down a small corridor toward the noise. Another door, and I was in.

There were about twenty people in the small room, seated around a long picnic table. Benches on opposite sides provided just enough space for everyone to sit. I was greeted with friendly cheers; many familiar faces were smiling at me, some with a surprised look. But everyone scooted together to make room for me. And that's how I ended up sitting next to Rich and opposite of Dickie and his girlfriend.

Rich was one of those guys who would talk to anyone, but who was also shy at the same time. Well, mostly he was shy, but with alcohol consumption, he would come out of his shell and turn on the charm. Rich, having enjoyed a few beers by the time I got there, wasted no time.

"You're one of the Weiser girls, right?" he asked.

"Yup, I'm Petra."

"Well, nice to meet you."

"I've seen you around. You're Rich."

He smiled. His eyes were glassy. He seemed pleased that a girl would know his name. Dickie had told me about Rich in previous conversations. He had said he was a good guy and that he desperately needed a girlfriend. He was just too shy to initiate things. I wondered about Rich's shyness. He was good looking and shouldn't have to worry about approaching girls. Brown hair, brown eyes, 5'8", with a good strong physique. Being scrunched together on the bench, our thighs touched. Every time he moved, I could feel the tightness of his muscles through our jeans.

I realized that he did not mind the contact; he occasionally bumped my leg to make sure I was still there.

"I gotta take a piss and get some cigarettes," he said suddenly and turned to face me, "Want to come with me?"

"Sure." I jumped at the chance. It was a good sign. He was interested in me; Dickie had been right.

We got up from the table. He seemed vertically challenged, and I offered my hand for support. He took it without hesitation.

Once outside, he put his right arm behind my back and his hand on my waist, while I did the same on his left. It wasn't easy to sturdy him as we walked down the cobble street toward the cigarette machine. We took our time; uneven stones can be challenging for the inebriated. At the cigarette machine, Rich took some coins out of his pocket, put them into the machine, and made his selection. Marlboros. *Yuk*. I did not smoke, nor did I care for it. But everyone smoked then; it was the social thing to do. Sure, I had tried it at fourteen—at the urging of my friends—and had ended up feeling sick. Not to mention that me and my girlfriend had been caught smoking in her parents' bathroom, and I had never heard the end of it from mine. I knew it wasn't for me for all those reasons. Financially, it made no sense either - it was expensive.

Rich put the small pack in his shirt pocket. With dreamy eyes, he said to me, "I think you deserve a kiss for coming along."

The words had barely left his mouth, when he pulled me into his embrace with surprising precision and kissed me. I let him. This was different than what I had experienced with my last two teenage boyfriends. With them it had been all about wet, sloppily planted kisses with a tongue forced into my mouth with crude choppy movements. Rich's kisses were tender and considerate. His tongue was not an intrusion. It was playfully exploring. His moves had purpose. They stopped suddenly.

"How old are you?" he slurred.

"Sixteen in a week," I answered.

He took a step back, almost tripping over his own foot.

"I,…I didn't know you were… that young," he finally got the words out.

"It's not that young," I protested.

He stood opposite me, his face clearly showing his disapproval. Finally, he took a slight step toward me and reached for my hand.

"I'm twenty-three," he said.

I took his hand and we headed back in the direction of the party, not saying anything. We were both processing the age difference. I wondered why it would matter to anyone. Love is love. I had fallen for Rich. Yet I realized that he had withdrawn himself despite his feelings that had just spilled out. The age difference apparently did matter.

In the basement, Rich stopped to use the bathroom and motioned for me to go back into the room without him. I took my seat at the table, in the same spot. Dickie threw me a questioning glance, and I nodded. He smiled. I shrugged. I was unsure of what would happen next. Dickie kept his concerned eyes on mine. We could easily communicate without saying anything. He smiled, offering reassurance as Rich returned to sit next to me. Rich started to talk about soccer and acted as if nothing had happened between us outside. However, our thighs remained in contact, and I knew that not all was lost. I mirrored Rich's behavior and proceeded to sip my cola-beer[9] while talking to some of the other guests. The night was still young. I knew that I would get another opportunity to make Rich see what he was missing.

Just before midnight, we all stood up to count down the seconds to the new year. Rich was unsteady, but he kept his position in front of me, rocking slightly back and forth in his fight with gravity. I was fully aware that he wanted someone to kiss when the clock struck midnight. I was ready.

"Five, four, three, two, one... HAPPY NEW YEAR!"

The room exploded into cheers, hugs, and kisses.

Once again, Rich drew me into him. We kissed. I was unaware of my surroundings. I was focused on convincing Rich to fall in love with me. I tried very hard.

Then, Rich pulled back with a concerned look. *Not this again*, I thought. Rich opened his mouth to say something, when someone bumped into him.

"HEY, watch where you're going," he slurred as he turned to face the person who had interrupted us. "What's your problem, man?" Rich tried to make himself taller, which was a pitiful sight since he could barely stand. His eyes were searching for the guy who had bumped into him. He looked like a rooster preparing for a fight. I stepped in.

"Rich, leave it be, let's go outside and watch the fireworks."

I grabbed his hand and headed for the door, pulling Rich along. Once outside, I hugged him tightly and said, "You don't want to start the new year with a fight."

I could feel the tension in his body. I kissed him, and he did not shy away from me. He too seemed to be more committed than before, remaining in the embrace. He was still a good kisser. I was happy, I had accomplished my task. He was mine. There were enough fireworks for everyone.

The rest of the group had joined us by now, oohing and awing whenever there was an especially colorful explosion.

It was cold, but we did not care, our heated breaths visible whenever we took a break from kissing.

"Yeah, you're right," he finally said. I could feel his tension dissolve, "I'm really not the type of guy who would fight anyone."

Everyone else had gone back inside. We were alone again.

He looked at me with sad brown eyes.

"Tonight...errr... *this* is it, it can't continue after this," he said out of the blue.

My mind was reeling. *Hadn't we just kissed? Didn't that mean that he liked me? Why would he say something like that?*

"What do you mean?" I asked.

"It's not okay. You're not even sixteen, and I'm twenty-three. It'll never work."

"You don't even know that."

"It won't work."

Tears filled my eyes. I couldn't hold them back. My hands formed fists.

"How can you say that, when you haven't even given it a chance?" I threw my arms up in frustration.

"Besides," he said, "I got someone else in mind. There's this girl I want to pursue, she's older."

"Who?"

"It doesn't matter," he avoided eye contact, "I can't be going with a sixteen-year-old. I can't."

I was balling. Life was unfair. I hated my age. *Why hadn't I been born sooner? Or better yet, why did age matter to older people?*

"I'm really sorry," he touched my face with his index finger, tracing one of my tears down to my jaw. "I just can't."

And with that, he walked back into the basement.

I stood outside a while longer, unable to comprehend this huge unfairness. I did not see an age difference that mattered. I thought it was all an excuse.

"You okay?"

I had been lost in my agony when Dickie came out of the basement.

"I saw Rich come back in without you and wanted to make sure you were okay," he said.

"He says it won't work because of my age," I cried.

"He's just drunk. Come here," he opened his arms to me.

I stepped in. His body heat offered a welcome change from the cold. It felt safe.

"You know what?" he asked.

I shook my head and looked up at him.

He kissed me, ever so gently. It was our first kiss.

"I like you."

I was overwhelmed and confused. My heart had just been broken by Rich. At the same time, my heart was euphoric. Dickie had just taken a big risk for me. He had acknowledged that he had feelings for me. But... there was no future with Dickie. Where did this leave me? Rich had been my way out, my distraction from Dickie. Instead, Rich had driven me closer to Dickie.

Dickie looked around. It was only us out there. He kissed me again before stepping out of the embrace.

"C'mon back inside. Maybe Rich will change his mind?"

I didn't have to think about it long. Dickie was right, Rich had fallen for me twice that evening. I could do it again. And Rich was one of Dickie's best friends. Dickie would know what his friend thought of me, he wouldn't encourage me otherwise. Based on tonight's reaction, Rich had feelings for me. *Wasn't it true that people showed their true state of mind when they were drunk?*

"Thanks, Dickie," I said, drying the last of my tears.

"Anytime," he winked at me.

We went back inside. We let go of our hands when we reached the door to the party.

Rich held firm. He would not look at me again for the next few hours, while he proceeded to get completely shitfaced. My heart was aching, I felt like a martyr observing Rich, who purposely ignored me; the pain pushed deeper and deeper by the realization that Rich would not break his new year's resolution of not dating a sixteen-year old.

I finally went home around three that morning. I cried the entire way.

How cruel life could be, slapping me in the face twice that night with the fact that I liked two unavailable men.

♀

THE PETER PAN

Dickie and I finally made our date. We had been meaning to go on it for a while, but something always came up, and we had to keep moving it. That night, he decided to take me into Kinzigstadt, about half an hour away from our hometown. We were walking, hand-in-hand, on the uneven cobble streets in the old part of town, which boasted a multitude of stores. We were enjoying the mild spring evening; it was unusually warm. It was dark. All the shops had closed for the night. It wasn't busy, especially since we stayed on the side streets, away from the main hustle.

Dickie, at age twenty-two, was a dream to look at. He was a bit taller than me, maybe 5'7". He was the perfect height; I did not have to stand on tiptoes too badly to kiss him. He had straw blond hair, a round face with an incredible smile, perfect teeth, blue eyes, a smooth tan body, and he was fit from playing soccer. I had been lucky enough to explore some of his best body features in previous get-togethers. He was soft spoken, considerate, and I had had a crush on him for a while. Dickie was a local, and we hung out in some of the same circles at the social club, at parties, or at the local watering hole[10]. I also ran into him frequently while I was delivering weekly advertising fliers on my bicycle. His house was on my route. So, while I had known of him for quite some time, I had started to know him more intimately only a few months ago; some time after the New Year's Eve party.

Before the walk, we had gone to an ice cream parlor near the busiest part of the city. It was run by Italians and known to have the best gelato around. This wasn't your typical ice cream parlor offering cones and various flavors in scoops. This place rivaled a restaurant with comfortable seating around tables with linens. The serious ambience showed that this was a place for high quality ice cream not to be confused with a Baskin Robbins. The menu showed artfully arranged ice cream dishes with homemade whipped cream and tasteful toppings. Your order would look exactly as pictured. It would cost about the same as a real meal.

Dickie and I were seated inside, close to the entrance. The big glass windows ensured we could watch people outside going about their lives. Some were on their way home from work, others just arriving to spend a night on the town like we were. The main bus terminal across from the ice cream parlor provided a steady stream of passers-by.

Silently, we hoped not to be seen by anyone who knew us. We did not want our date night spoiled.

"She bitches about everything," he said.

She - was his fiancée, soon to be wife.

I leaned forward, ready to hear more, *This is good. She's bad, I'm good.* I scooped up a nice heaping of chocolate ice cream on my spoon. It was incredible.

"Last night, she complained about the toilet," he continued. "I mean, c'mon, I'm a man, I don't sit down to pee. It's only natural that things don't always land where intended. She makes a huge deal out of it; it's nothing!"

I nodded my head in sympathy. We kept eating. We were lucky that the parlor was open to enjoy this cold goodness. Typically, they didn't open until the weather stayed hot after the winter break - closer to May or June. It was April.

"She doesn't listen to what I have to say!"

I was an excellent listener. It all went down easy: the ice cream, the complaints, the joy of being together.

"Take out the trash, pick up your clothes, rinse your dish, don't hang out with the boys again, don't drink so much; it's always something. It's not right. You," he looked straight at me, "you don't care about these things. I can just be myself - with you."

I kept nodding. I knew what it was like to have rules.

"Have you realized what we are doing?" he asked out of the blue. "I mean, we haven't done anything bad yet. It will be bad once we do something bad. That would be bad." He smiled.

I loved his wittiness. But I remained silent.

"I have thought about stopping it," he admitted.

Of course he had, because which engaged idiot wouldn't have second thoughts about dating a sixteen-year old on the side at this point?

"But then, I wonder what you are doing, and I want to see you." He sighed.

It was the first time he had mentioned it to me. I knew our thing, whatever it was, would end eventually. My reason for sneaking out was sitting across from me with a worried look on his sweet face; he had a lot more to lose than me. I could live with the consequences.

"Besides, we haven't done anything bad yet!" he repeated his earlier statement. It sounded regretful. I was willing and ready under the right circumstance (all it would have taken was a romantic place and more than a few hours of his time to make it seem like a normal relationship).

He licked his spoon perfectly clean and put it on the empty plate. My mind went to a dirty place having observed his tongue sweep across the surface of the spoon.

Interrupting my thoughts and seeing that our edible indulgences were gone, he said, "Let's go for a walk."

We took to the streets, window shopping, giggling like young teens. Our intertwined hands were swinging carefree with our synchronized steps. The air embraced us, and I was a bit warm in my jeans, T-shirt and a pullover, which tied at the waist and did not let any air flow through. It was too many layers.

Unexpectedly, he pulled me into a recessed shop entryway, away from the streetlights and the crowds. It was a perfect spot. We took position behind a column surrounded by three sides of display windows, which protected us from the few people passing in the front. As he drew me closer into him, I had to think about his eyes, which consisted of shades of blue with hints of green; they were unusual. I was disappointed that I could not see their color in the dark.

"This is so nice." He kissed me. It was passionate and honest. My knees buckled. My heart fluttered. I was in love.

We stayed embraced for a while, kissing and not hiding our feelings for each other. He finally retreated his lips from mine.

"I gotta get you back," he said. He removed his pager[11] from his belt and tried to see if he had received any messages during the distractive activities. The pager was his fiancée's way of exerting some control over him while he was out and about without her. Originally, he had gotten it for work, but having it meant that he could be reached—if only one way— if she wanted to. If it went off, he would have to scurry to a phone to return her page for his next orders.

"C'mon," he said, dragging me out of the safety of our hiding space. I gave him my best pouting face and he laughed.

"Don't be silly. You know this isn't the best place for us to be. Besides, we can make out more when we get back to your house." He smiled his mischievous smile. It was so him!

He was right, of course. Fortunately, the pager had remained silent. I still had his full attention. We walked back to his car, which was parked in one of the parking garages in the area. We listened to the soccer match during the drive home. He had to know the score as part of his alibi. He had told her that he would be watching the game with his buddies. We held hands, unless he needed his for shifting or steering or other explorations. We made a good couple, two flirts speaking in innuendos at every given opportunity. I did not want the night to end.

I was glad when he did not stop in front of my house and instead, proceeded down the road next to the cemetery toward Main Street. After three hundred yards, he made a left, then another, and then another onto a dirt road; effectively having executed a full circle while not placing us directly in the line of sight of my house. It was close, maybe two hundred yards diagonally to our left, but it was hidden by trees and a garden fenced in by tall lush evergreens. We were parked on the dirt road that lead to the dairy farm where I had spent a lot of time during my early teens.

He turned off the engine and then the lights. We were immersed in darkness. My skin and senses were at high attention, sensitive to his every move. We reclined our seats to a parallel position. He moved over as best as he could. We proceeded to make out. Time seemed to stand still. His hands weren't still, and I did not mind.

"Can't really get to you today," he complained as he fumbled with the tied pullover waistband.

He was correct, once again. Besides the tie-me-at-the-waist pullover, I was also wearing suspenders (they were cool back in the day), and a tall-waisted stretch belt (also cool back then). There was no getting into things too deeply. He settled for kissing and trying to get some type of feel over all the layers. I had never given my wardrobe much thought in that sense, until that night.

Finally, he had to go home. The soccer game had ended.

"I liked it much better when you lived with your parents," I said. He had recently moved in with his fiancée, taking the next big step in his transition from boyfriend to husband.

"Don't I know it," he replied. "My freedom is limited."

One last kiss and we returned our seats to their upright positions. I opened the passenger door and stepped outside, then I turned back around to take one final look at him.

"I'll see you soon," he said.

I closed the door and started walking home. I sure hoped that we would meet again soon.

Safely back in my room a few minutes later, I wondered about what Dickie had said in the car about freedom. Unlike me at sixteen, Dickie, at twenty-two, was an adult. He could make decisions without parents deciding differently for him. I did not understand relationships and the commitments that came with them. I knew Dickie was torn about his feelings and that he did not want to risk his current relationship. He was emotionally invested in it, also financially. Plus, I could relate to liking two people at the same time. Sometimes I had multiple boy crushes in the same week. I was easily falling into the "I-love-him" pattern once a boy, whom I had a crush on, paid any attention to me - stalkers excluded. I would have had a hard time choosing one of my crushes over another if they had thrown themselves at me at the same time. Love hadn't defined itself clearly to me yet.

The one thing that was clearly defined was: no matter my crush, I always came back to Dickie when given the opportunity.

We met secretly a few more times over the next months before "we" finally fizzled out for good. By fall, before starting business school, I gave up my paper route. I haven't run into or seen Dickie since then.

We never had intercourse and kept the physical stuff light. I was a virgin, and I had ideas of saving myself for the right guy. Dickie could have been the one, but he never tried or asked. I am thankful for that - as surely, he is.

Dickie was the man who was a constant in my life from the age of fifteen until seventeen. For him, I was the person who let him relive his wilder, younger, carefree years – a time period he wanted to hang on to for as long as possible. Sex was not an important factor for either of us, more so him I assume. He just wasn't ready to become a responsible adult. Time spent with me was a trip to Neverland for him. And he was too weak to face his feelings about his life with his significant other.

For me, he was the safe choice. Out of all my boyfriends, he was the one that I felt closest to, even though he was in a committed relationship with someone else and not accessible to me. It was safe in the sense that *I* did not have to commit to him. I had never had a constant male presence in my life. With Dad working rotating shifts, he wasn't visible enough to show his emotional, loving side to teach me about relationships. Additionally, neither of my parents had grown up with expressed physical or verbal love, and the concept of hugging, touching, and expressing love in spoken words was foreign to them.

And so, I was accustomed to more of a hands-off approach when it came to love and relationships.

♀

THE BOY NEXT DOOR

Summer that same year, I ran into Rick at a birthday party for a mutual friend. Rick was a local guy, twenty-two, making him six years my senior. We knew each other casually; the way you do when growing up in the same town and running into each other at the grocery store, bakery, etc. We had talked in the past, and I considered him a pal. He was laid-back and easy to talk to. Typically, when I saw him, he wore blue overalls covered with grease and oil spots and a white shirt underneath. He worked as a mechanic, but I knew that he also liked to tinker with his motorcycle when at home. To me, Rick was average looking. He was about six feet tall, and his physique was slim. With his red hair and freckly face, his wide smile was his best asset. I had never paid him much attention.

The weather was beautiful that night in June. It was my good fortune that my parents had made plans to attend a festival with another couple. They knew the birthday party was only a few blocks away from our house, and they knew a lot of people who would be at the party and who would keep an eye on me. My curfew was midnight. It took me only fifteen minutes to walk there. Wooden party benches and tables were set up outside. The party was in full swing. A DJ was playing the latest hits. Between the loud music and the drinking crowd, it was hard to have a conversation with anyone. I sat down on one of the benches, trying to blend in – I was the youngest one there. A movement to my right caught my eye. It was Rick, who had just arrived. He was moving confidently through the crowd, greeting his friends, shaking hands, and making small talk.

It was a revelation: *this* wasn't Rick, my buddy, who I run into occasionally and talk to. *This* guy, who was moving in slow motion in front of me, I did not know. *Who was this stranger, this man in tight jeans with cowboy boots tucked under his pant legs?* The way the boots peaked out from underneath the jeans, and the way the jeans bunched together at the point of his ankles, made his legs look longer than they were. A crisp green and white checkered cowboy shirt was tucked into his jeans. But not too tight, that would have been uncool. The shirt was unbuttoned at the top. As he stopped and turned to speak to one of his friends, I was treated to an unobstructed view of his butt. The jeans were perfect in showcasing his other, previously unnoticed, very fine asset. He looked like he had just dismounted a horse. His walk had swagger and purpose. He turned back around and continued toward me.

Still in slow motion.

My heart skipped several beats.

Did anyone notice me blushing? I wondered. *Was it hot out here?*

As he nodded a *hello* my way, I was captivated by the freckles dancing around his incredible white and broad smile. His red hair was thick and fell naturally to his ears; perfectly framing his oval face. His brown eyes sparkled with amusement.

Did he see me blush?

He passed by me and took a seat a few benches over, turning his back toward me. I realized I had never seen him so cleaned up. So... SEXY.

Where had I been?

Where had he been?

What the hell just happened?

I was confused about my newly discovered feelings. *Why hadn't he stopped to talk to me?* He had greeted, what seemed like, EVERYONE but ME! He had walked straight past me, barely acknowledging me with that nod. I looked good in my extra tight jeans with the dark blue V-neck that accentuated my tiny waist. The remaining curls in my permed brown shoulder-length hair gave the perfect amount of flowing shape around my face to highlight my own cute freckles around my awesome broad smile.

Don't be upset that he didn't stop to talk to you. It's not like you talk every time you run into him. And why would he pay you any attention now, when he's here with his friends? Calm down. This is normal. This is just Rick.

I knew I would never look at him the same old way again.

I spent the next hours trying to stare a hole through Rick's back, hoping he would come talk to me. The clock was stuck in slow motion. Rick seemed to enjoy himself without me. By 11:30 P.M., the police had been called twice for noise disturbance, and so the party came to an end. Ready to walk back home, I got up from my seat.

"Can I drive you home?" a voice asked.

I turned to see Rick standing behind me.

I was taken by surprise; after all, he hadn't acknowledged my presence all night.

"Sure," I said as casually as possible. Internally, I was jumping with joy. *He had noticed me!*

His car was parked on-street, and we walked the short distance in silence. He opened the passenger door for me and grabbed something from the front seat.

"Here, you look cold," he said as he placed his jean jacket around my shoulders. The night had gotten cool, and he had seen the goosebumps on my arms.

I got in and he closed the door. I watched him go around the hood of the car, still looking sexy.

He opened the driver door and sat down behind the wheel. He smiled at me as the dome light went dark.

"Pretty nice party, don't you think?" he asked and turned the key. The engine sprang to life.

"Uhm, it was alright," I replied.

"I thought so for sure," he continued. "Michael always throws great parties. He's such a nice guy. I am leasing his garage space on the weekends to fix cars and motorcycles."

"That explains why you always wear those blue overalls," I said.

He laughed, "I know, they are not the best outfit, but man, they are comfortable and practical."

"Sure they are, they look it too."

Another honest laugh escaped his lips.

We had arrived at my house.

"So, what are you up to these days? I hear your sister moved out?"

"Yeah," I replied, "she boogied out of here as soon as she could. Works at the bank now as a teller."

"C'mon, it cannot be that bad at home with your parents?"

He turned off the engine.

I couldn't see his face clearly in the dark. Which also meant that he could not see mine. I had blushed again when he mentioned my parents. Talking about my parents made me feel like an adolescent. I wanted to talk about serious things. Things that showed my maturity. I did not want him looking at me as a child.

"Strict parents are not that bad," he went on, "mine were really hard on me too, but only because they wanted the best for me. If they can push me a bit more to get me further down the road to success, then that's okay by me. You know, I still live with them too."

There was a short silence. I did not know how to respond or if I even should.

"So, what about you? What are you up to these days?" he asked again.

"I just enrolled in a trade school," I answered, "I'm going to become a Foreign Language Secretary. School starts in September."

"Are you excited?"

I nodded and then realized that he could probably not see me in the dark.

"Yes, but it's also disappointing because I wanted to become a Foreign Language Correspondent. It would be so much more interesting than just secretarial work. But that would have been a private school, and we can't afford it. So, I had to settle on the secretary school. It'll be alright," I paused, "My English is excellent, and my French is good. If I can keep using my languages in my professional career, I'll be happy. I love English especially. It has always been easy for me."

We kept talking. Time went by.

"I got to be in by midnight," I bolted upright in the passenger seat, realizing that I hadn't paid any attention to the time. "What time is it?

"Few minutes till," he said.

"Shucks," I whispered.

Sensing that I was about to get out of the car, he quickly asked, "Wanna go out next week sometime?"

It surprised me.

"Sure, just call me," I tried to sound as casual as possible.

"I will."

I exited the car. The dome light came on.

Facing him to close the door, I said, "Okay then."

Both of us smiling our biggest smiles. I couldn't tell who had the larger one; they seemed to match.

After that night, Rick and I went on multiple dates, but we never called them that. It was normal to me since my last "boyfriend" and I hadn't been in an official relationship; I did not think this to be unusual. We saw movies, went to an amusement park, or went to the local pub to hang out. The whole town thought of us as an item, but we weren't then, and Rick hadn't made a move yet. He was, I assumed and hoped, too shy. I was ready, but I expected him to initiate physical contact.

In July, we drove to Emperortown for some window shopping. It was my idea based on my previous positive experience with a love interest and window shopping. I had made plans to take the initiative this time; I wasn't willing to wait any longer.

Walking along the row of shops, I peeked to my left and said, "Hey." When he turned his face toward me and said, "Hey you," I reached for his hand and locked my fingers into his. He held my fingers tightly and exhaled, "Nice!"

"I've been wanting to do this for a while," I admitted, "and I figured I'd have to make a move if you weren't."

"Thanks," he said with a big grin.

It was contagious. The Cheshire cat had nothing on our smiles!

When we were done window shopping, we decided to go to his house.

Rick's house had a similar set-up as mine, except it did not have a third floor. His grandparents lived on the first level. His parents occupied the second floor, where Rick had his bedroom.

In Germany, it was typical for the older generation to live downstairs and the younger one upstairs. It also wasn't uncommon to have three generations living in the same house. When the older generation turned close to seventy, the house was gifted to the child who would, in turn, let the parents live there rent-free. The child was also committed to take care of the parents in case of illness. This ensured that the elders could remain in their homes until they died without having to worry about the cost of moving into a senior care facility.

Once in the apartment, he took my hand and led me to his bedroom. "I don't want anyone walking in on us," he grinned. I grinned back, giddy with anticipation.

A battered motorcycle racing suit, hanging on a hook behind the door caught my eye. Next to the suit was a photograph showing a motorcyclist mid-race, going around a tight curve, his knee pads scraping the tarmac beneath. He was almost horizontal to the ground.

"That's me," he simply stated the fact.

Gosh that is so hot, I thought.

"I didn't know you raced motorcycles," I said.

"Yup, I like to work on them too, not just cars. You know, I spend a lot of weekends going to motorcycle races."

I didn't. I shook my head. I kept staring at the photo. I couldn't believe that unassuming Rick had such an exciting and dangerous hobby. *What else was there for me to discover?*

"I know it's kind of weird that I still live in my childhood room in my parents' apartment at my age," he said as if to apologize. "I'm saving up enough money so that I can add on a third floor to live in. I'm almost there."

I thought he was very responsible.

We sat on his bed. My stomach fluttered. We kissed for the first time. *Fireworks!*

I felt wanted, and I wanted more myself. I had waited for this moment too long. Our kisses said as much, but we kept to kissing only; still worried about his mom getting back from grocery shopping.

When she did, we scrambled to pull ourselves back to reality, adjusting our clothes, slowing our breaths before Rick made the formal introduction with me as his official girlfriend. I was thrilled to be in a serious and public relationship for the very first time.

Rick was a most generous boyfriend. We went out a lot, and he always paid for everything. He even bought matching jean jackets. "So you don't get cold," he said. He opened doors for me. He spoiled me with attention when we were together. He was proud to be seen with me, I could tell, always touching me and stating how much he liked me. We could talk about anything. I was smitten. I had never experienced so much goodness all at once. It was overwhelming.

And then one morning, just three months after the birthday party, I woke up with the instant knowledge:

I did not love him.

The three months we spent together already felt like a lifetime. Him letting me know that he liked me at every opportunity did not help with the pressure of being too committed. I sensed that his expectations of where our relationship was going, were larger than my own.

My heart ached for him. It was unfair. I did not want to hurt him, but he was just too nice to be led on.

Soon after this realization, we were back in Emperortown one late August evening for a stroll, and I broke the news to him before getting back into his car.

"Rick," I started, "I can't do this anymore. I can't see you anymore."

"What? Why? What's going on?" he asked.

"This is too serious. I'm not ready. I really *really* like you Rick," I scrambled, "but I have to be honest. I don't think that I love you."

It was a horrible thing to say. I started to cry.

"I'm sorry Rick."

He took me into his arms and then cupped my sobbing head in his hands, holding me softly to his chest, my tears soaking his shirt.

"It's going to be okay," he said. He sounded sad.

Then he drove me home.

Rick eventually built a third floor, got married, and had children. I hope that he is happy.

Timing had been off for us. I hadn't been ready to appreciate his niceness or the constant attention he had given me. I had suffocated in the offered commitment and love that he had been willing to share. I had fallen in love with the idea of *us* more than the actual *us*. He had seemed perfect. Older, mature, and open to a commitment in public. He was the boy next door, all grown up, and he was loved by everyone. He was the one I thought I had been looking for. He was the one other people had hoped for me to be with. Completing the perception of unity to the outside world. Fulfilling the expectations to society.

Within just a few months, the thought of being put in a box of expectations seemed unattractive. Things could not be that perfect, it was too easy. I did not give myself a chance to dive into my emotions trying to determine if I was being fair to love.

I had fallen out of love as fast as I had fallen in.

♀

THE PLAYER

W e all have met this person. The player who has a current love interest, a past devastated one, and a future one in the works. Or potentially even more than that. Good looking and full of confidence, he is always able to find new victims.

The thing that did not help in my case was the fact that this dick wore a uniform. Something about a man, all clean-cut and neat looking that just gets me all goo-goo. The honest truth, which probably does not need to be spelled out, is that uniforms represent authority and order, and I was naturally drawn to that, because I was raised to obey. There was safety in the familiarity of obedience.

If there was a convoy of U.S. Soldiers driving down Main Street during maneuver time, then you could find me glued to a bench on the sidewalk, drooling over the eye candy passing by. I often wondered if German soldiers would have had the same effect on me, but somehow, I think not. English had been easy for me to learn, and I loved the way the Americans slanged their words; they just seemed so cool. Americans also chose to go into service. German men were drafted. Being drafted did not mean that Germans enjoyed wearing a soldier's uniform. American soldiers always behaved confidently anywhere they turned up. Cocky. Sexy. In charge.

In September of 1988, I started the Foreign Language Secretary School in Kinzigstadt at age sixteen. The city was full of American soldiers, courtesy of the United States Armed Forces with their large military base, Fort Apache. On my twenty-minute walk from the bus station to school, I couldn't help but notice them: the green, brown and black fatigues, the black polished lace-up boots, the small textile caps, and just below the caps, the shaved thick necks of strong, fit GIs. It wasn't hard to spot the soldiers out of their camouflage either. The haircuts made them easy to spot. As did their cocky and loud behavior.

I became infatuated with them. I wanted to be one of them.

My poor teachers watched in horror as I transitioned from a modest German girl to an androgynous all-American:

I cut my hair short, buzzed all the way to the ears. From there on up, the length was layered, maybe three inches at its longest at the very top. I wore jeans, white sneakers, sloppy T-shirts, and a baseball jacket. To complete the outfit, I purchased a baseball cap. The cap was made of mesh, except for the bill, which showed the F-14 Tomcat with its two tails, wearing a six-shooter. It had a large opening in the back for adjusting the size. It was perfect for showing off the blonde "P" that I had dyed into the back of my head.

Not exactly the poster child for secretaries.

In the fall of 1988, I met Wanker in a dance club, a favorite hang-out spot for any U.S. soldier stationed in Germany. My father had loosened up the restrictions, and I was allowed to go out until midnight with my friends.

At the club, the music was blaring, and lights above the large dance floor were encouraging the crowd to join in the celebration of the pounding beat. I was too insecure to display my dance moves in public and had decided to stay in the darker area that provided seating. It was close to midnight, a time when the club would really come alive, which I would miss out on due to my curfew. There were no empty booths to sit in, and so I tried to look cool leaning against the wall near the bathroom. A short, pimply faced guy kept creeping past me; he was trying to get my attention. It was hard not to make eye contact because he was obvious about his intentions, passing by every five minutes, staring in my direction as to force a reaction from me. I realized that it would be a matter of minutes before he would approach me. He wasn't my type—he was around my age—and I panicked at the thought of him starting up a conversation. I looked around for a way out. Getting on the dance floor was out of the question. He would just follow me there, and that could be embarrassing. There was nothing smooth about his movements, and surely his dance moves were a whole lot more awkward than mine.

The booth closest to me drew my attention. *Americans!* A bunch of loud, rowdy young men were clinking beer bottles and laughing, "Cheers." I felt myself drawn to their sounds and looks. One of te guys, seated near the end of the booth, was especially attractive. I liked the way he smiled, it looked mischievous. The decision was made. I walked over and sat down next to him.

"Hi," I said, smiling.

He smiled back.

"Well, hi there."

We laughed, our faces just inches from each other. His brown eyes looked like they were challenging me to something. He had freckles, and his hair was red. He instantly cast a spell on me with those deep eyes and boy-next-door smile.

"So, what's the deal with that guy?" he asked. "Do you like him or what?"

He was referring to my stalker, who was making a beeline toward the exit. He knew he could not compete with this bunch of handsome, clean-cut, confident Americans.

"Nah," I said, "I just wanted to get rid of him."

I remained seated.

"I'm Wanker," he said.

"Petra."

I did not know what else to say. While I had admired Americans from afar, I had never had the opportunity to actually talk to one of them until that point. I was unsure if my English was good enough to carry on a conversation.

Wanker and his friends returned to their friendly banter while I tried to understand what they were saying. We had learned British English in school, and I wasn't familiar with some of the American words. Plus, they were speaking way too fast for me.

"You're so quiet," he said. "Say something."

His arm was touching mine.

"I have to go now," I blurted out.

"Whoa, you don't have to go because of me," he jumped in quickly. "That's not what I wanted to hear when I said to say something."

Cool, he wanted me to stick around.

"No, sorry," I stammered, "I do have to go now. You are here next week, yes?"

I got up and looked down at him.

"Sure will, you too?"

"I will now."

And with that I left him at the table and headed home.

I later learned from my neighbor Melanie, the one who had dumped her controversial boyfriend and was looking for another one at the same club, that Wanker was twenty-two and single. And that he was interested in me. Melanie knew Wanker and said that he was a good, sensible guy. Of course, I had already fallen in love with Wanker by then.

The following Saturday night, I found him sitting in the same booth at the club. I was happy that he had shown up, true to his word.

While sitting next to each other, shoulder to shoulder, one of Wanker's friends came up to me and whispered in my ear.

"You like him, yes?"

"I do, yes."

"Wanker says that you should kiss him – IF you like him."

I turned to face Wanker. *Gosh his face was so adorable with those freckles.*

"Is it true that you said that I should kiss you?" I asked him.

"Yes, I did say that."

"You did?" I couldn't believe my ears.

"Yup," he responded with a smile.

And so I did.

"Do you like me?" I asked.

"Yes."

"Really?"

"Yes."

And to me this meant that he was my boyfriend.

That night I learned that he only had eight months left in his deployment. He would have to return to the United States in June, around the time of his birthday. I vowed to try to get to know him better. Eight months seemed far away, yet I knew that it did not give me a lot of time to establish a strong relationship.

The night ended, once again, with me having to leave due to my curfew.

"I'll call you next Saturday at 1400," he said as he kissed me good-bye. It struck me funny that he said 1400 and not 14 o'clock, as Germans would refer to two o' clock in the afternoon. I was not aware of military time then, but I knew what he had meant. Germans do no refer to mornings or evenings in the A.M. or P.M. format. If its midnight is "24 o'clock". To me, it seems like such duplicate effort to have to clarify A.M. or P.M. Military time, like German time, is clear without needing further explanation. Why bother with the add-on only to reuse the same twelve numbers? It still makes no sense.

The week went on forever. When Saturday arrived, I hung out in the kitchen, where our rotary phone was located. I was ready for Wanker's call. It never came. I was crushed and disappointed.

That night, back at the club, Wanker did not show up. I had been ready to confront him about not calling me. Germans take promises very seriously and find it very offensive when someone does not keep their word.

"He's not coming today, he got hurt playing football," one of his friends told me when they arrived. *Really?* I thought. That wasn't even very original. Phones still existed and that did not explain why he did not call.

My friend Melanie stepped in.

"Don't worry, Wanker's not one of those guys. If he can't come, then it's because he can't come."

Wanker's friend also commented, "He's not like that. He wanted to call. He'll call you tomorrow, promise."

I believed them.

And he did call the next day, explaining how he couldn't come because of work, then the game, and then the hospital.

Of course, I believed him.

He called the following week, explaining that he may not make it to the club that Saturday because of assigned duty. We agreed that we should go to the club on Friday.

My sister ended up going with me that night. When Wanker showed up, I knew something was wrong. He did not kiss me, did not hold my hand, or talk to me. He stayed with his friends and all but ignored me. When I asked him what was wrong, he would only answer, "Nothing". I went home that night not making sense of anything. I couldn't sleep all night.

The next morning, I called the barrack phone and asked the soldier on duty to get Wanker. When he finally made it to the phone, he wasn't very nice, but said that we would see each other that night at the club to talk.

I waited for him anxiously. I had made the decision to call it quits if he acted weird again. When he showed up, it was a repeat performance from the night before. It got worse when Wanker started talking to another girl. Melanie, who was with me that night, said, "Petra, talk to him. What he's doing to you, that's not fair. That's not a relationship."

She was right. I confronted him.

"Tell me the truth about our relationship."

He took a moment and said, "It's hard."

I was prepared for the worst.

He continued, "I don't know what to do. I'm much older than you."

I couldn't believe his words. Age again. It had not bothered him previously. I continued to stare at him. He shuffled from one foot to the other.

"It's hard to have a relationship when I have to leave in June," he finally said. "I don't want to hurt you."

"But you are already hurting me."

"I don't want to hurt you now, but I think it will hurt less now than it will later."

"Then why don't you try to make me happy now?" I asked. And he took me in his arms and kissed me.

We were back on again. I was happy.

When it got time for me to go home, he said, "I'll call you tomorrow."

I waited three days before I placed my call to the barracks.

"You didn't call," I accused him right away.

"I got promoted and got drunk," he responded.

"Congratulations," I said and shrugged off the fact that he did not want to share the good news with me as it had happened. We exchanged some pleasantries before ending the call.

Days, and sometimes weeks, went by without any word from Wanker. Yet I heard from his friends, and mine, that they had seen him at a concert or other events. Wanker did not have a car, which was not uncommon for soldiers who lived on base. I figured he took every chance he could to get out of base. It meant that he had to go where the opportunity took him. I never considered that Germany had a great bus and rail system, which theoretically would have enabled Wanker to come meet me during his free time.

So, I only got to see him one or two nights during the weekend at the club. By December, Dad had learned about my American love interest. And I learned about Dad's disapproval of anything American.

"I remember American soldiers with their cigarettes and chocolates when I was a teenager, growing up after the war," he would say. "They would rather throw away their cigarettes than share them with us Germans. I watched them destroy a cigarette right in front of me when I asked for one once. Americans are rude and arrogant. They are always starting fights. They are nothing but trouble. I want you to stay away from them."

It wasn't a good enough reason for me to consider stopping my relationship. I can still see my dad waving his index finger at me.

"They are only here short-term, and they only want one thing. It never ends well. You're only setting yourself up for heartache. Don't ever bring one of them home. They are not allowed in my house."

He couldn't tell me anything. I was almost seventeen.

With Dad imposing sanctions on American boyfriends, I finally realized that Wanker had never mentioned the desire to come to my house. We only ever met at the club to hang out and make out. But other than kissing and a bit of groping, we had never advanced beyond that point. Wanker seemed quite content with our situation.

After two weeks, and multiple tries to reach Wanker through the shared phone in the barrack, a friend of Wanker's finally confided that Wanker did not want to talk to me over the phone.

Friday night, back at the club, I was hanging out with a schoolmate when Wanker showed up. He came directly to me and said, "I want to talk to you."

I figured he would tell me it was over.

"I know you're angry at me," he said.

"I'm more than angry."

"I understand, and I'm sorry for what I have done. You know the problem we had before? When I told you that I did not want to be involved with someone when I have to leave next year? Well, now I know it won't bother me. I'm going to enjoy every minute that I have left in Germany."

He took me in his arms. I was crying. He was so sweet.

"Everything is going to be ok," he said.

"Do you want to come to my house one day?" I asked.

"Sure," he said. "We'll make it happen."

I believed him. When I had to go home, he promised to call the next day.

He did not. He finally called a week later, a few days before Christmas.

"How about New Year's Eve for a visit?" he asked.

It was music to my ears. We could take our relationship to the next level.

"Sounds like a plan," I practically sang the words. "I'll pay for your taxi."

He laughed.

"You might not have to," he said after a short pause.

"What?"

"I may rent a car."

I was ecstatic. Renting a car was expensive. *He would do that for me! How could I ever doubt him?*

He continued, "Let me talk with Ryan, he's coming to Melanie's house for New Year's Eve."

Melanie had recently hooked up with Ryan, an older American soldier.

"We could hang out with them?" he asked.

It would be perfect. And that way, I was not going to break any rules, bringing him into "Dad's" house while my parents were celebrating the New Year off-site, like they had last year.

When New Year's Eve arrived, I was overjoyed. Wanker confirmed that he would come. We would spend the night partying with Melanie and Ryan at her house next-door. I figured that Wanker would get a ride with Ryan, who had a car. He hadn't told me what time, and so I sat in the kitchen, near the phone and the window overlooking the street.

I waited and waited.

By nine o'clock, I was desperate and disappointed, but I hadn't given up hope. I called the barrack phone and was told that Wanker had left some hours ago. I grabbed my coat and my house key and went to Melanie's house. My heart started beating faster when I realized a car was parked around the corner, near her front door. It had an American license plate. *Wanker was here!* I raced up the front steps and impatiently rang the doorbell. Once the door buzzed open, I ran up the stairs and into the kitchen where Melanie and Ryan were talking. I looked around the tiny room with its slanted ceiling. *No Wanker!*

"Where's Wanker?" I planted my eyes on Ryan's face.

He shrugged, "I dunno."

"Where is he? Did you not see him? Did he say anything to you? Why did he not come with you?"

It came blurting out, I had no control over it. The last hours of waiting had stretched my anxiety to its limit.

"We never agreed to come together," Ryan said.

I had assumed they would.

"I did not see him today. Last time I saw him he said that he may get his own car for tonight."

There still was hope. Surely, he had rented or borrowed a car. He would still come. He was probably stuck in traffic. He had run out of gas. The car broke down, there was no way to contact me. There was a perfectly fine reason why he wasn't here yet.

"I'll go back to my house in case he is trying to call me," I said, turned around, and ran back home.

I took position next to the phone. And waited. In agony, yet with the belief that he had promised to be there. And so he would. He had given me *his word*. In Germany, *giving one's word* was more than a promise: it was a commitment. A man is only as good as his word. I wanted to believe he was a good man. I wanted to believe that I was worthy of his word.

Was I not worthy?

When the clock mocked me by turning eleven, I conceded. I decided to go back to Melanie's place to see if they had any updates. I knew they wouldn't, but I did not want to be alone. This would be my second disastrously disappointing New Year's Eve in a row.

Melanie and Ryan did not look excited as I meandered up the stairs. I slumped on the kitchen chair, elbows on the table, face supported by my hands.

"What an asshole," I said.

"Wanker's a bit of a player, I'm sorry," Ryan offered, drinking Budweiser out of a can.

"I wish someone would have told me that sooner."

"Sorry, but it is what it is. You know, he's going home in June, so he was never in it for a real relationship. He just wanted to have fun."

Melanie jumped in, "Hey now, what does that mean for us? You just want to have fun with me?"

"Never, babe," Ryan planted a kiss on Melanie's cheek. "I'm different. I'm older and wiser. Wanker's an asshole. I'm not. We're gonna make it."

My stomach felt sick. I hadn't eaten since lunch. And this sweet talk between the two lovebirds did not help.

"Want a drink?" Ryan asked.

"I don't like beer. And I don't like how the strong stuff tastes," I said.

"Awh, you won't even taste the liquor in this drink. It's called a screwdriver. It has vodka and orange juice, but you'll only taste orange juice."

It sounded good. I liked orange juice.

Ryan fixed the drink in a pint glass and used a spoon to stir up the mixture. He had been wrong. I could taste some of the vodka, but the orange juice flavor was also there, and so I kept drinking.

"Can you make one more?" I asked when I had finished.

"Whoa little one," Ryan said.

"I just want another one to take home, to start the New Year with," I assured him.

I went home with my refill. I sat in the kitchen, staring at the phone. There still was a glimmer of hope left. I extinguished it with my second screwdriver. It went down easy.

Fireworks went off. I jolted up. I had fallen asleep.

My head felt heavy. My stomach was upset. I was nauseous. The New Year was spinning.

Make it stop!

It didn't.

It was time to go to bed. But not before I paid a visit to the toilet bowl, trying to eliminate the fluid contents of my otherwise empty stomach. Exhausted, tired, and defeated, I crawled upstairs, hoping that the sky would not fall on my head. Once under the covers, I prayed for sleep. I wanted this night to be over, the world to stop spinning, and my worthiness to be restored.

Happy fricking New Year....

A week later, I turned seventeen. Deep down, I had hoped that he would call me on that important day. If not to apologize, then to offer me his birthday wishes as any good, decent person should. When he didn't, I knew it was over – for real.

Up to that point I had had no reason not to believe what I had been told by a man. Dad always followed through on what he said. And since Dad rarely talked to me, his words, when he did, were given serious attention. He was a man of his words. Threats as well as promises were always kept. I could not imagine a world where someone would lie to me. When I gave my friendship, I expected honesty, and with it, integrity. Because that was who I was. I hadn't considered or experienced men yet who wanted to hide their intentions for selfish reasons. I thought lying and deception required too much effort, as did the upkeep over weeks or months. Why would anyone want to bother when they could just be honest, get to the point, and know where they stood?

Maybe only American men acted like that? Dad had warned me about them. He had called them rude and arrogant, both proven by Wanker to be true. Could he be right? Dad was rarely wrong about things.

I hated the thought. I had to prove him wrong.

♀

THE ALCOHOLIC

a.k.a. THE TATTOO ARTIST

I n February, after the disappointing start into 1989, I met my future Mr. Dick at the same night club. It wasn't love at first sight for either of us. I thought Dick, despite being shy in his demeanor, was annoying. He would constantly ask me to dance or if I wanted something to drink. I did not find him very attractive, and he wasn't the type of guy who demanded presence when he entered the room; but he was easy enough on the eyes. He was in good shape, more wiry than solid or defined, about 5'9", blue eyes, with a cautious smile. The fatigues helped make him sexier than he was, and I think he purposely wore them to the club for that reason. His brown hair was like every other American soldier's: buzzed on the side with a little flat fluff on top; Germans commonly referred to Americans as "flatheads" for that reason. Dick was nineteen and with that on the younger side for me.

When Dick first saw me, he thought I was a guy. Granted, I could have passed for a flathead myself with my copied hairstyle, tight jeans, and baggy shirt. And... since my chest hadn't developed quite like some others had, I can see why this assumption was made.

What finally drew me to Dick was his persistence and the fact that I could not get any other (better looking) American to pay me any attention. Plus, I was impressed that he pursued me consistently, and it wasn't in an offensive, aggressive way. He showed true interest in me, despite my physical shortcomings. Dick was quiet and prone to mumbling. At times, I had to lean in closer to be able to hear his words. He lured me in, slowly. When he said he would call, he called. I started to believe again that a man's word defined his character through his actions. Dick was a good man in the sense that he was always there as promised.

By April, we were seriously dating. At first, we would only see each other at the club. Dick lived on base and did not have a car. Once the weather got warmer, he bought a bicycle, and he would ride to my town from base, about ten miles one way. While my father stood firm that no American would enter his domain, he did not forbid the relationship. Also, since my grandmother lived downstairs, I had found a true ally in her. "You can't tell me not to let him into my apartment," she would firmly tell her son. "Dick is welcome in my house." Dad surely did not like it, but Grandma was feisty and stubborn, and so we did have an indoor space to hang out in. Unfortunately, Grandma barely left us by ourselves. She knew not to push the boundaries too hard with Dad. Therefore, our one-on-one time was mostly spent outdoors, weather permitting.

"What's that on your chest?"

I had noticed it the second he had taken off the jacket. It was mid-May, and the morning had been cool when he left the base. By noon, the temperature was supposed to climb to seventy, and we had planned to go on a picnic. Getting off his bike, he had wiped the sweat of his face, placing his backpack on the ground to remove his jacket, which now was partially hung over his right shoulder, obscuring my view. He was wearing a V-neck, and I had seen something on the left side of his chest, a couple of inches above his nipple, just before he had swung the jacket into its current intended position. He probably hadn't washed his other T-shirts that he normally wore underneath his fatigues, which had crew necks, and which would have completely hidden that something from my view.

"It's nothing," he replied, annoyed.

"Well, if it's nothing, let me see," I challenged. I reached for the jacket, trying to get a better view. He pushed my hand aside.

"No, just let it be," he insisted.

I did, knowing that it would be best not to upset him further. He had just bicycled ten miles to see me, and I was sure he would turn right back if I kept at it. I did not want to miss out on this opportunity to spend more time together.

It was a beautiful day. We were going to have our picnic somewhere by the woods, which started just a mile up the hill in front of my house. Dick picked up his backpack and quickly, in what seemed like one fluid movement, removed his jacket from his shoulder and replaced it with the wide strap of the rucksack. The strap obstructed any view to the area in question. It was irking me a lot, because he was just prolonging the inevitable. But... I had patience. I would see what I wanted to see eventually.

We walked on, not speaking, the only sound being our steps on the pavement heading toward the forest, and once there, the crunchiness of gravel on the nature path along the tree line. A while later, we had wound our way to the other side of the forest, with no houses in sight for a few miles. We stopped to look for potential picnic site options. Behind us was the forest with its large beech and oak trees, offering shade and soft footing. In front of us were fields of tall grasses and wildflowers. Fruit trees were scattered in no discernable pattern. We opted for a spot in the center of a field to be able to soak up some sun, and with-it warmth; the forest would still be too cool. The grass was tall enough to offer some visual protection; if in a lying position.

Dick laid down his jacket and removed the backpack. He quickly tucked his V-neck into the back of his jeans, so that the front part moved up higher onto his neck. *Damn, why was he being so deliberate in hiding whatever IT was?*

"Let's see what I got for us," he said with a smile as he reached into his backpack. Dick had promised to provide our picnic items, and I was looking forward to experiencing unknown American goodies he had bought at the PX[12]. The first item was a small blanket for us to sit on. I thought it was weird that he would pack the blanket on top of the other items, since it was bulky and had made the backpack tip over when placed on the ground. It would have made more sense to place it underneath all the other items. We sat down on the blanket, leaving enough space in the center for the food.

"Saltines…," he looked at me, "…those are crackers. We need those to eat the…" he paused and did a pretend drum roll. "Peanut butter!"

I squeaked in excitement. *PEANUT BUTTER.* I had read about peanut butter in my romance novels. It seemed to be mentioned a lot, and I figured it had to be really good. A rush of affection came over me. Dick had remembered. I could not wait to try it.

"And, most importantly, Bud-*WEISER!*" He thought it was no coincidence that two of his favorite things shared the same (last) name. "The *real* American beer!" he proclaimed, proudly presenting a six-pack of cans, which sported American colors.

I wasn't crazy about beer, but since he had not brought anything else to drink, it would have to do.

He pulled one of the cans from the pack and popped it open. Foam started exploding from the top of the can. Dick jumped up and tried to catch as much of it in his mouth as he could. I laughed out loud. *What did he expect after having jarred the cans during the bike ride and our walk?* I pulled a can for myself, pointed the opening away from my body, and slowly popped the tab. The can made a soft clicking noise and a small amount of foam dispersed. I let it settle and then took a sip. *Wow, not what I expected.* It tasted so different from German beer. The beer flavor seemed watered down yet pungent at the same time. There was a hint of bitterness. I did not care for it. I reached for the peanut butter jar. It was huge. Same with the box of crackers. I realized that there were multiple layers of crackers inside the large box. Americans did not seem to do anything small. I opened the first batch of crackers and kept staring at the small piece wondering how I was supposed to get any decent amount of peanut butter on it. And just as I reached into the jar with my cracker, it broke into a million crumbly pieces.

"That's why I brought this," Dick laughed, handing me a large plastic spoon.

I tried to pick out all the cracker pieces as I dipped the spoon into the brown mess. It ended up being quite a large scoop. Dick looked at me, his eyes huge.

"You're gonna eat…" he tried, but I had already shoved the spoon into my mouth in anticipation. I puckered my lips around the spoon, then removed it while scraping off its contents. I soon realized my mistake. This was quite dense. Memories of the carrot salad incident came flashing back. I was quickly distracted by the flavor: this was SALTY! I had expected something sweet. I lived in Nutella country. It never occurred to me that this famous peanut butter would be salty, even though I knew what a peanut tasted like. Nutella had hazelnuts. But it also had chocolate. The color of the peanut butter should have been my first clue. There was nothing chocolaty about this. The salty crackers did little to improve my experience. I took a hard swallow and washed the rest down with the unpleasant beer. This was not the picnic I had hoped for.

Sensing my disappointment and carefully opening his second can, Dick said, "I got some good news though."

I needed some good news. "Yeah?"

"I'm moving off-base in a week. Darryl is renting an apartment in Fort Apache, and I can live with him. We finally have a place to…" he did another air solo, "…*be* together."

This was huge. I beamed at him.

"That is great news." And with that, I took the chance, leaned forward and pulled down his V-neck. I could make out dark blue individual dots—each about 2-3 mm in size—and I realized that they formed letters. I could make out a few of them F, U, C, before Dick pulled back. It didn't leave any question as to what the last letter of the word was.

"Is that…" I didn't want to say the word. "Is that F U C K on your chest?" I had spelled the letters. "Who did that to you? Why would you put that on your chest? That is so offensive! Does it come off? Please tell me, will it disappear with time?" He just looked down. Then it hit me, "Is this a real tattoo?" I was horrified.

Dick nodded.

"Who did this to you?" I asked again. It wasn't his first tattoo; he had two of them on his left arm, but this, this had to be a mistake. Surely, someone had knocked him out, strapped him to a chair, and tattooed the most horrible four letters onto his chest that anyone could think of.

"I did it." He held up his hands. "I know. It's the stupidest thing I could have done." He reached for his third can. "Just, sometimes, I can't stand the pressure of it. I can't stand the thought of what I'm doing in the service. I'm playing war games every day. I practice aiming and shooting that big gun at different targets in the distance, killing people. People I can't even see." Dick was in the field artillery division. "And the worst part of it is that I know, should I ever do this for real—and there's always a chance that we will go to war with the Russians—that I only got twenty minutes to live before retaliation. Once they fire their missiles, our lives would be over in about twenty minutes. And there's nothing I can do about it."

I had never thought about what he did in the Army.

He continued, "You don't know the things that I know. What I can't talk about. Day in, day out, do this, do that, follow orders." He sucked in a breath along with more Budweiser. "A few days ago, I couldn't take the pressure anymore. After dinner, I just drank and drank, trying to forget. I was in a dark place. Some of my buddies showed me how to self-tattoo using a needle and ink. It hurt like a motherfucker. I wanted to tell the whole world to fuck off. It's how I felt at that moment. Trust me, it helped get my mind off it." He tried a sad smile.

"We have to get this fixed," I said. "You can't walk around with THAT on your chest."

"I know," he said. "I can't risk getting discharged for this. There's this famous tattoo artist in Mainhattan. I am sure he can cover this up with something."

We decided that we would go the following weekend.

"Maybe you can get one too?"

I had never thought about getting a tattoo. Germans weren't into them, and they were more commonly seen on Americans.

"Yeah, maybe." *Now, there was an idea.*

THE ALCOHOLIC

a.k.a. THE PUBLIC OFFENDER

We arrived at the main train station in Mainhattan by 10 A.M. on a sunny, warm July day. It had been three weeks since Dick had gotten his tattoo outline done; the one that would eventually conceal the disgraced four letters. Due to the size of the cover-up, which would be an eagle with its wings spread, the tattoo could not be done in one sitting. Today, the magnificent eagle would get its internal colors and come alive. We were both excited.

When we had walked into the famous tattoo shop for the first time, I had been smitten by all the displayed artwork. The British owner, Art, had recently won some big tattoo title, and with it, the right to treat other humans as lesser beings. His time was precious, after all, and not to be wasted. He hated people loitering in his shop and discouraged it by prominently displaying the following rule: *If you don't want a tattoo, fuck off.* If he thought you could not read (the signs were only displayed in English since Art spoke no German), he would make sure to yell at you in words similar to the current tattoo he was going to cover up on Dick's chest.

Seeing that it would be a difficult environment for me to stick around to watch Dick get his tattoo, I had decided to get a little one myself. I hadn't wanted anything large, and so I had settled on three little butterflies. I had chosen a spot on the outside of my upper right arm. It was a place where it would hurt the least, I had been told. The tattoos had been done while Dick and I had been seated next to each other in hair salon-type chairs. Dick had gotten the Grandmaster, Art, for his tattoo, and I had watched him squirm in pain while my tattoo artist had done my butterflies. I had been pleasantly surprised that I liked the feeling of being tattooed. There had been little pain, only a warm burning sensation. I had started to understand what people meant when they said, "Once you get one, it's hard to stop."

Given the small size of my tattoo, my artist had been finished in no time. Before Art had had the chance to tell me to go fuck off, Dick had told me to go wait for him at a nearby pub, which he had spotted on our walk from the train station to the shop.

At the pub, I had ordered a Coke and waited for Dick. When the outline had finally been completed, he had joined me, his face all red and contorted in pain. "Nothing a few beers won't take care of," he had gritted between his teeth. He had been wrong; it had taken more than a few.

I was worried that Dick would want to drink again this time; a fear which was confirmed as we continued walking toward the shop. Dick was getting fidgety, realizing what he was about to do.

"I think we should stop by the pub first. I can't take that much pain again without something to help me along," he said. I frowned, having recalled that another sign in the tattoo shop had clearly stated that no tattoos were done on drunks. Seeing the look on my face, Dick continued, "Last time was just the outline. Today, he's filling in all the areas. That's a lot of ink that has to go in. The pain is going to be unbearable."

With this explanation, it was settled. We stopped at the pub for Dick's *Morgenschoppen*[13], and, after Dick popped a few pain pills for the long-term torture he was about to endure, we proceeded to the tattoo parlor right down the road.

I had decided that I wanted to get another tattoo on my upper left arm. A peacock had caught my attention during our first visit, however, since it was larger than the butterflies, I had not had the guts to go through with it then. Today, this beautiful bird would find a new home on my skin.

Art was in a great mood that morning. He was the only one there, and he told me that he would do my tattoo after he'd finished Dick's. And that he didn't mind if I stayed to watch him fill in the glorious eagle. I was happy to hear it as I hadn't wanted to go back to the pub by myself. I watched Art complete the eagle, alongside Dick's face getting redder and redder by the minute. I was sure Art could smell Dick's beer breath, but he remained silent, focused on his work.

After three hours, we all marveled at the artful piece on Dick's chest. There was no way to tell that the eagle was a cover-up. As Dick paid for his tattoo, still red-faced and with a clenched jaw, Art told him, "Now go fuck off while I do her tattoo."

Dick looked pissed. "You know where to find me," he said while he glared at Art, and then he left.

Art proceeded to clean up his workstation to get things ready for my tattoo. "What's a nice girl like you doing with an arse like him?" he asked. I could barely understand his fast, British dialect. I just shrugged my shoulders.

An hour later, I was done. With the tattoo covered in petroleum jelly and a bandage, I walked to the pub.

Dick was seated at a table near the door.

"That fucker did my tattoo extra slow, so it would hurt more. What an asshole," he said as soon as I sat down.

It wasn't the conversation I had expected. I thought we would check out our new body art. He didn't even ask to see mine.

"Can he do that?" I didn't know that tattoo needles could be operated at different speeds.

"Of course," Dick sneered. "He probably hates Americans. British fuck."

"I don't think he likes anyone. He probably smelled beer on you. You know the sign said that he won't tattoo if someone's drunk," I tried to explain.

"I wasn't drunk."

"Maybe he could still smell the beer on you. And to him, it probably meant that you can't take pain."

Dick took a long sip of his beer, thinking about what I had just said. "That British fuck has no idea the pain that I can endure. And have endured. He's got nothing on me," he spat out the words.

It probably wasn't a good time to bring up the fact that Art had been covered in tattoos.

We sat in the pub for another hour. Dick continued to complain about Art while drinking a few more beers. I was unfamiliar with Dick's behavior and did not understand the root of his displeasure. I had never seen him this way. Unsure of how to handle the situation, I decided to remain quiet.

Back at the train station, we sat down on one of the benches on the platform. The benches were located underneath a partial roof, providing shelter from the sun, which was now offensively hot. Humidity clung to the air, and the only occasional breeze came from passing trains, slinging a hot, heavy dust cloud through the station. Our train was due to arrive in fifteen minutes.

"That fucker…" Dick kept on. "First, he deliberately hurts me, and then he's got the nerve to tell me to go fuck off. Who does he think he is? Like his shit don't stink. He let *you* watch *me*. Why the fuck did I have to leave? He was probably hitting on you the entire time, wasn't he? If I ever run into him again, I'm going to give him a piece of his own shit."

"That doesn't make sense," I replied. It was the only thing I could master after the barrage of words he had just thrown at me.

"What the fuck did you say?" he demanded.

"I… I did not understand what it means," I tried to explain, realizing that I had set something in motion. I had never heard of someone giving someone else some of their own shit.

"Naw, that's not what you said." He got up from the bench and started pacing in front of me. He was slightly unsure of his steps thanks to the many beers he had consumed. His voice had gotten louder. I looked around to ensure that the other people on the platform had not heard. All was good. They weren't looking at us.

"You just said that I'm stupid," he jabbed a finger toward my face, just stopping short. "You stupid fucking cunt. How fucking dare you call me stupid? All this pain I'm in and you have the nerve to treat me like that?" He was now yelling at me. "That motherfucker did that to me," he pointed at his chest, "and now you fucking decide to take his side? What the fuck happened at the shop? Did you make out with that asshole or what?"

I blushed, my face a deep crimson. I had never been talked to that way. I didn't know what to do. All I wanted was for this to end. The other people were now staring at us.

"I'm sorry. Nothing happened. Please, believe me." My voice was breaking. "I would never do that to you."

"You're damn straight you won't," he screamed.

"I'm sorry, please... please sit down with me," I pleaded.

"Yes, you are. Sorry excuse of a girlfriend. You shouldn't have been left there alone with him. I can't believe you did that. Just left me to suffer by myself. Knowing that I'm hurting so bad. Fuck, my chest is on fire. I need a beer. Fuck. Let's go back to the pub."

"We can't," I almost whispered, not wanting to upset him more. "I told my parents that I'd be home in time, so we can go visit my mom's parents tonight."

"ALWAYS," he proclaimed to the world, "always with the parents. You can't do this, you can't do that. Fuck them. You're with ME now, they can't fucking tell you what to do. You understand?"

I nodded, trying to hold the tears that were welling up.

"I do, I'm so sorry, please come sit with me."

He took in a long breath. Looked around. "What the fuck you looking at?" he yelled as he turned in a circle to examine his surroundings. Then he sat down next to me. "Fucking nobody cares about me." He took my hand and stared ahead into nothingness.

I was beyond embarrassed. This was so much worse than the only other experience I'd had with a person close to me being drunk. Once, when I was around six years old, Dad had gotten stuck at the bar during the town's carnival party, while Mom, my sister, and I had been enjoying ourselves. We were with our friends, dancing to the carnival music, singing along the famous songs, all dressed up in our costumes. I had been an Indian, and my sister had been a Cowboy. When it had been time to go, it had taken Mom a while to locate Dad. He had never been prone to hang out with the other men at bars during these occasions. When the three of us finally had found him, Dad had refused to leave. It had taken Mom's persuasiveness in the end, and he had pushed himself off the bar in protest. He had staggered to the exit in Mom's arms, singing and waving to the people around us. It had felt like the entire dance hall had been watching us. I had cried because I had never seen Dad act this way, and because he had brought shame on us. I had been mortified.

Still, that was nothing compared to what I was feeling currently. This was a different man. What had I done to set him off? Dick had to have been in a lot of pain. That was the reason why he was acting this way. I was too sheltered to imagine the amount of pain he was experiencing for real, otherwise I would have been more compassionate. I should have been more supportive.

Our train pulled into the station. We got in and found seats. Dick passed out. I was relieved.

THE ALCOHOLIC

a.k.a. THE WAYWARD SOLDIER

D ick and I got engaged that same month, mid-July. I had lost my virginity to him only a few months ago after concluding that we were in a committed relationship, and Dick had mentioned jokingly that I was his. We had talked about marriage previously, especially since he would not remain in Germany indefinitely.

Dick's enlistment would end in August the following year, and it seemed only natural to both of us that we would get married before then. We would also need time to obtain and prepare the legal documents in order to get married in Germany. Dick never considered staying in Germany post enlistment, and neither of us ever brought this option up in conversation. I was okay with moving to the States. Anything to get me out of my parents' house. I could not be an adult as long as I lived with my parents.

Dick proposed unceremoniously one evening. I had bicycled over to his apartment earlier in the day. The apartment had turned out to be the perfect place for our more intimate get-togethers. We were putting our clothes back on in anticipation of Darryl's return. Darryl had offered to drive me home when he got back from his "errand". We appreciated the alone time and had made good use of it.

"So, what do you think, when should we get married?" Dick asked while he was searching around the room for his socks.

It startled me, but then, we had talked about it before.

"I don't know what's involved with getting a marriage license," I replied. "And let's not forget about my dad. He will not allow it."

"What about him? There's nothing he can do. You'll be eighteen in January. We don't need his permission."

I sighed. It was a sore subject for both of us.

"I know we don't. But, he's my dad. If he forbids the marriage, it will tear my family apart. He may never speak to me again; he may throw me out of the house. I'm not sure I'm ready for that."

"You can move in here with me if that were to happen. And we cannot wait forever to get married. There's a process to get you a green card[14], and we cannot proceed with that unless we are married," he said.

I sighed again. He was right.

"So, you're going to ask him?" He had bragged about walking up to my dad and asking for my hand in marriage. "You're still going to do that, aren't' you?"

Dick picked at his fingernails.

"I will… I said I would," he quickly said.

And he did. A few days later, Dick stood on the steps leading up to the main entry of my house. He asked me to get Dad, who was upstairs in the living room, watching soccer.

"Maybe we should wait until the game is over? You know how important soccer is to him," I suggested.

"No," Dick said. "It's now or never."

I drudged upstairs, my heart beating out of my chest. I hated the idea of interrupting one of my dad's favorite past times, but I was also worried about his reaction to Dick's question. I knocked on the living room door before entering.

"Dad, can you please come downstairs for a minute?"

"Why?" he looked at me. He knew that Dick had arrived.

"Dick wants to ask you something."

"So?"

"Well, he can't come up here since you forbade him," I reasoned.

"And?" He wasn't moving.

"He can't ask you if you don't come downstairs."

"What does he want?"

"I can't tell you. Will you please come?" I begged.

He paused. He considered my request. He must have known what was coming. He stood up, slowly, and gave me a serious look as he passed me on his way downstairs. I watched from behind him as he faced Dick, who was still positioned on the steps below. Dick squirmed; his eyes fixed on the ground.

In my spot, with my stomach clenched into a tight ball and my fingers curled into my sweaty palms, I anxiously waited for Dick to start speaking. I noticed that I had an urgent need to relieve myself; a sure sign that my nervousness had gotten to my bladder.

This is it, I realized. I knew this was one of those defining moments of my life, no matter the outcome.

Dick started, "Sir, I love your daughter. I will promise to take care of her. We want to get married, and I would like to ask for your approval. It will mean a lot to us."

Dad understood no English. In addition, Dick had mumbled, his words barely reaching my ears. But, since Dick and my dad had never spoken previously, it was obvious what Dick had just asked.

There was no response. *Maybe he did not understand.*

"Dad, he wants to know if you will allow us to marry," I said quietly. I held my breath. Time stood still. I could not see my dad's face. All I could see were Dick's eyes still looking down at the ground, waiting for an answer. Expecting the worst.

Finally, I saw Dad's shoulders drop. He extended his hand to Dick.

"Ja," he said in German.

Dick looked up, taken by surprise. He quickly accepted the handshake with an uncertain smile. I couldn't believe Dad had faltered. I hugged him.

He nodded, turned, and went back upstairs to his soccer game.

Dick and I were officially engaged.

From that point forward, Dick was allowed to come into the house. There were no more sanctions. Dick could even spend his weekends with me, staying in my room. He brought steaks from the PX, knowing that my dad loved to grill. Most Germans loved American steaks. They were larger and juicier than what was available at the local German supermarket – plus, steaks were expensive. But steaks weren't that expensive at the PX, and Dick took full advantage of my dad's love of anything meat. It didn't hurt that he occasionally brought Crown Royal Reserve either, which was my dad's favorite liquor at the time.

Despite the language barrier, my parents, Dick, and I sat together on many weekends, savoring the steaks and trying to bond. I was ecstatic with Dad's complete turn-around. He and Dick would often stay up late into the night, drinking. Drinking always improved communications between the two.

I fully accepted it all without question. Life was good.

Early in September, after the summer break, I returned to the Foreign Language Secretary School for my final year. I would graduate the following May, and we planned to wed after that. Dick's enlistment would end in August. We thought that we would have enough time for the paperwork to go through after the wedding to ensure that we could move our belongings from Germany to the U.S. via an authorized military transport.

One evening, while I was doing homework, Dick called.

"I can't talk long," he said.

"What's the matter?" I asked.

"I'm in the hospital."

"You're in the hospital? What happened?" I started to panic.

"Nothing, they put me here for my own safety. But I'm okay. Will you come visit?"

"What happened?"

"I'd rather not talk now, and I don't have much time. Will you come visit me?"

"Where are you, which hospital?" I managed to say.

"I'm at the military hospital in Mainhattan. It's not far from the tattoo shop. You can take the train and then walk. Don't tell your parents, okay? Will you come see me? I need to see you," he said.

"It will have to be after school. Late afternoon."

"Just get here as quickly as you can," he sounded desperate. Then he hung up.

The next day, after school, I walked to the bus terminal and located the bus line that would take me to the main train station. There, I found a kiosk that sold maps, and I bought a city map for Mainhattan. Then, I purchased my train ticket, boarded the train, and studied the map for the best way to get to the hospital on foot. The walk took an hour, and it wasn't too difficult to find, thanks to the map. Unsure where to go once inside, I approached a large reception desk in the lobby.

"Excuse me," I said to the woman at the desk. "I am here to see a patient, but I don't know where to go."

"What's his name?"

"Dick Smith."

She looked through some lists.

"Yes, indeed," she said as she pushed her large glasses up her nose. "He's on the third floor. Psych ward. Take the elevator over there, hit three for the third floor. Then you will have to get buzzed in. What's your name?"

"The what?" I asked.

"Psych ward. What's your name, dear?" Her voice sounded softer.

"Petra Weiser," I responded in shock.

She looked at another list.

"Yes," she said, "you are on the visitor's list." She picked up the phone. "I will let them know you are coming up."

"Thank you." I moved toward the elevator. *He's in the psychiatric ward. Isn't what were they put the lunatics?* I entered the elevator, hit the button for the third floor, and tried to ready myself for what would come next. Exiting the elevator, I faced two large reinforced glass doors. They were large enough to move a hospital bed through. There was a call button, which I pressed. A voice crackled through the speakers, "One moment." The doors buzzed, and a nurse appeared on the other side, pulling them open.

"Petra?" she asked.

I nodded.

"Follow me, I will take you to Dick's room."

The double doors clicked shut behind us as we moved down the long corridor with rooms to either side. The nurse turned to her right, and I followed. The room had no furniture other than a hospital bed. Dick lay in it, arms crossed over his chest, staring at us. I noticed the leather restraints on the bed frame. They were empty, but they had been used, I deduced as much.

"You have thirty minutes. The door has to remain open." And with that, the nurse left.

"What happened?" I asked.

"No kiss, no hug, no, how are you?" Dick looked tired.

"Sorry," I went over and kissed him. *What's that smell?*

"What's that smell?" I had to know. Dick rolled his eyes.

"It's me, two days without a shower that is," he said. "That and the remainder of my drunken stupor."

I sat in silence. Dread had gripped my heart.

"They put me in here because I threatened to kill myself. I was really drunk. I got in a fight with the MPs[15]. They said I had passed out and then stopped breathing. All it was… well, I was just really drunk. And I was sleeping. When my buddies tried to wake me, I flipped out. I don't think I stopped breathing. They were messing with me. They couldn't just let me be."

I sat down at the foot of the bed, puzzled. *They? MPs? Where had this happened?* I needed more details.

"You weren't in the apartment?"

"No, my buddies were celebrating a birthday on base and wanted me there. They said I could spend the night if I did not want to walk back to the apartment. I had planned on walking back, but I passed out on John's bed. Of course, that idiot tried to wake me. He said I had stopped breathing. I think he just wanted his bed back. I got pissed, you know how I don't like to be messed with when I'm sleeping."

I didn't, but I kept it to myself.

"I kinda jumped him, when he finally did wake me up. He must have shoved me out of his bed. At least that's what someone said. That he pushed me to the floor and then I woke up and charged him. I can't remember anything. I must have beaten the shit out of John 'cause they called the MPs on me," he smiled. "Assholes. All of them."

"What happened when the MPs got there?"

"I must have freaked out more. I had been in trouble before - for drinking. They had warned me in the past. I can't believe they called the MPs on me. I took a razor blade and threatened to cut myself." He must have seen my worried expression. "I would have never done it. I was just being dramatic. Trying to protect myself. Better to be considered mentally unstable than to face a court-martial for disobeying orders or smashing someone's face in," he smiled a crooked smile. "I made a smart move without even realizing it."

"What's a court-martial?"

"It's like a trial, but not really a trial. Well, sort of like a trial, but not fair at all. You can get a dishonorable discharge."

"And what does that mean... a dishonorable discharge?"

"It doesn't look good on your record. Like, when you want to apply for a job back in the States. They want to see your discharge papers before they hire you. I would lose some veteran benefits as well. Plus, the word *dishonorable* alone, it's a stain on your personal record."

"What happens next?" I asked.

"They said, I'm on probation. And they will put me on some drugs."

"What type of drugs?"

"Some drug that makes you really sick when you smell or drink alcohol. So, you can't be wearing any perfume around me anymore."

That was disappointing news. I loved to spend hours at the famous Douglas[16] fragrance store with my friends, trying out the latest perfumes. Girls my age liked to smell good. A good perfume was like your signature scent.

"I gotta take those drugs for four weeks. And I have to do some counseling for the suicide thing. No biggie."

Seemed like a big deal to me. But I wasn't going to tell anyone. *How do you explain to any reasonable person that your fiancé had just lost his marbles, got in a fight with the military police, and tried to kill himself?* Things were going so well with my parents. I could never tell them.

As if he was reading my thoughts, Dick said, "Guess, no more cookouts and drinking with your family for a while. We'll have to meet more at my place. And with your dad's shift schedule, he won't even realize that I haven't been around as much. Good thing it's getting too cold out to barbeque. Plus, field maneuver is coming up, and I'll be gone a while." He shifted on the bed. "There's one more thing though," he started. "Part of the deal is that I will get discharged by next March or April."

This was huge. We had planned to get married in June, after my graduation! He wasn't due to exit the military until August.

"But that's not possible. Why would you get discharged earlier?" My brain was trying to make sense of his words.

"It's part of the agreement. They will give me my treatment for the alcohol and suicide thing while they process my early medical release paperwork. That can take some time. But, most importantly, it will not be a dishonorable discharge. I guess, they just want me out at this point."

The nurse came into the room and motioned for me to leave. I wasn't ready to go yet, but the nurse remained in the room and gave me an insistent look.

Dick and I locked eyes.

"I'll be out in a day or two. I'll call you then, and we will figure it out," he promised.

Once outside the hospital, I zipped up my jacket. It had gotten cold. I tried to process my swirling thoughts during the long commute. I didn't know if Dick had told me the whole story, but he hadn't lied to me before, so I had no reason to doubt him. I could probably sell the medical discharge to my parents if I could come up with a good medical reason, other than psychological. One that was more acceptable, but not debilitating or life-threatening. Maybe asthma, but the fact that Dick smoked made this potential alternative problematic. I had to come up with something. Anything not to ruin the good thing that I had going.

It was dark when I arrived back home. By then, I was determined to find a way out of this mess. We just had to do some damage control and readjust our wedding plans.

THE ALCOHOLIC

a.k.a. THE GAMBLER

Somehow, we pulled it off. Maybe it was because I didn't give out any information, other than the fact that Dick would be discharged in March. Nobody knew that I couldn't have given more details even if I wanted to. Without understanding the military process or the backdrop of what had really happened for Dick to be in that situation, I was incapable of explaining. I was forced to accept the reality of Dick's early discharge, without questioning, alongside my family.

Life normalized in the following months while we maneuvered through the bureaucracy of obtaining a marriage license and tried to arrange transport of our belongings to the States.

We had decided to keep the wedding date as planned. The first and official one was going to be at the courthouse. Due to the court's schedule, this date was set for the end of May. Our church wedding would happen a few weeks later in June. This meant that Dick would fly back to the States in March and that he would have to return, as a civilian, for the wedding in May. Our marriage paperwork had to reflect that Dick was no longer in the military, and it made things a bit more complicated, but not impossible.

However, in order to get our household moved for free, Dick had to be a service member. This meant that we had to see about getting our belongings moved before Dick's discharge and before our wedding. According to Dick, we didn't have to be married; we could get a free military transport as long as we were engaged. He ensured that he had taken care of the application. Granted, we did not have many belongings, but some of my family members—mostly my parents—organized several household items for us: dishes, utensils, linens, towels, pots, and pans. Naturally, I had planned on sending some of my clothes along, since it would be impossible to fit all of them into two suitcases.

In February, Dick said that we could bring our belongings to the barracks. There, they would be consolidated with other couples' belongings and then transported across the ocean. Their arrival would coincide with Dick's return to the States, so that he could take them to his mother's house in South Carolina. During the time before the wedding, Dick could check out the job market and get things situated for my arrival. His mother would let us stay at her house until we could afford a place of our own. She lived by herself as Dick's parents had divorced when he was a little boy.

After the wedding, the graduation, and the green card approval, I would fly to the States with him to start our life together as a married couple.

"Don't you want to see where you'll end up living before you get married and move away?" Mom asked.

"I would love to, but I don't have any money," I said.

"Your father and I think it's important that you at least see the place. You know, see if you like it," Mom continued.

"Why wouldn't I like it?"

"I don't know. But that's the point. You should really go to make sure you'll like it. Don't you have some money saved from your part-time cashier's job?"

"I do, but it's not much, and we'll need some money for when we will actually live there. It's February now, and I'll be going there in June. Seems wasteful to have to spend money on two tickets when I only need one."

"How about we split the cost of this ticket?"

I was surprised by this generous offer. Unquestionably, I wanted to see my future home. I couldn't wait. I had heard South Carolina had great weather. I hated the cold winters in Germany.

"That would be awesome, thank you very much," I said. "You don't have to though. I know I will like it. Dick's told me all about South Carolina. It sounds great."

Mom shook her head, "It's okay; we want you to go."

"I could go the first two weeks in April, over Easter vacation. School will be out, and Dick will be there. It'll be perfect. He can show me around," I was already making plans in my head.

"We'll call the travel agent tomorrow then," Mom said. "Hopefully, we can get a decent price for that time period."

In April, I flew to Palmetto, SC. Dick's mother, Erlene, would pick me up from the airport. Dick had flown to the States two days earlier, and he was getting his discharge paperwork completed. Since he wasn't being processed in South Carolina, we would pick him up, the next day, at the same airport.

I had seen photographs of Erlene and she of me, and we had no difficulty finding each other at the airport. People, back then, could still go through security and to the gates in order to accompany travelers before boarding their flights, as well as meet them as they deplaned.

Erlene was about my height, with curly brown hair to her shoulders. She was of medium-build, and her features were soft and pleasing.

"Darling, so nice to finally meet you," she drawled as she pulled me into a tight hug. I could barely understand her thick Southern accent.

She pulled back and gave me a broad, open smile.

She talked to me the entire way home. I had a rough time understanding anything, so I just smiled and nodded when it seemed appropriate.

When she pulled into her driveway, she said, "The yellow ribbons are for Dick. It's a welcome home sign for when soldiers come back from service."

I wasn't paying the ribbons any attention as my eyes had been drawn to the object in front of me. I had never seen a house like *that* before. *That* looked like a super-sized sardine can. With windows and a door. The door was decorated with a yellow ribbon. I thought it looked like something that Gypsies would live in. It was a conclusion made after I had seen, what must have been the front end of the home which sported a steel extension that could be hooked up to a vehicle. Clearly, this home was movable. I knew only of Gypsies that took their caravans with them when they moved from one location to another. I wondered if Dick's mom moved her home from time to time, which probably was quite an undertaking, considering the size of this—I still had no name for it—container. I couldn't imagine a contraption that was capable of moving such a large structure.

"Welcome to your new home," Erlene said happily. She grabbed my suitcase and motioned me to follow. "You and Dick get situated real good, and then you can get your own place down the road. I know it ain't much, my trailer. But it's mine. I'm just so excited to have y'all here. It's been so lonely without my son."

Erlene's "I"s sounded like "A"s. I had never heard English spoken in such musicality. It sounded like Erlene was singing and stringing all the words together into one long exhale. Dick's accent wasn't as thick, nor did he have that many pronounced ups and downs in his tone when he spoke. I could understand him well enough to carry on a conversation.

I got settled in quickly thanks to Erlene. I could tell that she was truly pleased about my presence. "I always wanted to have a little girl. Guess I do have one now," she would beam at me.

We picked Dick up the next day, who was a bit embarrassed about the yellow ribbons tied to the many pine trees in Erlene's front yard.

"You shouldn't have," he mumbled.

It didn't take long for him to take down all the yellow ribbons. I didn't understand why he had to do that. His mother had gone through the trouble of buying and placing them, honoring him, and he hadn't thought twice about her feelings when he had removed them. The trailer sat on a small piece of land surrounded by thick pine forests. The nearest town, Localyokel, was ten miles away, and there hadn't been but a few cars passing all day. I had never seen a place as remote as this, and there wouldn't have been many by-passers who would have seen the yellow ribbons to warrant any feelings of embarrassment.

I didn't know what he had told Erlene about his discharge. I could only imagine that she knew as little as me, or potentially less. Dick was very quiet in our new surroundings, which wasn't unusual for him. But I had expected him to be more caring and forthcoming toward his mother. However, Erlene didn't seem to notice, she was full of energy and loved to talk.

Later in the evening, as Dick and I lay in our bed, he turned to me and said, "Got some bad news."

"What is it?"

"They didn't have our stuff," he simply said. "They said it never got picked up."

I knew instantly that he was talking about our belongings.

"What do you mean?"

"Our stuff wasn't on the plane. They said they picked up everything that was due to be transported from Fort Apache. But our belongings weren't there to be picked up."

"How can that be?" I didn't want to believe it. That was all we had to start our new life. My family had spent a lot of time and money getting us some of the essential household items. "How can stuff just disappear? From base? It was in a locked room. You showed me!"

"I don't know," he shrugged his shoulders. "All I know is that it's gone. I can't explain it. They can't explain it. Someone must have stolen our stuff."

How do I explain this to my family? I thought in panic.

"Can you file a report or something?" I asked. "Stealing is a crime. It's not different in the military, right?"

"No, it is not, and I have filed a report," he said impatiently. "But in all honesty, even with the report, we'll never see our stuff again. It's gone. Let it be and quit asking more questions. I ain't got no answers."

"My parents are going to be so mad."

"Don't worry, we'll get new stuff. We don't need no charity from your parents anyways. I'll buy us better stuff once I have a job. Promise."

I wasn't happy with his promise. We should have had *our* stuff. Things that reminded me of Germany and my parents.

Dick must have sensed my sadness, and as he turned off the lights, he said, "Now, what kind of a welcome home present are you going to give me?"

Returning to Germany two weeks later, I broke the news to my parents, who were extremely upset by this development.

"I'm not sure that there wasn't something else going on," Dad said, his face in a grimace. When I pressed him on the matter, he just looked at me and answered, "I meant what I said."

I had no clue what Dad was hinting at; until about six months later. After the wedding, while waiting on my green card, Dick remained in Germany. It would take about three months for my visa to be approved, and my parents had agreed to let us stay at their house until then. Dick obtained a work permit and found short-term employment at a large chemical plant in Kinzigstadt. I had found a temporary job assignment in Mainhattan, and while we both commuted by train, we did not have the same work schedule. Dick would often come home much later than me, despite his earlier shift end. He did not like to be at the house by himself when I wasn't there. Besides, he had found like-minded colleagues, and they would spend their time after work going to pubs to drink and play pool.

Our income was decent, considering our lack of work experience and Dick's non-existing German skills. We needed every bit of money to give us a decent head start in the U.S., especially since we had lost our previous household items.

I tried to figure out how much money we had saved up one day in early August.

"How much have you got? I have about $1,000 saved so far," I looked at Dick.

"I don't have any savings. The money I make, we use for paying rent and going out."

The statement was only partially true. Both of us contributed money toward the small amount of rent that my parents had asked for. There was plenty of money left after that.

Petra Weiser

I got irritated. "Why don't you have any money saved up? We make about the same, and I was able to put money aside after paying rent. Sure, you spend more going to the pub almost every other day, but still. And how about our next Consulate visit? We've known for weeks that I have to have a physical and that the application costs over $100."

The visa approval was dependent on the results of the physical, as no green cards would be given to applicants with HIV. I would have no issue passing the physical exam, which would mean that we could leave for the States within weeks. While I had the money for the Consulate visit, it didn't seem fair that we would always use my money when it came to official expenses.

"I just don't have it," he said.

"How come you don't have any money saved up? We just got paid."

"I spent it."

"But we *just* got paid. Where could you possibly spend that much of your money, two days after getting paid?"

Since Dick did not have a bank account in Germany, he received his pay in cash on pay days.

He avoided looking at me.

A lightbulb went on. I realized his lack of funds seemed to coincide with his pay days.

"When you go to the pub after work with your colleagues," I cautiously started, "and you play pool with them, do you bet money on it?"

"Sometimes," he replied.

Of course he had. I had been with him on several occasions when he had tried to entice complete strangers to a friendly betting game of pool while we were hanging out in pubs. Typically, excessive beer consumption had been the trigger.

The timing, the circumstances - it now made perfect sense. He liked to gamble when drunk. I had no idea how long this had been going on or how deep this problem had manifested itself in Dick's everyday life. *Is this what happened to our stuff?* It was the first time that thought had entered my mind. But I never asked Dick about it. I was afraid of his reaction. My question would be viewed as an accusation, and he would not take lightly to his wife questioning his integrity. And in a way, I didn't want to know. I didn't want to open the door to something I wasn't prepared to face.

"Don't give me that look," he said after I had been quiet for a while. "You have no idea what it's like for me. I can't speak the language, I have no real friends, and I can't just sit and wait for you at your parents' house. All I got are work friends. I can't help it if they want to go out after work. And I can't see why you can't understand that it's the only thing I enjoy doing over here. Playing pool is what I do at home with my buddies; it's the closest activity that reminds me of home. How can you be so selfish? Don't you want me to be happy?"

"Of course. I'm sorry that I was upset with you."

"I need you to be on my side, babe," Dick pleaded. "I can't stand it here much longer. There are too many rules in Germany. Don't stomp out cigarette butts on the sidewalk and leave them. Don't cross the street if the light is red. Turn off the light, even if you only leave the room for a minute. Put down the toilet seat... How ridiculous. I'm so tired of rules."

I completely understood. We both wanted to get out of Germany for the same reason. Additionally, it was the only way to get Dick away from his gambling cronies.

THE ALCOHOLIC

a.k.a. THE NO-SHOW

Once back in Germany, after my short visit to South Carolina, I was fully focused on our wedding preparations. By the middle of May, I was filled with excitement. My parents had helped to make most of the arrangements for our wedding. They would pay for everything: my dress, the flowers, the church service, the wedding hall rental, food, drinks, etc.

Dick was scheduled to fly in just a week prior to our court wedding at the end of May. I couldn't wait. We had found a cheap flight from the States, but it meant that Dick had a long journey ahead of him. He would have a layover of several hours in Capitol City, U.S.A. From there, he would fly to Biervaria, which was a four-hour drive from my parents' house. He would have to take a train from Biervaria's airport to my hometown once he arrived.

He called me the day of his departure to go over the travel details one last time. He was nervous about finding the right train since he spoke no German. Smartphones did not exist, and one had to rely on being able to read the displayed train schedules, which could be quite complicated. We could not talk for long as international phone calls were very expensive. With the time difference—Germany was six hours ahead—and the combined flying time of twelve hours (not counting the layover), Dick would leave the States that afternoon and arrive into Germany the next morning, local time.

I knew I would not hear from him until his arrival at my house, which would be sometime in the late afternoon. We had agreed that he would take a taxi from the train station to my house, since there was no way to call from the road to let us know about his exact arrival time.

When the phone rang around two o'clock, I picked it up, absentmindedly.

"Weiser," I answered.

"Babe, it's me," Dick said, his voice sounding small and far away.

"Where are you? Are you close?"

"I'm in the States."

"You're in the States?" I repeated. "Why?" I panicked, *Was he pulling out of the wedding?*

"I'm in Capitol City. They detained me."

"Who?"

"The fucking Capitol City police," he whispered.

"What did you do?"

"Nothing. While I waited for my next flight, I had two beers. When I tried to board the plane, they wouldn't let me on."

I had never heard of someone not being let on a plane.

"Why would they not let you on the plane?"

"I don't know. Because she was stupid. She made something out of nothing."

She? "Who's she?"

"The stupid bitch at the gate. She said I smelled like beer when I handed her my boarding pass."

"But you said you only had two beers," I argued. "Two beers is nothing. Were you acting weird?"

He ignored the last question, "Well, that bitch acted like I had fifty. Said I was drunk and that she could not let me on the plane."

"TWO beers?" I tried again.

There was a short pause.

"Are you on my side or not? Why can't you just be supportive for once?" he sighed in disappointment. "Listen, I can't talk long. This call is going to cost a fortune. I had a few beers to celebrate our wedding; people were buying them for me. They were being nice. That bitch wasn't nice and called the cops on me. They treated me like shit. Even cuffed me. I had to spend the night in jail." He took in a breath to calm himself down. "They told me that I can take the same flight today without paying any penalties. I'll be there tomorrow. Okay?"

I didn't say anything.

"Please don't make this harder than it already is on me. I had to spend the night in jail. JAIL," he repeated. "Don't make such a big deal out of it, and *don't* tell your parents. Just tell them my flight got cancelled. It happens all the time. I swear, I will see you tomorrow. I've got to go. They'll take me back to the airport in a bit. Okay?"

"I don't know, I guess," I finally said.

"Babe, last night was rough. The whole last month without you was rough. I need you by my side. I can't function without you. I promise, everything will be fine once I get there. Then it will be me and you, forever. I love you."

"I love you too. Just get here," I said, confirming my allegiance.

I kept a straight face as I informed my parents of the delay.

"Better late than never," Mom reassured me. "Right?"

I nodded. Crisis averted.

THE ALCOHOLIC

a.k.a. THE HUNTER

We quickly settled into our new lives in the States. I soon realized that Localyokel, South Carolina, had no public transportation system in place. Far from it. Walking to the store was not an option. Localyokel was ten miles away. We lived in the middle of nowhere; our only visible neighbors were trees and squirrels for miles. It was quite unsettling that I was stuck at the house with nothing to do and no way of getting anywhere fast. If I wanted to go for a walk, my only option was to head into the woods, which would eventually lead me into the swamp.

Dick got a job at a textile plant, about thirty minutes from home. It was the largest employer in the area, and its various plants ran three shifts during the week. Dick, being a newcomer, had to settle on the graveyard shift, which was from 10 P.M. until 6 A.M.

Erlene moved out soon after Dick and I had settled into her home permanently. I missed her company the most during my solitary evenings. Her gentle smile and positive attitude had always been able to cheer me up when I felt sad or lonely. She did most of the cooking and cleaning, and she mothered me in a good and generous way at any given chance. She would buy me clothes and fake jewelry, and then tell me how nice I looked in them. She was instrumental in getting me acclimated to the way things were in the States. She took me to the grocery store, showed me how to work the simple washer and dryer, and even tried to show me how to cook Southern food. Which meant, how to fry everything in Crisco without burning down the house.

While I was sad to see her move in with her boyfriend, I was also relieved. Erlene and Dick had been getting into fights more and more as time progressed. She did not approve of his drinking and kept saying how much he was like his father.

"Imagine, growing up like that," Dick said out of the blue after one of their fights. "She says, you're like your father, go live with him. And then I do, and he says that I'm just like my mother and to go live with her."

With Erlene gone, it became even more important that I should get my driver's license and my own car. Only then could I search for a job. Dick had told me how easy it was to get a license in the States, and I was glad when this turned out to be correct. With a written test passed, I was given a permit, and I took the official driving test soon thereafter. In Germany, the legal driving age was eighteen, and all applicants had to attend driving school. A certain number of theoretical hours had to be met in addition to a required number of practical hours. Practical hours reflected certain driving conditions: country roads, interstate, as well as night driving. Not only was this process time consuming, it was also very expensive. It wasn't uncommon to spend anywhere from $1,000 to $3,000 for the license.

Once I had my thirty-dollar driver's license, I started looking for employment. This turned out to be very challenging. There weren't any companies in the immediate area that could have appreciated my German education or that would have had a need for someone with German language skills. My English, while decent, wasn't perfect, and I had no work experience other than three months of part-time work in Germany.

Erlene helped with my résumé and cover letter. After some research, I was able to locate and call the nearest German Chamber of Commerce in Regent City, across the State line. For a small fee, they sent me a book listing all international companies in the metropolitan area. I started sending out letters to the German firms first, and eventually was offered a clerical job with a company that made and serviced testing equipment. There were two downsides: one, the commute was almost one hour one-way, and second, it only paid $5.50/hour. I accepted; it had been the only reply and offer to my applications, and I was ready to explore the *new world* on my own.

Dick purchased a second used vehicle. His mom, once again, came through for us. Not only did she rent out her trailer to us for a small amount, she also sold us her older model Buick.

I was off to start my professional career.

While I now had employment, I was still lonely. I had no friends and no way of easily making them where I lived. The few colleagues at work were much older, had different interests, and lived too far away. Dick kept mostly to himself, and his idea of going out was a trip to Walmart, where he loved to pick up more hunting and fishing paraphernalia. He was my only companion, my sole source of entertainment. He tried to make me feel better by letting me participate in all his hobbies.

His hobbies though weren't of interest to me, but it did not matter. He especially liked to hunt—as did everyone else in Localyokel—and he was insistent that I would learn how to hunt with him. On one of our visits to Walmart, he bought me a shotgun and a hunting rifle.

I was amazed how easy it was to obtain weapons. In Germany, unless you were an official game hunter or in law enforcement, you could not own a gun or rifle (other than a pellet gun for bird control). Here, we had walked straight to the gun department at Walmart and walked right out with both weapons and enough ammunition to supply an army.

Dick already had his own shotgun and hunting rifle at home. We spent the next several weekends shooting targets in our backyard. During the week, I was focused on resting my sore and discolored shoulder for the next practice session.

I was not surprised that I wasn't a very good shot. My heart and my mind weren't in it. I did not see the purpose of killing an animal when there was perfectly good food to buy at the store. I didn't understand how anyone could shoot an animal under the pretense of needing food in today's abundant society. Dick seemed to take more pleasure in talking about how he could kill a deer running through the woods two hundred yards away than about how we would store the unpleasant tough meat in our freezer for the next four months for ample food supply.

I also couldn't dare think about what had to be done to the animal in order to get to the meat. I purposely was never present for "field dressing" of any of the animals that Dick had killed. I later realized that the best part of field dressing for most hunters was the drinking. It was quite a lengthy process and therefore needed lots of beer.

I hated everything about hunting: from getting up early, being out in the cold for hours, being hungry about one hour into getting situated on the tree stand because I didn't eat anything first thing in the morning, to waiting for an animal to come by that I wouldn't shoot. I once did see a little buck, who was just starting to bud his antlers. He had probably smelled the nasty pee concoction that we had poured onto the ground earlier. It also seemed silly to rattle deer antlers together in order to attract a buck to come near so that he could be shot. I didn't understand why humans had to set traps. *Wasn't that cheating?*

When we went deer hunting, Dick would get me situated on a fixed hunting platform while he would move on to set-up his portable climbing tree stand somewhere else. I was not comfortable sitting ten feet up in the air with my shotgun on my lap and the realization that there was no one else around. I felt isolated and forgotten, but at the same time, I enjoyed the peacefulness and the quiet that the woods offered. It was a place where I could be without any thought and simply enjoy my surroundings. At least, for a little while. After a few hours of nothingness, it was tough to ignore the boredom. Granted, I loved being lazy and to have to do as little as possible, but typically, "me being lazy" involved a book to read, a TV to watch, and a couch to sleep on. Obviously, there were no couches or TVs in the woods that could have made my situation more comfortable. Dick would not allow me to bring any books along, since the rustling of the pages would alert the deer to a human presence. The purpose of hunting was to sit completely still (in uncomfortable places) and to observe and listen, and to kill unassuming prey. I was stuck, having to wait for either a shot, indicating that a deer had been killed (Dick was an excellent sharpshooter), or for Dick to return when he thought it was an appropriate time to go home.

Dick never stated when he would be back after getting me settled on the platform. I often worried that something had happened to him, especially after many hours had passed. I was unsure at what point I could assume that my worries were justified. I did not know if I could find my way out of the woods by myself. I feared that I would end up sitting in my spot for days, unsure if I should move or stay. Dick had only laughed when I told him about my fears. "I'm an excellent hunter, and I will always come get you," he had promised.

I was always cold, despite my thickly insulated hunting overalls, warm socks, and waterproof hunting boots.

I found turkey hunting to be quite entertaining; and stupid. We would cover our faces with camouflage paint. "Turkeys have great vision. You can't show any skin, or anything shiny," Dick would say. I thought we looked like Rambo going to war.

When he showed me how to work the turkey call, I almost fell over with laughter. "That's NOT what they sound like, is it?" I didn't believe it.

"You shoot turkeys in the head as not to mess up the body with your shotgun pellets," Dick explained.

I stopped laughing.

Dove hunting turned out to be extremely annoying. A bunch of men and one woman, me, would gather in a large open field near a tree line. When pigeons were spotted flying in the distance, someone would call out. As they approached, gunfire would erupt all around us. It seemed chaotic and very unsafe. *There's no meat on a pigeon, why would anyone want to shoot them for food? Americans surely have funny traditions.*

In order to go rabbit hunting, Dick bought several beagles, which he locked into a small kennel behind our trailer. They sure made a lot of noise. We only went rabbit hunting together once, and I remember walking through acres of thorny fields, tearing up my clothes and getting scratches all over. Dick tried to get the dogs to do their job, but we eventually figured they had never been properly trained, despite what the seller had told him. Dick and the useless dogs got to go rabbit hunting by themselves after that. He soon got rid of them; they were too much trouble.

Dick never could convince me to go squirrel hunting. Granted, you could do that from your front porch; they were all over the place. But I had no interest to use the poor squirrels for target practice. With my aim, I'd just be shooting pellets into trees. *Is there anything edible on a squirrel?* I wondered. I knew I would never eat one. They looked too much like climbing rats.

When the term coon hunting came up one day, I wasn't sure what it was, until someone explained that coon stood for raccoon. (I later learned of its secondary meeting and refused to believe it.) Dick had bought a Bluetick Coonhound, a dog that had been trained for racoon trapping. The dog would be let loose at night, track down a raccoon, and then chase it up a tree. The dog would bay[17] once it picked up a trail, and the bay was an easy sound to follow for the hunter, especially once the raccoon was treed and kept in place by the dog. The raccoon, with nowhere to go, could then be shot without much trouble.

I quickly realized that hunting was a year-round activity and that hunting regulations weren't taken seriously or necessarily observed around our parts. At times, Dick would use the hound for illegal deer hunting activities, along with other hunters and their dogs. Hunting dogs were set loose in a pack in the woods, and the hunters would disperse in their trucks in different directions, trying to anticipate by the dogs baying where a deer might run out of the woods to be shot.

Some hunters went out at night to look for deer using their four-wheel drive trucks and bright lights mounted atop a rack. A deer's eyes are optimized for very low light. With its eyes fully dilated at night to capture as much light as possible, it cannot see anything when confronted by bright lights, and it freezes in place. The goal of the illegal hunter was to be able to shoot the deer before its eyes could adjust so that it could escape.

Another unpleasant nighttime hunting experience was frog gigging. Considering the amount of meat on a pair of frog legs, I really had no interest. But Dick insisted, and I had to admit, I was curious about the flavor. Anytime anyone mentioned frog legs, they would say, "Tastes just like chicken."

I wondered, *Why not just eat chicken?* There had to be some difference, and I wanted to find out what the big deal was.

Late one evening, it was probably around midnight, we left the trailer and headed into the woods toward the swamp. Dick was leading the way; he was holding a flashlight in his left hand while carrying the frog gig and net in the right. The frog gig was a long wooden stick with five prongs at the end of it – to jam into the frog to kill it. I carried a large bucket for frog collection.

As we arrived at the swamp, Dick turned to me and said, "We'll have to wade through this mess until we get to the boat." Our feet would be submerged in a foot of swampy water. We were both wearing sneakers.

I had never been *in* the swamp before. I also figured that nighttime was not my preferred time for watery explorations. This was confirmed by Dick's next words, "Watch out for water moccasins[18] and copperheads."

I swallowed hard. I hadn't thought about snakes up to this point. I had been more concerned with spiders and snapping turtles.

"You should be alright, just stay behind me," Dick instructed.

I stayed on his heels until we reached the small jon boat[19] that he had tied up to a stump. The swamp opened up from that point on, and we were able to proceed in the boat. Relieved, I got in, my feet slopping out swamp water from my now ruined sneakers.

"Watch out for snakes near low hanging branches or at the edge of the water," Dick said, once again jarring my survival senses alive with a shot of adrenaline.

"Here, take the flashlight. We'll glide through the water slowly. I'll tell you where to shine the light. I'll need my hands for the gig and the net," Dick handed me the flashlight.

I took the flashlight and continued my prayers for a snake-free event. As luck would have it—it clearly was on my side that night—Dick was unable to find many frogs. The few that he spotted escaped, thanks to Dick's unstable gigging skills and correlating bad aim from a swaying boat. Or it could have been because Dick had been swaying himself.

We soon called it a night and went home.

I never could make friends with the swamp. Yet, Dick loved to fish in it, and we spent many hot and miserable afternoons in the jon boat, roasting, and getting eaten up by mosquitos.

As I looked around, wiping the sweat off the tip of my nose in the heat of the August afternoon, I wondered if fishing in the swamp was for beginners. The small aluminum craft, which barely had room for me and

Dick and all our gear, reflected the rays of the sun in a way that made it hard to see without sunglasses. I pushed mine back up my sweaty nose and hoped, at the same time, that my baseball cap would prevent my face from getting too sunburnt.

Looking at the scenery, I saw nothing but straggly trees and shallow water with what seemed an endless number of tree stumps and roots; some visible, some hidden. At times, I could hear the boat hitting them as we drifted through the swampy pond. I wondered how a place so remote could have that many tree stumps; it seemed a hostile place for logging. Other than the trees, stumps, and roots, one also had to worry about weeds, shrubs, and snapping turtles when fishing. And, of course, water moccasins.

"This lure here is one of the best ones for gliding through shallow water like this," Dick said as he affixed a small, rubbery worm lure to the end of the line. "Just be careful where you cast your line." He handed me the fishing rod.

Just be careful where you cast your line, I sarcastically repeated his words in my head. I had never cast a line.

Dick must have seen the worried look on my face.

"Let me show you," he said as he tried to get situated behind me to help demonstrate the proper arm movement needed for casting the rod. I was careful not to release the line while we practiced swinging my arm in a sideways wave.

"You're too stiff," Dick laughed. "Watch me do it."

He moved to the back of the boat, readied his fishing rod, and in one easy movement had flicked his line fifty yards into the swamp. The bait had barely made a splash or sound as it had entered the shallow water. He reeled it back in.

"Just like that," he said.

Sitting at the front of the boat, in the immediate line of his sight, I held out my rod and gave it a good fling. My lure landed on a tree trunk not five yards from the boat. It was stuck.

Dick maneuvered the boat over and set the hook free.

"Try again," he encouraged me while trying to reel in his laughter.

I did, over and over with the same result; if it wasn't a tree stump, it was a tree limb, or a root, or just weeds. I could tell Dick was getting frustrated with the many hook removal disruptions. I was throwing him off his game.

"I think, I'll just watch you," I finally said, laying the rod down inside of the jon boat.

"Sure?" he faked his concern.

"Yup," I replied, "I'm no good at it. I'd rather watch you. You make it look so easy."

"Practice makes perfect," he bragged.

He grabbed another Budweiser from the cooler. Then he cast his fishing rod in one perfect swing, cracked open the beer, and forgot that I was even there.

THE ALCOHOLIC

a.k.a. THE CONTROLLER

In late 1993, three years after my arrival into the U.S., the General Manager of the German company announced that all employees had to take a 10% pay cut. Things were tight, for the company and myself, and I could not afford to make any less than my already puny salary. I had worked there for more than two years, and I figured that the work experience gained in such a small company would count for something. I began searching for other employment opportunities.

In January 1994, I started a new job with a young, progressive company that was into virtual kiosks, using phone and internet lines.

I wasn't familiar with the term "internet" or "world-wide web", nor did I understand the company's visionary product. Such matters were of no concern to me in those days. I had been offered a lot more money and that was all I cared about. Unfortunately, my commute also increased to ninety minutes one-way since the job was in Regent City, North Carolina. I didn't give the distance much thought as the increase in my salary was substantial enough to justify it. I could have never earned the equivalent in South Carolina.

The company was in its infancy stage. Nonetheless, the company's size was considerable with over one hundred employees. I was hired as an Executive Secretary, supporting three Executive Vice Presidents with their presentations, travel arrangements, and other administrative tasks.

I enjoyed going to work every day. Most employees were well under the age of forty and very young at heart and mind. It was a vibrant place, and while I felt out of my league around these intelligent, nerdy brains, they did not seem to notice or care that I was just a secretary. What mattered most to them, was that I was the "Donut Girl", and they liked me for that.

Every Friday morning, I would go to Krispy Kreme near work and buy ten dozen donuts, courtesy of the company. Waiting for them to be boxed up, I would watch the donuts' journey down the conveyor belt, getting their final bath in the sugary icing. The smell in the bakery was amazing.

The scent of freshly baked donuts would quickly breeze through the company, announcing their arrival, and most employees would soon flock to the large break room to enjoy them with coffee. It was the largest social gathering I had experienced since coming to the States, and the first time I could observe and partake in normal conversations. There was no talk about deer, fish, palmetto bugs that liked to sneak rides on clothes, or who got arrested for drunk driving, and who beat the snot out of someone else. It was different from home.

I had told Dick about my work environment and how everyone talked to one another, not just on Friday mornings.

He had just shaken his head in disapproval.

"Office people," he had sneered.

One Friday, while I was returning to my desk after the donut break, I heard my phone ringing as I neared my station. By the time I got there, it had stopped.

I sat down at my desk, looking at the three empty offices in front of me. All my bosses were at a conference, and so I had enjoyed a longer than usual morning break, eating several donuts and chatting with some colleagues.

A presentation was due by Monday, and I tried to focus on the task at hand.

The phone rang again. It was Beth, the receptionist.

"Glad you're there. This guy seemed annoyed you didn't answer the last time, and he said to page you if you didn't answer this time," she said. "I'll hang up and you've got him, whoever it is."

"Thanks," I responded, feeling bad she had to go through trouble for me. I knew how busy the phone lines were, I had sat in for Beth during some of her lunch breaks. The volume of calls during lunch seemed excessive, and I couldn't imagine what she dealt with during normal business hours.

"Hello, this is Petra," I said into the mouthpiece.

"Where were you?"

It was Dick.

"I was here," I responded.

"No, you weren't, I just called."

"Well, I was on my way back from my break. You know we have donuts on Fridays."

"I don't understand why you can't eat them at your desk."

"Since I pick them up and take them to the break room, it's easier to eat one while I'm there."

"Who'd you talk to?"

"Nobody."

"Don't lie to me. I know you were talking to somebody."

"Why does it matter?"

His voice went up, "Of course, it matters. Did you talk to another guy? Tell me. Why would you not be at your desk, otherwise? That's it, you talked to another guy. I knew it."

"No, of course, not."

It wasn't the truth, but I did not want to upset him further.

"Then who did you talk to? If you don't want to tell me, you must be hiding something."

"No, of course not," I quickly repeated. "I was talking to Paige. Remember me telling you about Paige? She's the black woman from Accounting."

"I don't want you talking to her either," he scoffed.

"Honey, I've got to talk to somebody some of the time. It's a big company, and people come to my desk all day long."

"Then that's where you should be. At your desk. So why aren't you at your desk when I call? The only reason for you not to answer your phone is because you are off somewhere else, meandering around, and flirting with other guys. I trusted you. You should not be talking to other guys. It's not right. People always talk about other people having affairs, especially when it's a man and a woman in an office."

"There's nothing going on here with any guy," I tried to assure him.

"Well, I don't want you away from your desk. You need to answer when I call."

"I will try to be here next time, when you call."

"I mean it, stay at your desk and answer your phone."

"I will do better," I promised. I could not find a way to explain to him that I could not be at my desk all the time. But I vowed to myself to limit any excursions in the future to prevent Dick from getting upset with me. I wondered what I had done to cause his distrust.

My ninety-minute commute home gave me plenty of time to contemplate the root of Dick's behavior. He had called me on previous occasions, but his calls had been infrequent and mostly to ask a question about one of our bills. Since he worked the graveyard shift, I did not see him much. When I got up in the mornings, he was still at work. Due to my long commute, I had to leave the house before his shift ended, and when I got home from work, we would only have a few hours together before Dick had to go to work.

I could only imagine that he just did not know how an office worked, since I had no experience with a production environment in turn. He was an operator at a textile plant, and he would refer to himself as a blue-collar worker. He was always complaining about his bosses, who wore white collars. It sounded funny to have a blue-collar or white-collar job. I hadn't known jobs were defined by color (or collar).

Maybe he was feeling insecure. My time away from home, my new "work friends"; he was not part of it. Before I had found work, I used to be home during the day when he was there. *He must miss me terribly.* I remembered how uncomfortable I had felt about his work friends in Germany, and how I didn't like him hanging out with them. It must be the same thing.

I felt bad for Dick. He never talked nicely about his work or his colleagues. He was always tired. And now, I wasn't there to comfort him when he got off work. I had chosen this far-away job, and he had tried to talk me out of it. My commute took three hours each day. Considering that nine hours were spent at work, three additional hours seemed unnecessary to Dick.

"It's good money," I had argued.

"Not more than I'm making," he had rebutted. "You can find a job around here. And then you can be home more."

"I could never make that much money around here. We bought this new trailer, new furniture, and we have new cars, thanks to both of us earning good money."

"We can get by with less," he had said.

"Can we? You're already working double shifts every chance you get. I will not go flip burgers for minimum wage. Or work at the grocery store as a cashier, just to see us struggle even more with our bills. I can't help that all the high-paying companies are in or near Regent City. There is nothing around here; no companies, other than textile mills or chicken processing plants. They don't want someone like me."

"But, it's so far away," he had argued. "There's wear and tear on the car, and Regent City isn't safe. Small towns are safer, and people are much nicer."

He had been correct, there seemed to be a lot more crime in the big cities. I had seen it on the news and heard others talk. However, I hadn't been able to find a person who had ever driven further than thirty miles from their home, and who could confirm this through live accounts.

"I'll go straight there and then straight home," I had said. "I won't stop anywhere for anything, and I will keep my doors locked. Gas is much cheaper around here anyway, so there's no need for me to stop on the way."

And so, he had given in and agreed to let me start my new job in Regent City.

One year later, during the night, the phone rang.

Before it got to its second ring, I had the receiver in my hand and up to my ear.

"Hello?" I was now wide awake.

"Just wanted to make sure everything's okay," Dick said on the other end.

I could hear machine noises in the background.

"Everything is good," I replied.

I realized, I had fallen asleep before midnight this time, which was when the TV stations signed off playing the National Anthem. I was staring at a black and white speckled screen with static noise coming from its speakers.

I had just recently started to sleep on the couch in the living room. I did not like the quiet, the dark, or being home alone after Dick had left for work. A bonus to sleeping in the living room was the proximity to the only phone in the house. I had conveniently placed it on the floor next to the couch, near my head.

Dick did not like it if I didn't pick up immediately. He was always concerned with my safety. And since we didn't see each other a lot during the work week, Dick wanted to make sure that we stayed connected somehow. The phone was the easiest way to accomplish this. He knew that things were good when we talked on the phone. He needed to hear my voice so that he could stop worrying.

"Okay," he said. "I'll call you again in a little bit."

THE ALCOHOLIC

a.k.a. THE RACIST

B y early 1995, at age twenty-three, I had become accustomed to my American life and my daily routine. I would rise early in the mornings and head to work. I loved my long commute, and I would crank up my hyped-up stereo system on full blast; two ten-inch subwoofers with amplifiers supplying a beat that one could hear from miles away. I would sing along to the latest hits at the top of my lungs. It was a time and place where I felt free from any worry.

At work, I would try to anticipate Dick's phone calls: his first one would typically come around the time when I arrived; to make sure I had made it. There would be more during the day, but I would usually get a break for several hours while Dick slept. If I did not make it home within a ten-minute window, he would question why I was late. Then, I would prepare our dinner, we ate, and watched some TV, before Dick headed out to work.

I would do some household chores when I felt like it. Our house was a mess most of the time; clothes, magazines, shoes, and miscellaneous items spread carelessly throughout the trailer. At night, the TV helped lull me to sleep eventually, only to be interrupted by Dick's multiple phone calls, confirming that I was at home.

During the weekends, we would do either one or multiple of the following: hunt, fish, visit a friend, or go to Walmart. We never went to a restaurant, a movie, or to social functions, other than family reunions. Three out of the four weekend activities involved drinking, and our refrigerator was always stocked full of beer, with an extra case waiting in the wings for refilling purposes.

Occasionally, I did not have to go hunting or fishing with Dick. Sometimes, he would find a friend or two, and they would stay out for hours, only to return drunk with the kill of the day. During those times, I would worry about Dick's drinking because he was also driving. But driving wasn't my only concern.

Dick could have a temper, one that could not be easily contained once he started drinking. There was no "off" button; he kept on and on as if he was a supernatural being. He did not easily pass out, and he seemed very much in control of his mind and surroundings. When he did pass out, he sometimes stopped breathing for what seemed like lengthy periods. I would spend many nights sitting next to him in bed, ensuring that he kept breathing. If he stopped, I would nudge him until he took another breath, and then he would curse me for interrupting his sleep.

It was amazing that he never once threw up after drinking himself into a stupor.

This was normal life for me. And I assumed that it was a normal life for everyone who lived in America.

Beer was a secondary activity for the men with anything that they were doing. Women, however, had their place in the kitchen, supporting their men by providing meals, washing their clothes, and doing all the other household chores. And sex, whenever the men wanted it. Women accepted their fate; it had always been like that from generation to generation.

"Dan beats his wife when she's being stupid," Dick would explain to me when I asked why Dan's wife had bruises all over her arm. "She was looking at another guy, and Dan had to put her back in her place."

I saw it everywhere. I felt lucky that Dick did not hit me. I was only slightly familiar with the concept of physical punishment. My parents, on rare occasions, had used a wooden spoon on my behind when I had done something bad, like lying. I knew that I had deserved it when it happened. I assumed that nobody just punished others for the mere pleasure of it.

I had seen some of Dick's relatives use a belt or their hands on their children. Hitting someone when they misbehaved was an acceptable consequence. Surely, they must have done something wrong to warrant such a reaction.

Dick had never raised a hand against me, and I would do anything to ensure it stayed that way. Even when he turned into a paranoid, belligerent, calculating über-drunk, he would direct his physical anger at others, or punch his fist through a wall near my face, or throw some plates past my head.

"You up?" Dick barged into the living room, where I was sleeping on the couch.

It was in the early morning hours of Saturday. Dick had gone to work Friday night, and he wasn't due back home until about seven.

"What are you doing back home?" I sat up from the couch, rubbing my sleepy eyes. It seemed like I had just fallen asleep.

"Don't you want me home? Were you expecting someone else?"

He wasn't kidding.

"Of course not," I quickly replied. "You know I would never cheat on you." I tried to divert, "Is everything okay?"

"Peachy babes," he slurred. "Machine broke at work, and they sent us home. So, Dan and I went to Jack's."

Jack's was a country bar seven miles down the road. We sometimes stopped there to pick up beer on Saturdays, as there were no beer sales on Sundays in the county. A Sunday without beer was considered a tragedy, especially since such an event was completely preventable.

Jack's was the epitome of a run-down dive bar; the fading white color on the building underneath the dirt gave an appropriate backdrop to the spray-painted offensive words and symbols in multiple colors. A Confederate Flag hung from a low flagpole on the side of the building, partially covering a black swastika. The KKK supposedly held a rally in Localyokel every year, so it wasn't an uncommon sight for the area. Two large dirt-streaked windows offered a view inside. Jack's was occupied by a long bar counter, mismatched tables and chairs, and two pool tables. The lighting was low, the floor sticky, and the place stank of stale cigarettes and spilled beer. I had only been allowed to go in it once. "It's no place for a woman," Dick had stated.

"What time is it?" I tried to make out the numbers on the clock on the wall.

"S'is early yet, babe, only 2 A.M.," Dick announced, "we got some driving to do."

I was confused, "Driving?"

"Damn straight, get some clothes on, you're driving. I'm gonna keep drinking, and we have to find some people."

"Why don't we just stay here? You can drink here, and we'll put in a movie to watch. We could watch *Bloodsport* again. You love that movie," I tried.

Dick had moved to the refrigerator. He opened the door to look inside.

"Damn it. Fuck, only two Budweiser left."

I hadn't moved from the couch.

"What the fuck is wrong with you? Are you deaf? Go get your clothes," Dick bellowed, and then he explained, "We don't have time to waste. I need more beer. Get dressed while I get the rifles and shotgun."

I scurried to the bedroom to pick up some clothes from the floor. As I got dressed, I watched in horror as Dick got our two hunting rifles from the closet alongside his 12-gauge shotgun. He put them on the bed and continued rummaging in the closet until he found the shoebox with his handgun. All weapons were fully loaded, but he grabbed some additional ammunition.

"Just in case. Help me get them in the car."

"What do we need all these guns for?" I asked, dismayed.

"You never know what you'll run into at night. Or who. Those black sons of bitches don't like us white folk. Gotta be prepared."

I knew there was no stopping him. Dick was determined, drunk, and on edge. My heart was pounding out of my chest, and I clenched my ice-cold hands into fists, trying to keep them from shaking out of control. My mind was blank, yet my thoughts were going a million miles an hour, searching for something sensible to say to stop this nightmare.

On the way out, I grabbed my wallet with my driver's license before locking up the house.

Dick's Buick was parked by the steps leading up to our front door. It was an old model, the year unknown to me, but it had a foot-operated dimmer switch for engaging the car's bright lights, which I had never seen in any of the cars I rode in my entire life. I did not like the car, it was huge and heavy, but Dick had recently purchased it from his father, and it had sentimental value to him.

Pushing the driver's seat forward, we placed the rifles and shotgun on the floorboard in the back. Dick moved over to the passenger side, got in, and placed the handgun in the glove compartment.

I cranked the engine and awaited my orders. My body was shaking, and I had broken out in a cold sweat. I had no idea what Dick had planned, and I knew that I had no control over him, myself, or the events about to unfold right in front of my tired eyes. *God, please help me*, I repeated over and over in my mind, as I placed my hands on the steering wheel to keep them steady. I knew that we would be in huge trouble if the police stopped us. I needed to calm down so that I could drive without getting noticed. Our chances were good considering the remoteness of the area.

"Drive me to Jack's, I need a refill," Dick said.

Once there, Dick commanded, "Stay in the car. I'll be right back."

I watched him go inside and then observed him through the two windows as he approached the bar.

Two men in hunting overalls, seated on barstools, immediately started a conversation with Dick, who had just opened a can of Budweiser. It appeared that they knew each other. Dick said something to the scruffy, but large bartender, who nodded. I noticed that the bartender, who had just placed a twelve-pack on the counter, returned it to the cooler. Dick and the two hunters proceeded to the pool tables, laughing while sipping from their cans.

Good, this is going to take some time, I realized. Maybe Dick's attention would be diverted from his original plans. I sighed in relief and made myself as comfortable as I could in the car. I turned off the engine and killed the headlights. It was going to be a long night either way. We had been on similar excursions before.

An hour later, Dick returned to the car with the twelve-pack under his arm. The look on his face told me that he had not won the multiple pool games and that he was not happy. I had lost count how many beers he had had while inside. It was a lot, and the smell drifting my way as he opened the car door only confirmed it. Of course, confirmation had not been needed after I had observed him stagger out of the bar, barely standing upright.

In the low dome light, I could see his glassy, heavy eyes, before he placed the twelve-pack on the floor and took his seat. I hoped he was too tired to continue.

"Fuck, fuck, fuck," he screamed, beating the dashboard.

"What is it?"

"Nothing, other than I just got cheated out of a hundred bucks," he slurred. "I swear they were moving balls around while I wasn't looking. Two against one. If it was just one, I'd have started a fight. Did you watch them, did you see them cheat me?"

I shook my head, "No, I didn't see anything. Ready to go home?"

"Home? Nah, drive," he answered.

"Where to?"

"Just drive. But stay on the back roads." He tore into the twelve-pack, grabbed a can, and popped it open.

Staying on back roads wasn't difficult. They all seemed like back roads around where we lived; only the road leading in and out of town could be considered a main road.

Some of the roads weren't even paved. They weren't gravel though, they were sandy and dusty.

I tried finding the foot switch for the bright lights. I had a hard time with it, but eventually managed to hit it. The bright lights barely made a difference. The night sky was without stars, the moon only showed a tiny sliver, and with trees on both sides, I tried keeping the heavy beast on the road in the darkness.

Neither Dick nor I spoke. The only sounds were made by the car's engine or the empty beer cans as Dick threw them on the floor. After each "clunk" to the floor, I would hear a "click" with each full can.

"Go to Coontown," Dick suddenly said as if he had remembered his original plans.

"Dick…"

"We're going on a real coon hunt."

Horror gripped me. *Please, God, no*, I prayed. My mind raced with many thoughts, but none I knew would convince him to stop where we were heading.

"Gonna shoot me a nigger," Dick opened another Budweiser. By now, several empty cans were piling up around his feet. He rolled down the window and threw the empties out. He took long gulps from the fresh can.

I did not understand his hatred for blacks. I knew Dick worked with them at the textile mill, and he would often remind me that it was not by choice. He was forced to have to interact with them there, to have to breathe the same air as *them*. All of Dick's friends were white, and they all were prejudiced to any skin color other than white.

The only black guy Dick seemed to half-way tolerate, was Deon, who had installed the stereo systems into our new cars. It was a "friendship of convenience", as Dick had put it.

Dick turned his upper body to his left, toward the backseat, and I figured that he was going to grab the shotgun. A shotgun, in most short to mid-range encounters, would offer the best assurance for success.

I hit a hole in the dirt road. They were hard to see in the yellow soil.

"Fucking watch where you're going, are you retarded, or what?" He loved to say retarded when he was drunk. He chuckled, "Fucking RETARDS, them niggers."

He leaned back in his seat, looking ahead. He had forgotten about the weapons for now, and I was thankful. He seemed lost in his thoughts.

I took any sandy road that I knew would keep us as far away from civilization as possible. I had sensed that Dick was winding down, not because he wanted to, but because his body was about to give out. I knew that if I kept driving, with some luck, the monotony of it, the slight swaying of the car, and the silence could put him to sleep.

A few minutes later, I could hear slow, consistent breaths coming from the passenger seat. I didn't dare to look over. I kept driving, my eyes fixed ahead, my heart sputtering a million prayers into the night, until I pulled the car into our driveway.

"Honey, we're home," I whispered into his ear, lightly shaking his shoulder.

He slowly opened his eyes, "Hmphh, home?"

"Yes, just like you asked me to," I assured him. "Let me help you out of the car."

"Don't need no fucking help," he mumbled and then grinned, a piece of spittle stuck to the corner of his mouth. "We'll get 'em next time," he slurred, opened the car door, and stumbled toward the trailer with a beer in his hand.

By the time he reached the bedroom, the can was empty.

He fell onto the bed, belched, and passed out.

I went back into the living room. My body and mind had been on edge for hours, and exhaustion was setting in. I lay down on the couch, reliving the night, and wondered how many different endings it could have had.

If he stops breathing now, he's on his own.

THE ALCOHOLIC

a.k.a. THE DESTROYER

"If you are going to shoot yourself, please get out of my car first," I said.

It was in the late spring of 1995, when I was twenty-three, and I had packed up some of my belongings, mostly clothes, into my car. Sitting behind the wheel, parked outside of the trailer's front door, I had been ready to leave, when Dick had entered the car and sat down next to me.

He was crying and held his Magnum revolver in his right hand.

"Please don't leave me, babe," he pleaded.

But I was ready. I had waited too long for this moment, had become stuck in the routine, scared of the uncertainty of the consequences this step would bring. I could wait no longer.

I couldn't tell for sure when the curtain had lifted. Maybe it was when I realized that I hoped for Dick to die in a car wreck on his drive to or from work, or for him to accidentally shoot himself while hunting, tripping over a tree root, or breaking his neck falling off his tree stand.

Dick had become increasingly unstable in the past months. I knew that he was taking uppers to manage through work. He was exhausted all the time and angry with the world.

With my hands wrapped tightly around the steering wheel, I wondered what would come next. It had taken me years to get this far, and the moment felt surreal. I let myself get lost remembering some of the moments that had finally led me here:

Friends and colleagues at work had started to notice that I had become more introverted than usual. I had lost weight and my face looked haggard. I rarely spoke or mingled. I remained at my desk, waiting for Dick's calls. There were only three reasons for me to leave my desk: to go to the front desk to have copies made, to go to the bathroom, or to leave for home at the end of the day. My co-workers tried to reach out to me.

"Petra, we are going out for drinks after work," Beth said one day while I was waiting on some copies. Beth was the receptionist and front desk clerk at my company.

"Who's going?" I asked, feigning interest, knowing that I could not go. Dick would not allow it.

"Robert, Rick, Paula, Veronica, and, of course, me."

"Not sure that I can," I said.

"Sure, you can," Beth encouraged. "It's just for one drink, it won't take long. It will do you some good to get out." She smiled and placed her hands on her protruding belly. At five feet tall, Beth was a good bit shorter than me, but her personality made up for it. She would often joke that she would get as wide as she was tall during her pregnancy. She was one of those people who instantly became your friend. She always seemed happy and at peace with herself and her surroundings. She was a great front desk person. Everyone loved her.

"What does your husband say about you going out with other people, especially since there will be other men?"

She looked at me with a confused expression.

"What do you mean?"

"Your husband doesn't mind you going out drinking with other people?" I asked, avoiding the reference to *men* this time.

She laughed, "Heck no, why would he? It's normal to go out with your friends after work. My husband doesn't need to be there, nor would he want to be there. He knows little about my work, and he doesn't care as long as I'm happy. Plus, it's not like we are going to get shit-faced and have an orgy."

Beth blushed and then giggled. She typically did not use such brazen language.

"And he's not jealous?"

Beth gave me another weird look.

"Jealous? Not at all. I'd never be with someone who's jealous. I mean, why get married in the first place if you can't trust your spouse? That's just non-sense," she laughed again.

It was a lot for me to process. I had never thought of trust and jealousy as being related.

"So, are you with us?" Beth asked.

"I can't," I said. "You know, I barely get to see Dick with my long commute and his night schedule. It would be too late by the time I got home."

The phone lines started ringing, and I was glad that Beth had to direct her attention away from me.

"Maybe next time?" she asked, handed me the copies, and then picked-up the phone.

It wasn't the only time I had been invited to social events by my colleagues. Seeing that they could spend time away from their spouses without jealous rants, time justifications, or repeated phone calls, I started to realize that my marriage was not normal.

The inner uneasiness that kept creeping in when I dared to compare my co-workers' relationships with my own had been a sign of a failing marriage. My attempts to fix my marriage had solely been focused on Dick's alcohol abuse.

Several times throughout our marriage, I had threatened to leave him if he didn't stop drinking. At times, this threat worked for a few months. But eventually, he couldn't help himself and reverted to the familiar - to drinking. Lately, he started to say that he would kill himself if I threatened to leave him again.

In March of 1995, Dick agreed to go to a rehab facility after a drunken night and threats of suicide. While at the facility, we met with a counselor.

He asked, "How do you feel, Petra?"

I had to take a moment. I hadn't thought of words for my feelings before.

"I can't trust you," I finally said, looking at Dick. "You say you love me, but you love alcohol more than me. How can you promise to stop drinking and then break that promise over and over?"

"I'm sorry," Dick said, his eyes avoiding mine.

"I can't believe anything you say."

"I love you," he said. "I really do."

"But you love drinking more. How can you choose drinking over me?"

"I don't," he answered.

"You have, you do, and you always will," I spat.

"I'm hurting inside… so bad," he said out of the blue. He was crying. "The pain is killing me."

I was angry. This had been about *my* pain. It was the first time someone had asked me about *my* feelings. This was also the first time I could verbalize my anger in front of Dick without having to fear his reaction. *How dare him turn this back on himself.* I had no sympathy.

The counselor chimed in, "Dick, I believe we should address this in our next session. This was quite a break-through. I think we should stop for now. You need to rest."

Dick looked miserably small in his chair. He nodded tiredly.

The counselor motioned me to follow him outside into the hallway.

"Petra, I know this was hard. Life has not been easy for you. But Dick has a problem that he has no control over. He has emotional scars that need to be addressed before he can start to heal himself. It is important for you to realize that Dick has got to want to make a change. He must admit that he has no control. I'm not sure that he is there yet. He may still hit his lowest low before he will want to change."

"I don't think he will ever change," I said.

"He may not." The counselor nodded his head. "I want to give you a book about codependence. It will explain your feelings and your behavior. You have to make peace with yourself and the situation. You cannot help others if you don't first take care of yourself. You must admit that you are powerless in the way that you cannot control him. You are in control of your own behavior and your responses to his. While Dick is dependent, you are co-dependent."

It made me uncomfortable to be referred to as controlling. I never had the feeling of any control when I was with Dick. The codependent part sounded right, even though it was the first time I had heard of the term.

The counselor went back into his office and returned with a book which he handed to me.

Codependent No More[20] was the title.

"Please, read it," he said. "And go home and rest. Dick will be fine, here with us. I'm not sure what the future will bring for both of you, but I can see that you are a strong woman. Trust in yourself."

He gave me an assuring smile.

It felt good, hearing his words. He had seen something in me that I had lost; or maybe not discovered yet. He seemed to think that I could be my own person. I held on tightly to the book. Without Dick's presence at home, I could read it without any distractions. There had to be something there that would help me understand the mess that I was in. The counselor seemed sure of it, and I trusted his sense of confidence in me.

I went home, tired and exhausted, but instead of sleeping, I started to read the book. I learned about the lives of people in similar situations. I read about the suffering of others, who had lost loved ones, who were beaten, and who seemed stuck in worse circumstances than me. I loved how the book did not judge. The examples were listed matter of fact. I started to recognize that I had been supporting Dick with my behavior. I had been trying to control Dick's life as much as he had been trying to control mine. My control issues had not been as obvious, as they had been about denial, damage-control, and self-preservation. It became clear that until I relinquished control of what was uncontrollable, I would remain stuck. It was then that I started to form the first thoughts of leaving Dick. With this vision and hope, I fell asleep.

The ringing phone jolted me awake. It was Dick.

"Come get me," he said. "I'm ready to come home."

"But, don't you think it's too early? You have only been there two days. The counselor said that it would be best for you to stay at least one week."

"We can't afford it. Besides, I promise, I'm better. I feel good, recharged. I have taken a huge step toward recovery. I understand that I have a drinking problem. We'll keep the house free of alcohol. I won't drink anymore. I can do it with your help. We don't need fancy counseling. You and I, together, that's all we need. Please?"

We really couldn't afford his treatment. We were barely scraping by as it was.

I picked him up and took him home. Everything I had just read in the book was put on hold for the sake of my marriage.

It didn't last. Dick kept on drinking. He started taking uppers so that he could stay awake longer. I assumed it was to make sure that I didn't leave him while he was asleep. The pills and alcohol were a bad combination. He seemed delirious at times.

He could feel me slipping out of his claws, and he did not know how to cope, or how to make me stay and love him.

Suicide became his favorite argument.

It was the very same argument he tried to jam into my face back in my car—in the shape of that Magnum—which jolted me back to reality. He kept waving his gun in front of my face.

"Please don't leave me, babe," he said again. "I'm going to shoot myself if you leave me."

"I don't care anymore," I said determined, surprised at the strength behind my voice. "If you must shoot yourself, then do it outside of my car. I don't want my car to get all bloody." Internally I was shaking with fear. This was it; I knew that this precise moment would be the end of our marriage, no matter what he was about to decide to do next. I was so tired of it all.

The risk that he could shoot me did not phase me that instant. I must have known that it was an available option to him. Me, leaving while he was home, surely increased my chances of getting hurt. I felt some danger, but it was more looming than immediate. Maybe it was because he had never physically hurt me before. He had only raised his voice to me, never his hand. I trusted that he would not change his mind today. Yet deep down, I was sure that time was running out on my survival options if I continued to stay. If I didn't leave now, there would not be another chance. I was determined, and he would not stop me this time. My suffering had to end; one way or the other.

We stared at each other. Dick looked down and sighed, his shoulders visibly dropping. We were both exhausted from arguing and worrying.

To my surprise, he exited the car without another word, closing the door behind him.

I wasted no time, cranked the engine, and headed down the driveway. Looking in the rearview mirror, I saw Dick get into his truck. I knew he would follow me; he would try to stop me. I sped up, literally racing the ten miles into town, and once there, stopped at the police station. Inside, an officer asked how he could help.

"My husband is chasing after me in his truck. I don't feel safe," I managed to say. My hands and voice were shaking. I was asked for a description of the truck and Dick, and the officer assured me that I could stay until I felt safe to leave. About an hour later, I was back on the road to freedom.

I had made plans to stay with a colleague in Regent City, North Carolina, until I could figure out my next steps. She had recently separated from her husband and was renting an apartment. It was only a two-bedroom apartment, and since her two children lived with her, I would have to sleep on the couch. It was enough for a new start. We weren't even the best of friends, but I was thankful that she was willing to share the little she had without an expectation of payment.

Within days of leaving Localyokel, I hired a divorce attorney, who filed the divorce on the grounds of habitual drunkenness, which meant that the courts could grant the divorce in as quickly as three months.

While my parents must have hoped for my return, I knew that I wanted to stay. America was my home, and even though it hadn't been the happiest place for me so far, I knew that I belonged here. Plus, I was too proud and stubborn to admit to my parents that I had made a mistake. I would prove to them that I could make it on my own; I was not a failure.

In July, Dick and I met at my lawyer's office in Localyokel to divide our belongings. Dick brought Erlene, who gave me a warm hug. I could tell that she was sad to lose me as her daughter-in-law. The meeting was amicable. Dick sat quietly and agreed to the split as per my proposal.

We did not have many belongings, and fortunately, we had always had separate bank accounts. Dick had lost his job in the meantime, and I took over the trailer payments since I had a steady income. I had always loved the eighty-foot-long, single-wide home. It was quite luxurious: it had a jetted tub and a fireplace.

We each kept our financed cars, and all that remained were clothes, household items, and guns. It was clear that Dick would keep the guns; I had no interest in them. All household items would remain with the trailer. I would be responsible for paying to have it moved to a new location.

The last time I saw Dick was in court at the final divorce hearing. "I won't fight it," Dick had said previously, and he kept his promise. When the judge asked each of us if there was anything that could be done to save our marriage, we both said, "No."

After the divorce was granted, I headed for the exit when Erlene stopped me.

"Darling, I'm so sorry for everything," she said and hugged me tightly. "I'm gonna miss you terribly. You were my little girl." She was crying. "Honey, let me tell you though, when you get to move your trailer," she continued, trying to cover up her emotions, "be aware that it's a mess."

I looked at her, confused, "What do you mean, a mess?" Dick and I never had kept an organized house, so I was surprised when Erlene made mention of it.

"Dick has raged around in there like a tornado. Everything's all over the place. All your wedding photos are on the floor, clothes, books, you name it. And Dick's put a few bullet holes in it too."

"He did what?"

"He shot at the trailer from the outside… Honey, it's a blessing that it looks like he did not do any major damage to anything on the inside." She gave me another hug. "By the way, the power's been out for a few months, too. It'll be hot and smelly."

She was correct. Early September, I drove to Localyokel to perform a major clean-up operation on the trailer. Thanks to Erlene's warning, I came prepared, the car loaded with large, heavy-duty garbage bags and miscellaneous cleaning supplies. And air fresheners.

The bullet holes weren't hard to miss. I counted nine, ten if I included the window by the front door, which had been partially shattered.

I unlocked the front door and was immediately hit by a rush of humid, hot air. Erlene had been right, there was stuff all over the place. There was not a single path to move about. I climbed over mountains of clothes, papers, magazines, video tapes, and photos. I went to each room and opened the blinds and windows to let light and air in. I surveyed the trail left by the bullets. None of them had hit any appliances, dishes, electric circuits, or water lines; the damage was purely cosmetic.

I went to work, throwing out most of everything in my way. The floor in the living room was sticky: Dick had torn out all our wedding photos from their albums and had doused them with beer before crumbling most of them in his fist. The photos weren't worth saving. I had no problem parting with them; I did not want to take these memories with me.

The worst part was the refrigerator. It had been loaded with deer meat in the freezer and regular items in the fridge. The smell of so many things that hadn't gotten proper cooling in months in the middle of summer was indescribable.

I made over five trips to a dumpster located four miles away, near a High School, and almost filled it up.

Finally, it was done. The trailer was clean, neat, and ready for its move the next day.

I was ready to move on with it and to close this chapter of my life for good.

The young woman stuck in a new marriage and new environment frustrated me throughout this chapter. Why was she so blind, so naïve, so powerless? Even weak. The warning signs had been there, yet I had chosen to ignore all of them in exchange for what? Love? Independence from my parents? A new experience? Anonymity?

In an abusive environment what may be perceived as weakness truly is strength.

It means sacrificing yourself for the benefit of another. It means keeping the faith in something that may be lost forever. It means enduring pain, from within your soul, your heart, and your body. It means staying strong when everything around you crumbles. It means managing the day despite the turmoil and fear. It means survival.

So, what constitutes abuse? For some, the answer seems crystal clear, and I would argue that those people have not knowingly experienced abuse or thought about it deeply.

Abuse is not a line that can be plainly defined, or can it? Is the line physical abuse? It seems that's where I had drawn it.

What about emotional abuse?

Or verbal abuse?

Or is the line, any type of disrespect? Raising your voice to others?

Or bullying?

Or is it taking advantage of someone?

How about manipulation?

There are many forms of abuse, and I speculate, it is experienced by many, unbeknownst to them.

I did not believe that I was in an abusive relationship.

There's a lot of gray between the black and the white. Denial sits in the gray zone, next to acceptance of the routine, next to fear of what will happen if we dare make a change. Uncertainty trumps abuse, most of the time.

I had grown up, trusting in authority and the righteousness of it. I took things at face value, believing the decisions of others. I had followed blindly in good faith.

My parents told me recently that they had been on the verge of driving to the barracks many a times in order to find out the truth about Dick. They knew something was off, they felt the danger their little girl was in, yet they knew there wasn't anything that they could have done to stop it without some major consequences. They did right by me, supporting me, letting me make my mistakes on my own. If they would have tried to stop me from marrying Dick, I would have cut them out of my life.

At that point, all I wanted was to move out. I longed to be a grown-up with all the freedom that came with it. And I did not realize until much later that I had traded my name for my freedom when I got married.

♀

THE ITALIAN STALLION

Working in Regent City in 1994 opened a whole new world to me. The simple act of picking up donuts on Friday mornings allowed me to observe normal interactions between colleagues in the break room. While eating their donuts, they spoke about their lives, their spouses or significant others, and they made plans for going out together after work or hanging out on the weekends.

Friday's treat was paid for by the firm's owner, Mr. Cazzo[21]. He had a large office near the lobby, and he employed his own personal secretary. My three bosses worked directly for him, and their offices were down the hall, about thirty feet from his.

One morning, I had to take documents to the front desk, where the receptionist would make copies for me. The front desk was in the large lobby area, which had a huge glass frontage and roof, and which was quite impressive to look at inside and out. The floor looked to be marble, and most visitors would stop upon entry, not knowing whether to look up at the twenty-foot glass ceiling or the beautifully patterned floor.

As I leaned on the front desk watching Beth, the receptionist, make copies, I heard a roaring engine sound coming from the entryway. The parking lot was located immediately outside of the lobby. I saw a bright orange Lamborghini pass by the front, and shortly thereafter, the engine sound stopped. I knew that this could only be Mr. Cazzo. The car matched his personality to the T: loud, stylish, and very Italian.

"Buongiorno, girls," he called out to us as he walked in.

Mr. Cazzo wore a tailored, dark blue pin-striped business suit with gold cufflinks peeking out from underneath the jacket's sleeves. His large, gold watch was hanging loosely around his wrist, the golden links barely preventing it from falling to the ground. His crisp, white shirt was unbuttoned at the top, showing off a matching gold link-chain necklace. His longer, salt-and-pepper hair was neatly combed backward from his large forehead. His tinted skin color made him look much older than fifty.

"Good morning," Beth and I chimed back.

"It's going to be a quite a day," he said, and as quickly as he had appeared, he was gone again.

We continued hearing his boisterous morning greetings to anyone he saw along the way to his office.

It was a big day for the company, and we could feel the excitement in the air. The company's name change was going to be made public. Press and other dignitaries would show up later for the official announcement.

A few days ago, we had been told to wear jeans for this occasion and that we would be given new T-shirts to change into before the guests would arrive later that afternoon.

The shirts were handed out just prior to lunch. They were white and showed the new company name and logo on the front in maroon colors. I changed in the bathroom and was pleasantly surprised how well mine fit. Typically, shirts, even in a small size, ran big on me.

Returning to my desk from my lunch break, and now in my new T-shirt, I passed Mr. Cazzo's office. The door was open, and I could see him sitting behind a large executive desk, looking out into the hallway.

"Ahhh," he jumped out of his chair when he saw me. "The new shirts are here, I see."

I stopped in the doorway of his office, not wanting to be impolite, and nodded, "Yes, we got them an hour ago."

He moved toward the doorframe on his skinny legs, his aftershave announcing the arrival of his larger upper body before it physically got there.

From three feet away, his eyes wandered up and down my body, resting on my chest a little longer than anywhere else.

"It's a little small up front," he said.

I looked down at my feet, trying to see what he had seen. Not discovering anything unusual, I stared back at him, not understanding.

"Don't you think, *it's* a little small up *front?*"

I wasn't sure why he was enunciating some of the words.

He giggled, paused, then sighed in frustration, seeing that I did not get the joke.

"You can go now," he said as he turned his back to me.

Back at my workstation, a colleague was waiting for me.

"I got the tickets for John, I was in the lobby when the travel agent dropped them off," she said as she handed me an envelope.

"Thanks," I said, lost in thought.

"What's the matter?" she asked. "You have a confused look on your face."

I put the envelope on my desk, "It's nothing. I didn't get the joke that Mr. Cazzo just told me."

"Maybe I can explain, do you want to tell me?" she offered.

"Sure, thanks; sometimes I'm not sure about American humor. I felt kind of stupid, you know?" I said.

She nodded.

"Well, I was passing his office with the new T-shirt on, and he said that it was small up front," I said. "And then, he laughed. I don't know why that's funny."

Her eyebrows shot up. "He said that about you?"

I hadn't thought about his comments being *about me.*

"I don't think it was about me. I think he meant the shirt was small, but I still don't get the joke."

"It's *not* a joke," she breathed out. "What a dog, he'll never learn. Are you sure that is exactly what he said to you?"

"Of course," I assured. *Why would I make it up?* I was still trying to wrap my brain around the insinuation that Mr. Cazzo had talked about my chest size. Admittedly, it had been an odd thing to say to me. Mr. Cazzo had never singled me out for any type of conversation before, other than the occasional greeting he extended to everyone.

"You have to tell Anne."

Anne was the Human Resources Manager. I had only talked to her a few times during the hiring process.

"I don't think that's necessary. It wasn't a big deal," I said.

"It is a big deal. If you won't talk to her, I will."

And with that she took my arm and pulled me with her to the personnel office. Seated across the desk from Anne, I cowered in my chair while my story was repeated by my colleague. Anne listened attentively.

"I would like for *you* to tell me what happened," Anne said quietly, looking at me.

I shook my head.

"You don't have to be afraid. We will not share this with anyone else. You're safe."

The possibility that this event could be shared with others had not even entered my mind. There was nothing to tell. I did not want this attention.

"Go on," Anne insisted.

I repeated what had happened, my voice small, and my bottom shifting uncomfortably on the seat.

After I finished, the Human Resources Manager took a moment before she replied.

"We are not a company that tolerates any type of sexual harassment. No matter if the intention was there or not, certain things are not appropriate to say. We will address this immediately with Mr. Cazzo," she said with a re-assuring look on her face.

"There's no need to talk to him. I'm sure he didn't mean it," I tried to convince her that his words had not harmed me. I didn't think it was a big deal. I had heard worse words spoken to me in the past. Not just in a personal setting, but also during my short-term job assignment in Germany. It wasn't unusual for the male boss to make rude comments to the female staff. It was just the way things were.

"It's no problem," she insisted.

I did not understand why she had to talk to Mr. Cazzo if it wasn't a problem. She was making something out of nothing.

Thirty minutes later, I was called to Mr. Cazzo's office, where I took a seat around a small conference table, alongside the HR Manager and Mr. Cazzo.

Anne began, "Earlier today, it came to my attention that some words were spoken in this office that were not appropriate."

She looked at Mr. Cazzo before turning her face toward me with a serious expression.

I blushed. I did not want to be there.

Mr. Cazzo cleared his throat as soon as Anne finished, "I meant no offense. It wasn't my intention to make her feel uncomfortable."

He then addressed me directly, "I'm truly sorry if I have offended you in any way."

"Okay," was all that I could manage in embarrassment. I avoided making eye contact.

"Petra, I want to thank you for having this brought to both of our attention," the HR Manager smiled at me.

I wished I had kept my mouth shut.

She continued, "As a company, we want to do right by our employees. Do you feel that we need to do anything else to rectify this situation? We both want you to be comfortable working here. If you need to talk more or need other actions to be taken, please let me know?"

The HR Manager tried to hold eye contact with me, but I couldn't give her more than two seconds.

"No," I said, staring a hole into the carpet.

Can I go now? I secretly prayed.

There was no *situation*, and without it, no need to rectify anything.

"Thank you, Petra, you may go back to your desk."

I scooted out of that office as quickly as I could, hoping for my red face to cool down soon. I did not want anyone else approaching me, asking questions.

Later, as Mr. Cazzo gave his speech in the break room to the press, dignitaries, and employees, I made sure to stand in the very back. I did not want him to see me. I wanted to see as little of him as possible. I would never be able to face him again without blushing.

Fortunately, everyone was caught up in the excitement, and nobody noticed me as I made my way back to my desk after the speeches were done. I did not stick around for any social interactions. I had had enough of those for the day.

Mr. Cazzo was like so many male bosses during that time.

This incident had not struck me as offensive. Especially in Germany, male bosses were known to be rude. I had observed such behavior while on my short-term assignment with the temp agency before moving to the States. An executive secretary had taken me under her wings, mainly because she realized that I had no real work experience. I would sit a few desks over from hers, and I would frequently listen to her boss yell at her. Nothing had ever been good enough, fast enough, no matter how hard she worked or how late she stayed. She just stood in front of him and took the yelling, the derogatory insults, and then went back to work. I had felt terrible for her and swore that I would never work for such an asshole.

Mr. Cazzo wasn't quite as abusive, and I felt lucky that I wasn't working for him. My three bosses were nothing like him. They had always treated me with quiet respect and talked to me in a professional way. I had little exposure to Mr. Cazzo on a daily basis and was not familiar with his management style, other than noticing that he had a good-looking secretary.

I had been intimidated by Mr. Cazzo. He had money, a fancy sports car, a huge office with mahogany furniture, designer suits, and above all, confidence and a loud presence that were overwhelming to me. He seemed so important.

In my innocence, I had wanted to ignore that I had drawn his attention. It had taken me a while to realize that in just a few non-offensive words, he had made an insulting statement about the size of my breasts. Would it have been different if he would have said something complimentary using offensive words? I would have felt the same, but in its core, an offensive compliment sure seems nicer than an offensive insult.

I definitely did not want any attention drawn to any of my body parts, no matter how small or large they were. It had made me uncomfortable and self-conscious. I already had enough going on in my personal life, and this incident was most inconvenient.

Life hadn't been about me up until that point. I did not want attention. I wanted to stay in my little world, which I took great measures to protect from everybody's view. I didn't need anyone asking me questions about me, my life, or my feelings.

However, subconsciously, I learned that certain behaviors were not commonly acceptable, and that actions could be taken to punish the offender. Today, I have respect for the HR Manager who addressed this issue right away; especially since it was with the man who signed her paychecks, same as mine.

It also taught me that there was strength in numbers and that the shame was not automatically assigned to the victim, despite the victim feeling as if all the shame was singularly placed upon her.

Just like I had learned that distrust in a marriage was not acceptable by most people; all thanks to the many colleagues who had made an effort to help me see the light.

♀

THE BLACK MYTH

By June of 1995, just two months after I left my husband, I had settled into my new urban life. Living in an apartment, with my friend Susan and her two young children, was a lot different from my former country setting. I did not mind the change of scenery one bit or that the place seemed crammed with four of us in a small two-bedroom apartment. There was no green space, just the multiple apartment buildings with adjacent parking lots. It was noisy and busy; people were always coming or leaving, and we could hear our neighbors move around in their apartments.

For the first time, I felt free. I had a key to the apartment and my own car. I could do whatever, whenever, without anyone asking questions or caring about my whereabouts. Unfortunately, I wasn't able to live out my new freedom to its fullest potential because money was very tight. Time on the other hand, I had plenty, especially since the apartment was located only ten minutes from work.

My financial responsibilities devoured my paycheck, such as making payments on the trailer, which was still in South Carolina. I had also taken over the credit card payments since Dick had lost his job. Dick and I owed a little less than a grand; an accumulation of stupid items bought together on credit, hoping those material things would fix our marriage. One thousand dollars was a large amount to owe, and the high interest rate ensured that repayment would be long and painful.

Susan was great. She did not ask for much money toward rent or food, and I was always welcome to eat or drink anything I could find in the refrigerator. At times, I would watch her children so that she could go out and party. It was a good arrangement for both of us.

When I started to look at rental lots for the trailer, I realized that real estate was much more expensive than down South. It was difficult to find a lot to rent for a trailer near Regent City. After some research, I found a trailer park in Peaches, South Carolina. It was so close to the border of North Carolina that I could have walked across it if I didn't mind sharing the road with the manic drivers on the busy interstate that connected the two territories.

I had to put down a two-month deposit to hold the lot until I could move the trailer. Between that and the lawyer, the credit card debt kept growing. Not to mention that it would cost me an additional grand or two to have the trailer moved, which was money I did not have. Before I could get any utilities hooked up, I had to pay the old bills which Dick had chosen to ignore. He had moved out of the trailer after the electric company cut off the power. I realized that my monthly credit card payments would increase substantially under these circumstances. I would be left with very little money to buy food or other necessities.

Since I had been with my company for less than two years, I doubted that they would increase my pay any time soon. And even if I received an increase, it would not be enough to cover all my expenses and leave room for other items, such as clothes, shoes, insurance, or emergencies. I would also not be able to save up any money for trips to Germany, not to mention make prolonged phone calls to my parents on such a meager budget.

I wasn't going to ask my parents to support me financially anymore. They had paid for a lot in the past: flights, phone bills, a new well pump, to name a few. I figured, my best chance for more money was with a new employer.

After a few weeks of sending out applications, I was offered a job by a Swiss company. They were looking for a German-speaking Executive Secretary for their President and two VPs. The offered salary was a considerable bump from my current pay, and I did not hesitate to put in my two-weeks' notice.

One Friday morning in July, after my last donut-run for the company, I was chatting with Beth about how much I would miss her smiling face when Dickson joined us at the front desk.

Dickson was one of the finest men I had ever laid eyes on in my life. Well over six-feet tall, he stood out from any crowd, but his height wasn't the only thing noticeable. He had soft, brown eyes and a mouth, so luscious and full, it begged to be kissed. All the women at work went goo-goo over Dickson. His voice was smoother than butter, and his complexion was a creamy cappuccino color. Sometimes, Beth could get Dickson to make announcements via the intercom, and when he did, all the women melted away at his velvety, angel voice.

Not only was he good looking, he also seemed super attentive to women's needs. He liked being around the ladies. It was too bad that he was married.

"I hear you're leaving us next week?" he said to me as he leaned on the front desk with his right elbow, turning his fit body toward me.

I forced myself to look up at his eyes, *Damn, that man is just plain gorgeous.*

"Next Friday is my last day," I replied, as nonchalantly as possible. In my mind, we were passionately making out.

His eyes mustered me, then they sparkled.

"That's too bad," he smiled.

It was like his eyes were undressing me, and he liked what he had seen.

"Yes, isn't it?" I smiled back.

Beth wasn't paying us any attention; she was busy with the phones.

"We should give you a good-bye present or something like it," he said.

"What do you have in mind?" I offered. I had no idea where this *new me* was coming from. I wasn't the promiscuous type. But I liked the giddiness of the situation, yet not quite certain that I had interpreted his intentions correctly.

"How about I give you my number, and you can call me later to find out?"

Bingo! I had hit the jackpot. I wondered what my prize would be.

He wrote his mobile number on his business card and handed it to me.

"Now, you call me, you hear?"

I nodded my sexiest nod.

Dickson departed with a smile and a wink, leaving me at the front desk, discombobulated and aroused. But mostly aroused. I had just successfully flirted with a married man, whom I was going to secretly meet at some later point, I was sure of it. I assumed and hoped our meeting to be of sexual nature. After all, what else was there?

It's time for an adventure, I assured myself. Dick and I were officially separated, and we would be divorced in a few months. I deserved some adulterated fun. My conscience was clear. I did not care about Dickson's conscience. That was his concern.

Dickson, however, did not have to worry about his wife answering my phone call later that evening. It was rare to have a mobile phone back then, but Dickson worked in the service department, and the company felt it was important that customers could reach him after hours. I was certain that I wasn't the first woman to use the number to set up an extramarital date.

When I got home that evening, I told Susan. I could not keep this from her. She had a huge crush on Dickson.

"Maaaaaaaan," she drawled. "I'm so jealous, he picked you."

I beamed. It had been a long time since I had felt attractive.

"You're going to have to tell me about his penis, okay?"

I almost spat out the beer I was drinking. It was surprising that I could make friends with this golden liquid after all that I had been through with

Dick. Susan liked to drink beer, and it went with her party attitude. It was infectious, and it hadn't taken long before I enjoyed a nightly brew with dinner. I had become accustomed to the taste. Sometimes, Susan drank too much, but she was always a responsible mom during the times the kids stayed with us. Every other week and weekend, her children would live with their father.

"What would be so special about his penis?" I asked after I had managed to swallow successfully.

"Girl, don't you know about black men?" Susan gave me a knowing look.

"Obviously not," I replied.

"Are you kidding me? Where have you been, girlfriend? Down in Localyokel, South Carolina?"

We both busted out laughing.

"Seems that I have. Seriously, what's the deal with Dickson's penis?"

"Well, you know they say, black men have large ones. I always wanted to find out myself. Especially with Dickson. Have you seen his feet?"

I was dumbfounded.

"What about his feet?"

Susan rolled her eyes.

"Lord, I'm starting to believe you lived on the moon, not in Localyokel. It is also said that men with large feet have large schlongs. You're two for two with Dickson."

I didn't know what to make of her statements. As a small woman, her words frightened me a bit. But, there was no turning back, I was going to find out the truth.

"There's no time like the present," I said as I picked up the phone and dialed Dickson's number.

He picked up immediately, "Hello?"

"It's me," I said.

There was a deep breath on the other line. Then, "I was hoping you would call soon."

"What do you have in mind?" I offered again, using the same words as earlier.

Susan was biting her fingernails as she watched me use my sexy voice.

"I was thinking you could meet me in the parking lot at work at ten tonight?"

"That might be doable. And then?"

"Then," he softened his voice even more, "we can go for a romantic walk behind the building and make ourselves comfortable."

We had a date.

At ten that night, I pulled into the parking lot at work. Dickson's car was all the way at the end of the building, near a path that would lead into a green area behind the office. It had plenty of trees to offer some privacy. With the company located in a business park, we did not have to worry about any traffic or people walking about at night. The green space was large, without any other structures nearby.

When I got out of my car, Dickson took my hand, and we started walking toward the back of the building. We didn't say a word. I couldn't believe this was going to happen. I could still stop it if I wanted to. Which I didn't. Dick had been the only man I had "been with". I was ready to expand my sexual horizon.

Dickson laid down a blanket on the grass. It was a beautiful, warm summer night, with many stars in the sky. The scenery was romantic enough for our purpose.

"I've been wanting to do this for a while," he said, leaned over, and then kissed me.

It was a wet kiss and not at all what I had expected. He used his upper body and continuous kisses to maneuver me into a supine position. It was happening very fast, but I knew that was to be expected, since we both only wanted sex. Granted, I had hoped to be taught a lesson or two, since Dickson always bragged about knowing how to treat a woman right.

I tried to catch my breath between the kisses. *Where did he learn how to kiss?* I was not enjoying this. His mouth was too big for mine; and that's saying a lot. He had no clue how to use his lips or his tongue, and he was just stirring a huge pot of saliva. Fortunately, the kissing soon stopped. I heard a zipper, and Dickson got up.

Disappointed at his kissing skills, I wondered about the other services I had hoped him to provide. I had come with high expectations for this occasion. But so far, Dickson hadn't walked the walk, and he had not done anything in the pleasure department to get me into a more accessible disposition. Everything was happening too fast and not in the seductive manner I had envisioned.

I watched from below as Dickson turned away from me in a sideways angle, then he stepped out of his jeans and his underpants. In the moonlight, I let my eyes wander up his lean body. The calves looked strong, the thighs powerful, the butt was well rounded. The stomach was flat, yet not particularly muscular, there was no hair on his chest, which I liked. He seemed comfortable with his nudity.

I blinked and let my eyes remain shut for a few seconds, processing the last visual and contemplating what I had set in motion. The humid night air settled heavily into my lungs and with it, disappointment, regret, and shame. As I opened my eyes, my body felt uncomfortable in its reclined position on the ground. And I wasn't comfortable anymore with the thought of giving myself to Dickson *that* way. The urge to take charge of the situation arose in a panic as I struggled to my knees. I still had all my clothes on. I wasn't planning on taking them off at this point.

"How about a blow job?" I asked. I knew, from experience, that married guys typically did not get many blow jobs from their wives. It would be a tough offer for Dickson to refuse.

"Sure… if that's what you want," he said, his white teeth showing in the dark.

Once done, he got dressed. We returned to our cars, said good night with a quick kiss, and left.

I couldn't wait to get back to the apartment.

As I burst through the front door, Susan jumped out of her recliner.

"Well?" she asked. "What was it like? What did you do? Where did you go? Was he good?"

I walked over to the fridge and took out two beers.

Susan followed me into the kitchen. I could feel her prancing around behind me impatiently as I searched one of the drawers for a bottle opener. My hands were too sensitive to twist off the bottle caps. I found the bottle opener and popped the caps into the trash.

As I handed Susan her beer, I said, "Well, *they* were wrong. On *all* accounts. It was the easiest blow job of my life. I thought I was sucking on a Dum Dums[22]."

It was the best laugh we had in months.

$\female$

JUST FRIENDS

I started my job at the Swiss company in July of 1995 at the age of twenty-three. My new work environment was good for me on many levels.

I loved the fact that my ex no longer knew where I worked or lived. Internet search engines and social media were still relatively young in their development and not in use by the general public. While Dick had not given me cause to feel endangered during our separation, I sensed it was safer for me having moved completely out of his sight. It was like I had entered the witness protection program.

I had a new job, a new address, and a new me.

The Swiss company offered a dynamic work setting with many young and progressive employees. While I supported two Vice Presidents as needed, my focus was to take care of the second-generation owner and President, Sigfrid.

The typical day was as follows: first thing in the morning, I loaded a document organizer with letters for his signature. The organizer consisted of many thick pages with protruding tabs, which served as separators from one document to the next. The binder was placed on Sigfrid's desk, and it was the first order of business he addressed when he got to the office. Then, I sorted last afternoon's mail into stacks of magazines and advertisements. General correspondence, which had also arrived in the mail, was placed into the document binder by matter of importance (person or content). The age of electronic mail had not yet fully taken over the world, and most business communications were still sent via the postal service.

When Sigfrid arrived, he quickly got settled in his office. He enjoyed his coffee while perusing the document binder. A short while later, the door to his office would close. It was a sure sign that he was about to read some trade-related magazines. It was my job to ensure that he was not disturbed during that time. Which was not difficult since everyone at the company knew about the private bathroom in Sigfrid's office. We were all aware of his morning routine. I felt odd and uncomfortable at my desk, which was immediately to the left of his office door and adjacent to the bathroom wall. I could hear the water running with each flush, and I had a hard time diverting my inner views to other topics. It was a little too personal, but I doubted that Sigfrid had ever given the noise issue any thought.

Later in the afternoons, Sigfrid dictated letters to me, which I would take down in shorthand and then type up on the computer, to be placed into the document organizer for him to sign the next day. "You schmooze it up," Sigfrid would say to me. He trusted me to interpret and translate on paper what he was trying to convey in his broken English.

The three executives were knowledgeable in the industry, and they were respected and liked. I was lucky that I had three bosses who entrusted more tasks to me as time went by. While I had several years of experience under my belt, I was still lacking independence when it came to research and decision-making. Without a controlling husband instructing me what to do and think, I was able to start spreading my wings.

The job was never boring. I was involved in most aspects of the business. Since everyone had a lot of freedom to operate, the mood in the office and on the manufacturing floor was light and entertaining. During breaks, everyone mingled in the break room, conversing about life while making plans for the weekend. There was laughter and comradery. Working there felt like being part of a family.

My trailer had been moved to "Double Oaks Estates" in early September, and I quickly moved out of Susan's apartment and into my own home. I got tickled when I had to state my new address to others. "Estates" sounded uppity, while the actual trailer park was not. The lots were barely big enough for the trailer and the car. There were so many trailers, the park seemed to go on forever. There was no privacy with such proximity to the next sardine can. My blinds remained closed most of the time. I did not want my neighbors looking in on me from their windows or while passing by outside.

Despite the small lot size, there was a tiny bit of grass around the trailer, and I was quickly informed that I was responsible to cut it myself or to pay someone to cut it for me. Seeing that I had no lawnmower, and no desire or knowledge to operate one, I paid my neighbor to keep my yard in compliance. It was another expense I didn't need, but I didn't see the value of me cutting my grass with a pair of scissors either.

In the late summer of 1996, less than a year later, I realized that I could not make it financially. While I made more money than in my previous job, my single income could not cover the debt that Dick and I had accumulated, not to mention the new debt that I had taken on in order to get away from Dick.

"What's wrong?"

I looked up as Iris sat down across from me during our lunch break. Iris worked in the engineering department at my company. She was German and spunky. We had hit it off right away, and we had become close over the last six months. She knew about my past, and she had confided hers to me.

"Oh, nothing," I said.

"Well, it can't be nothing with that look," she insisted.

"I'm broke. I'm always broke, no matter what I do, there's never enough money."

"I know," Iris sighed. Her husband had moved out of their house a while back. It was a three-bedroom house in Lowing, just fifteen miles north of work. "It can be overwhelming."

"I didn't realize how much things cost. The lot, the trailer payment, the old debt, the new debt, insurance…" It was my turn to sigh. "I'm living off toast and water it seems."

We sat in silence. I took a bite from the dry ham sandwich, which I had prepared the night before.

"You know, you could move in with me," Iris said. "I have this huge house. I could rent you a room, and you can pay part of the utilities."

"You're serious?"

"Yes, totally. It would help me out too. It's tough to pay for all my bills with just one income. And it gets lonely at times. I would love to have some company. The great part is that the house is big enough to have privacy when wanted. You would have your bedroom, I have mine, and if we feel like it, we can both hang out in the common areas, like the kitchen or living room."

A week later, I packed up my few belongings and moved in with Iris. I did not worry or care about what would happen to the trailer. I simply stopped paying for it, the lot, and anything else I had left behind. I didn't realize that there was a complicated credit system that would haunt me for years to come after making this very unwise financial decision.

Iris turned out to be a great friend and mentor. She was ten years older than me, and we talked a lot about everything; nothing was off-limits. Iris was interested in people, new thoughts, places, adventures; anything to stimulate her brain. She was very easy-going in her everyday approach to life. I admired her.

Next to Iris, I had another close friend who I could turn to for companionship and advice. His name was Ryker, and we had met at the virtual kiosk company, where he was still employed.

Ryker was around 5'8" with red hair and brown eyes. He had a trim body, yet he acted like he was unaware of his good looks. I had noticed him early on at work and thought of him as cute. Back then, it had been dangerous for me to look at another man, and I had tried to stay at my desk, just like Dick had demanded.

However, throughout my time there, it had been impossible to ignore each other completely. Eventually, we had struck up several conversations about cars. He drove an older rally car and seemed in love with it, despite it needing a lot of work. I had always felt at ease when around Ryker. His quiet mannerism and reassuring smile often brightened my day. Sometimes, we would go to lunch together, and our coworkers took notice and commented that we would make a cute couple. I felt guilty about going to lunch with Ryker. It was a clear violation of Dick's rules. And deep down I knew that Dick had been right about the danger of men and women "hanging out together" at work. But I wasn't going to tell him.

After I left my husband and the job, Ryker and I had stayed in touch. I couldn't deny that we had a connection, and I did not want to lose him as my friend. He knew about my marriage and my struggles. He always offered advice, support, and a shoulder to cry on.

Ryker would occasionally come to my new job to take me to lunch. It became easier and more frequent once he accepted a position with a company located in the same business park as mine.

We saw each other infrequently otherwise, but it was not for lack of trying on Ryker's part. I felt it wasn't fair that he was paying for everything all the time, so I often declined. At times though, he succeeded, and I ended up accompanying him to his friends' parties. I knew that there would not be an expense that Ryker would have to incur at those events.

New Year's Eve 1995 was such an occasion. We had just arrived, and the party was going in full swing, when he scooped up a silly party hat from the table and placed it atop my head.

"There," he said. "Now that's appropriate attire."

We laughed. We sat down on a couch. I wasn't much for dancing and felt more comfortable observing the crowd from a distance.

Ryker placed his arm around me, and I put my head on his shoulder. It felt safe.

"Hey, do you want to come with me to my company's Christmas party?" I asked and sat up to face him.

"Christmas party?" he chuckled. "Isn't it a bit late for a Christmas party?"

"They always have it after the New Year, because it gets so busy around the Holidays," I responded.

"When is it?"

"It's in three weeks. And it's evening dress required, speaking of appropriate attire," I smiled.

"But I don't want to wear a dress," he joked.

I snorted, "You know what I mean."

"I'd love to," he said.

Three weeks later, he picked me up at the trailer. He looked good in his suit, his tie matching the dark green dress I wore. *So that's why he asked about the color of my dress*, I thought.

"We clean up nice," I said after we hugged.

"You definitely do," he replied with a broad smile.

The evening was lovely. The Swiss sure knew how to throw an elegant, yet fun party. The three-course meal was excellent, and a DJ had started to play music. There was a huge dance floor, and before long, it seemed that everyone was dancing. Including me and Ryker.

We stayed until the very end, comfortable with us and our surroundings. I smiled and laughed a lot. I felt young and alive.

When we got back to the trailer, we sat in the driveway for a long time, talking and laughing.

I was about to say good-bye when Ryker leaned over and tried to kiss me.

I pulled back. I had not expected it. *Or had I?*

"What's wrong?" he asked.

"I don't know. I can't. I'm sorry."

"You have nothing to be sorry for."

I could hear the sadness in his voice.

"I like you a lot," he said.

"I know..." I paused. "I... I, err, I like you too... but it's..."

"I shouldn't have," he said. "It's too early, I shouldn't have pushed you. I made you feel uncomfortable. I'm sorry."

He had ruined the evening. Things had been so nice.

Why did he have to ruin it?

I asked, "Can we be just friends?"

I cannot say for certain if I simply rejected him because I was scared, or if I had known, just like with *the boy next door*, that I did not love him?

Ryker meant a lot to me. He had been the guy who had treated me the best throughout the time I was married to Dick and for some time after my divorce. I don't think I ever heard him raise his voice to others. He was sensitive while being sure of himself. I could not deny my attraction to him.

Early on, I realized that he wanted more than friendship. I ignored it, afraid to address the elephant in the room. I was worried about losing him as my friend. I tried to keep him at a safe distance.

Even so, I knew that he would attempt more at some point. I dreaded the day it would happen, as it would change everything about our relationship.

I had given "us" serious consideration. Our time spent together was natural, we were comfortable with each other. I felt safe. But I believed a relationship needed deeper feelings to develop into something more intimate. As hard as I dug for those feelings, they did not exist.

Also, because I held out hope for love for another.

♀

THE SUGAR DADDY

I held out hope for love from the man who had entertained me with excitement, laughter, dinners, excursions, companionship, gifts, and sex.

It had started quite innocently.

As part of my job at the Swiss company, I was tasked with coordinating Sigfrid's and the other two VP's schedules for travel and meetings. When such meetings took place at our facility, I would set up the large conference room with the essentials, such as refreshments, coffee, pens, notepads, etc. At times, I was asked to stay in the room while the executives talked about P&L, M&A, turnover[23]... all empty words to me. I did not mind, even though it was boring. I felt important to be part of it, if it was only to record the minutes of the meeting.

It was during a merger negotiation between a large domestic conglomerate and a British supplier where I met Tadger[24]. My company had offered to facilitate the meeting, and I looked forward to the event. During the preparation phase, Tadger and I had talked on the phone many times to secure the meeting date and to help with lodging accommodations. I had been smitten by his sexy, British accent. He had an easy way of conversing, almost jokingly discussing events, people, and places. We often ended up making small talk after the business matters had been taken care of; neither of us wanting the phone conversations to end. I couldn't wait to put a face to the voice.

The day of the meeting, I wore one of shortest dresses I owned, a sixties-inspired, brown-striped piece that could have been worn by Twiggy[25]. A belt with a golden buckle accentuated my small waist perfectly. I had dug out what I considered to be the sexiest, yet still work-appropriate, black heels. I felt tall, now at 5'5", the heels adding two inches to my height.

When the group arrived, I was waiting for them in the conference room in anticipation.

"Welcome, I'm Petra, please do come in," I said greeting the first person.

"I'm Jim, nice to meet you," replied the man in a dark blue business suit. He was short, about my height including my heels, and not very handsome. I sighed in relief as he said his name in an American accent.

"Jim, nice to meet you too," I said, ready for the next visitor.

He wasn't much taller than Jim. He too, wore a business suit, and its brown, checkered pattern seemed dated with the yellow dress shirt and dark brown tie with golden stripes.

"Well, hello there, dear," he said in a British accent.

My stomach dropped.

"I'm Paul Leads, and I'm the President of Leads Incorporated. It sure is a pleasure to make your acquaintance," he continued. "And this dapper fellow coming up behind me is Tadger, who will be the Managing Director of our new joint-venture… if things go well today."

I quickly shook Paul's hand, smiled politely, and replied, "So good to meet you Paul. There's coffee and tea to the left and some muffins and Danishes to the right."

I couldn't wait to meet Tadger, who was next in line.

Fortunately, Paul moved right along toward the counter where I had placed the refreshments.

"We finally meet. It is about time."

Despite his tall stature at 6'3", our eyes locked the instant he had spoken. I was drawn into them, admiring their solid and deep brown color, which seemed to match mine. My small hand had completely disappeared in his strong manly grip, his touch sensual on my palm.

I looked down at our hands, wanting to make sure that this was happening. *Was it hot in here?* I hoped my palm wasn't sweaty.

"It sure is a pleasure to meet you, Tadger," I said, hoping not to sound too childish. I knew little about Tadger, but there were a few things that I had been able to find out before the visit. First, he was twenty-one years my senior, which put him at forty-four. Second, he was married. "How was the flight?"

Our hands separated, which made me sad. I took the opportunity to look him over. He stood tall and sure of himself, his brown hair shimmering in a reddish tint, a curious look on his handsome face. His body shape was medium build, but solid.

"Ahh, you know, dreadful, sitting in a plane for that many hours. But I'm glad to be here in this beautiful country."

He hadn't missed that he had been under my assessment. I couldn't miss that he had given me the same treatment. We both seemed pleased with the results. We grinned at each other, as if we were in on a secret.

Our conversation was abruptly interrupted by Sigfrid, who entered the room.

"Tadger... welcome. I trust everything is okay at home?"

Tadger shot me an apologetic glance and whispered, "I will see you later." Then he turned his attention to Sigfrid, "Certainly, same with you?"

They started walking toward the long, rectangular table, where Paul and Jim were immersed in a discussion over American football. I overheard Paul say, "You can't call that football; only one guy is using his foot to touch that thing that you dare call a ball. It's not even round. That's no proper football. What you Americans call soccer... now, that's the real deal."

To which Jim replied with laughter, "YAWN, how dull. Soccer is so boring that you hooligans have to beat each other up just to get some excitement out of it."

The room filled with laughter. Everyone got settled around the table, and I knew it was my turn to leave. I stole one last glance at Tadger before closing the conference room door. I sighed, *See you later.*

Tadger was charismatic, and I could not deny his strong presence had power over me. I thought he was handsome in a very grown-up way. A serious man with worldly experiences. The age difference did not bother me. It never had before. I wanted to be with someone who would know how to push my buttons. But, I figured that someone of my lower professional standing would not have a chance at being with an executive like him. I was a nobody.

This quickly turned out, not to be true.

Tadger was very interested in me, and he made an effort to include me in as many corporate functions and events as possible. My crush quickly turned into something more serious. I wanted him, physically. A man like Tadger could teach me about a lot of things.

With the joint venture moving along, Tadger relocated to the States and leased a furnished apartment in Craighead. We laughed when his assigned parking spot had the numbers 07. We had previously joked that I was his Ms. Moneypenny, the infamous secretary to James Bond. We were always flirting. I had started to wonder if I would be like the actual Ms. Moneypenny, who longed to be with her 007, but never closed the deal.

Once moved into the apartment, Tadger bought a boat.

"Well, with such a beautiful lake and such great weather, why not?" he said as he showed off his new purchase one late summer afternoon. I was thrilled that he had asked me to come down to his apartment on the lake, where he would also keep his boat. He had mentioned that it was just going to be the two of us. Seemed that everyone else had other plans. Mine were clear to me. This was my opportunity to close the deal; Tadger was going to be mine by the end of the night.

"How about a refreshing drink on the veranda overlooking Lake Duke?" he asked while securing the boat to the dock.

It had been lovely out on the lake, just the two us, looking at multi-million-dollar mansions which lined the vast coastline. We had been on the water for hours, yet only seen a very small portion of the lake.

"I'd love to."

I felt a bit awkward showing off my body in a swimsuit, but Tadger seemed quite comfortable with it. He looked delicious in his loose-fitting surfer shorts, his mid-length hair all wind-blown and ruffled. I couldn't help but notice his solid legs. They were just the right thickness; I had never been attracted to skinny, chicken legs on men.

Once in the apartment, he opened a bottle of white wine, and we each got settled in comfortable outdoor chairs on the veranda. We were overlooking a small dock area to our left, where residents had tied down their boats in leased spaces. The sun was setting.

"… and that is how I ran into Bono while living in Dublin," he finished saying.

I loved listening to his stories. He had traveled the world, met interesting people, had eaten weird foods, and experienced other cultures.

"I could listen to your stories all day long," I said contently.

"You sure could, because it seems difficult to get you to say anything at all," he laughed. "I always seem to be the one chatting away, rambling on about old stories … stories from an old man."

"You're not that old, and you are not rambling."

"How nice of you to say. Now, how about some dinner? Would you like to stay for dinner?"

He knew the answer.

"Of course."

He went inside to order food for delivery. I joined him, and while he made the call, I walked through the apartment. There were three bedrooms and two full bathrooms. The place was tastefully furnished yet didn't show any character. The colors were neutral: the furniture, furnishings, and the few paintings on the wall were bland and nondescript in nature. It did not tell me anything about what he liked or what he was like. There were no photos.

"I think I'll start picking up bits and pieces of different artwork to make this more of a home than a rented space. Everything is just a tad bit vanilla."

I nodded in agreement.

Our food arrived shortly thereafter, which we ate outside. We had a good view over the common pool area, located to the right of the veranda. A few guys in their mid-twenties were splashing around, beers in their hands. I noticed that Tadger watched me watch them.

"Ahhhhhh, to be young again," he finally said as he observed the men return to their apartments. Then, he looked straight at me as if he was challenging me.

"If you like that sort of thing," I replied and held eye contact.

He smiled. He had understood.

We remained outside until it got dark, and the mosquitoes started to eat us alive.

"Ouch," he said as he slapped his arm in an attempt to kill one of the annoying insects.

I stood up, walked to the side of his chair, and extended my hand.

"Okay," I said, "come with me."

"Where to?"

He took my hand, and I pulled him up from the chair.

"I think it's time you showed me your bedroom."

Excited that we had reached the next level in our relationship, I jumped at every given opportunity to spend time with him. Life was great when with Tadger.

We went to the steeplechase where I participated in the hat contest, saw musicals, concerts, and plays, and he would invite me to corporate events. We weren't advertising our relationship, but we weren't hiding it either.

Tadger took me to the finest restaurants. He got a kick out of my newness to the finer things in life. I enjoyed getting dressed up for him. As did he. A small portion of my monthly paycheck went to Victoria Secret[26], and it was a worthwhile investment. Typically, by the end of our dates, he barely could keep his hands off me.

Life with Tadger was lived in another world. A world for the rich. I hadn't realized how much nicer life could be on the other side of the spectrum. Rich people had exclusive rights and privileges. They definitely had more fun and were more relaxed. They did not worry about bills. Tadger even had a cleaning person, which I thought was silly. He was barely home and was very neat. He could have cleaned his own apartment in an hour.

I was amazed how the rich wasted their money, yet they never seemed to run out of it. I could not believe that I was privy to that life. I wanted it to last forever.

One evening, Tadger took me to a classical concert in Regent City. We were dressed to the nines. I wore a long, dark green velvet dress that showcased the tattoos on my arms. It was the same dress I had worn to the Christmas party with Ryker. I loved presenting my tattoos to the conservatives who seemed to frequent such exclusive events. It was like bringing the trailer-park to the rich and famous. Proper human beings, especially women, did not sport tattoos those days. Tadger and I would always get a lot of looks and whispers, but it could have also been because of our age difference. I wanted to think it was because of my classy, yet sexy look with the offending artwork. My short legs looked incredibly long that night, courtesy of a side slit that ran all the way up to the middle of my thigh. The matching green, velvet stilettos completed the sensual look.

Tadger was wearing a black suit, white dress shirt, and a black bowtie.

"I love the way this dress feels," Tadger said as he moved his hands over my belly. He stood behind me in line, waiting to get drinks in the foyer of the theater.

"Does it now?" I leaned into him, placing my hands over his. "Tell me again, what are we about to experience in there?" I asked, pointing toward the open doors that led into the theater.

"Dvořák," he said as if I should have known the name.

"Okay, and…?"

"It's the *New World*," he said. "Only one of the most beautiful pieces of symphony ever written."

"Okay," I said again, unimpressed.

We finally got our drinks and went to our seats, which were a few rows from center stage.

The music started, and I couldn't help but be captivated. The orchestra was so quiet at times, I had to strain my ears to ensure that they were still playing. Other times, the music was so loud that I felt my soul was shaken to its core. Within the hour, I understood what Tadger had meant. The music moved me deeply. I could hear every emotion the composer had put into his labor of love. I did not withhold tears when the violin strings tried to reach for hope. They disappeared into silence, then re-appeared, pulling my heart through the roller-coaster of ups and downs. Some portions were simply glorious. I pictured myself as the victorious conqueror of this new world. It was magnificent.

After the concert, I stayed over at Tadger's house, which was not uncommon. He never asked me to leave and seemed happy waking up next to me in the mornings. Though, typically, he had more of a guilty look on his face the mornings after his wife called him during the night. I hated the nightly interruptions; they seemed too familiar for comfort.

"Doesn't she know what time it is over here?" I asked him when he came back to bed at three one morning. He had been on the phone for an hour.

"It's complicated," he answered.

"It's not that hard," I countered, "she's five hours ahead. It's simple math, really,"

"She's not well."

"What's wrong with her?"

"She has a lot of issues," he said, but he would never say more about his wife. He had made it clear that she was off limits in our conversations.

But she sure was interrupting my sleep, and I was known to be cranky if I didn't get eight hours every night. I also could not understand why he put up with it. *If my husband had lived thousands of miles away from me when we were married, I would have never answered the damn phone during the night,* I tried to tell myself.

Additionally, he had his independence, so it seemed. He had money, a powerful job, and distance going in his favor. At now forty-five years old, he didn't have to answer the phone unless he wanted to.

"I can't," he said after I suggested that he unplug the phone from the wall. "She takes care of my mother."

And that was that.

Since Tadger traveled frequently, it wasn't unusual when I did not hear from him regularly. We both understood it to be a relationship of convenience. Months, and then a year went by as we enjoyed our time together while living our separate lives.

I was relieved though when he called me at Iris's one August afternoon. It had been over a month since I had heard from him last.

"Want to meet at Chichi's?" he asked. Chichi's was a restaurant in Craighead.

"Sure, see you in a bit." I was excited to see him after such a long dry spell.

I should have realized that meeting him in a very public space after that much time, near the interstate, where I would have easy access to return home, should have been a clear indication of an imminent break-up. Yet, I went there with such naivety, expecting the best.

He was already there, waiting for me at a table outside. The noise from the interstate could not be ignored, but it also covered other people's conversations.

I ordered a beer, a Blue Moon, which seemed fitting for such a beautiful, warm day. The sky showed its famous Carolina blue. I sensed

Tadger's nervousness as we waited for my beer to arrive. As soon as the waitress had set it on the table and left, he spoke.

"I can't see you anymore," he simply said.

It was like I had been slapped in the face. I suddenly realized why he hadn't asked me to meet him at his apartment.

"Why?" I managed to ask, not wanting the next words to leave his mouth.

"It just has to end. I have to get my life in order."

"That's wonderful. Let me be part of it?"

"That's not wise," he said.

"Why not?" I asked. "Have we not had good times together? It's all been good. We're good for each other."

"It's been... fun," he admitted. "But like you have told me so many times, I have too many loose ends in my life. Too many unresolved issues. I've had my head in the sand for too long. I have started new things without ever making peace with the past. It is not fair to you anymore. It's not fair to me."

Now he was willing to face the past and clear up his conscience? And the consequence was him dumping me? I could barely take it. It was true that I had pointed out to him that he could never move forward unless he took care of the past. I just never envisioned a future without me once he actually got there. It was ironic.

"Are you okay?" he asked.

I was crying. Not just little tears, my face was wet as if it had just down poured, and I had chosen to greet the rain face-up.

Tadger was scrambling for some paper napkins, which he quickly scooped up from the adjacent tables. The container on our table was empty.

"Are you okay?" he asked again, handing me a bulk of napkins.

I thought it was mean of him to do this to me in a public place. I deserved better. It brought me right back to the train station in Mainhattan. I felt small and unimportant. And ashamed.

I nodded. I didn't move or speak.

Tadger got up, put a twenty-dollar bill on the table, gave me one final pitying look, and then left.

The waitress came and picked up the twenty without a word, avoiding eye contact. "Keep the change," was all I could manage between snotty breaths and quivering lips, trying to make sure she would not return.

I stayed at the restaurant until my feelings of shame subsided long enough for me to find the courage to leave.

I had viewed my relationship with Tadger as a good thing. Now, I am torn about it. Not because Tadger was married or so much older than me.

More so, because my relationship with Tadger deterred me from developing feelings for other men.

While I was with him, I did not consider other interested parties as potential matches. He had been the safe choice to protect myself from getting hurt again. Reserving my time and feelings for someone who I knew I did not have a chance with long-term, was an excuse for not wanting to risk opening my heart to love.

I had known that Tadger was married. Yet, I made the effort to pursue him, and I deliberately took the first step with sex.

I tried to tell myself that this was just a fling. It was an adventure. The nice car, the boat, the fancy dinners, going out to shows and concerts in style – who would not want to keep doing it? We had fun. It was easy.

I don't regret a minute, other than the final ones at the restaurant. I deserved better than the safety of a public space that he had chosen for this purpose. I had expected the decency of a grown-up conversation in another environment. In fairness, I'm not able to come up with a break-up scenario that would feel fair compared to what I thought "we had shared".

While I understood that I had been an escort more than a serious girlfriend, after almost two years of having these awesome experiences together, it felt wrong to be dismissed without having been given any heads-up warning.

It had been a dick-move in my view.

It affected me more than the actuality of him cutting me out of his life. We had had the best of times for over a year, and in the end, he had taken a shit on it.

♀

THE OVER-COMPENSATOR

"Hi, my name is Rikkard."

I looked up from my monitor to see a young man in his late twenties extend his hand to me. He was a tall drink of water, around 6'4", with a lean body, with beautiful blue eyes set deep in their sockets. His skin was flawless, as was his smile. He wore a crisp, blue dress shirt with a white t-shirt underneath, and designer jeans with an elegant leather belt. He was handsome and very poised. He smelled good, unlike so many other Europeans who came to visit and who didn't use deodorant. His straw-blond hair was longer on top, and he had styled it up and back.

Just like Elvis, I thought.

"You must be Petra," he beamed, his hand still extended from his initial greeting.

A set of white, perfectly aligned teeth emerged from behind his thin lips. His eyes sparkled at me.

"It says so on your name tag," he pointed to the plastic sign inscribed with my name, which was attached to the front of my desk.

I stood up, feeling stupid.

"Yes," I managed to say while accepting his hand.

The handshake was firm, our hands locked in a tight embrace. It was a good start. Germans considered soft, wet handshakes to be a sign of weak character.

In a confident voice, Rikkard announced, "I'm from headquarters. I'll be staying in the U.S. for three weeks to visit some of our customers. I work in the research and development department. Sigfrid wanted to see me the minute I arrived to talk about my schedule. So, here I am."

I couldn't help but smile. He was still holding my hand.

"Can I have that back?" I asked.

He looked down and released my hand. It had been odd having my hand held for so long over the edge of my desk.

"Sorry," he said.

"No worries," I emphasized. I hadn't minded. "He's not here."

"Who's that?" he asked. Then he laughed. "Sigfrid, you mean Sigfrid isn't here? Boy, you have made me confused."

We smiled at each other.

"How about later?"

"What about later?" I asked. "Oh yes, later, you mean, will Sigfrid be back later?"

"Exactly," he said. "I'm glad it's not just me."

I blushed. *What was happening?* I collected my thoughts.

"He should be back after lunch. Do you want to come back then?"

"Absolutely," he replied.

Within days, Rikkard and I were spending time together whenever possible, even if it was just by phone. His travel schedule kept him on the road for most of the week, and so we only had three short weekends for further physical explorations. We had agreed that we would enjoy each other's company with no strings attached. Neither of us wanted a serious relationship, especially not a long-distance one. It was August 1996, and I was still involved with Tadger with no intention of relinquishing the good times for another love interest.

On one of his last days prior to returning to Switzerland, we were lying on my bed, content after concluding our supposedly last sex act.

"How would you like it if I come back and spend my vacation with you?" he asked.

We typically spoke English to improve Rikkard's conversational skills. I found his nasally Swiss dialect adorable.

"That would be awesome. I'll check with Iris, but I don't foresee any problems with you staying here."

"Three weeks okay?"

"Yes, are you sure you want to hang around me for that long?"

"I think I can manage," he smiled. "Three weeks isn't that long."

"That's easy for a European to say. Americans don't get as much vacation, and when they do, they usually can't take more than two weeks at a time. That is, if they are lucky enough to work for a company that even gives two weeks of vacation. Most Americans don't even get a week's vacation until they worked somewhere for a whole year."

"That stinks," he said. "But you don't work for an American company."

"It's still an American company, despite Swiss ownership. We don't get Swiss benefits. Besides, I've barely been there a year. I can probably get one week off and maybe a day or two in addition. You'll have to keep yourself entertained without me while I work."

"I do mind you working, but it's better than nothing," he frowned. "I was thinking about coming back soon. What do you think about next month?"

"September is a great month," I said. "You know what? You'll be here about the same time that my parents are going to be in Florida for their vacation."

"Are they coming to see you?"

"No," I said and sighed. "They want to travel all over Florida. Coming to North Carolina would mean a detour. Plus, I did not want to impose on Iris. My parents can be a handful."

Rikkard laughed.

"Can you find out where they are staying and exact dates?" he asked.

"Why?"

"How about we go meet them in Florida for a week?"

I was blown away by his offer. I didn't know what to say.

"You don't worry about the money," he said as if he had read my mind. "It'll be my treat. This way, I get to see Florida, and you get to hang out with your parents."

"You don't mind meeting my parents?"

"Why would I? Didn't you say that they can be a lot of fun?"

"They are fun, now that I'm older and wiser and not married to an alcoholic redneck anymore…" I admitted. "But meeting one's parents sounds serious."

"I'm not worried about meeting them. You haven't seen them in a while, and I haven't been to Florida. We can kill two birds with one stone. Hey, how about we also head up to the North Carolina mountains for a night or two? I heard it's beautiful up there. We could go check out Lake Lure, where they filmed *Dirty Dancing*?"

"That's too much," I tried to say.

"Nonsense. We'll have the time of our lives."

The date of Rikkard's return couldn't come soon enough. I took off early from work and was impatiently waiting for him at the house. When he finally drove up in a red convertible Ford Mustang, I noticed that he had colored his hair. It was now black, still styled away from his forehead.

Even more like Elvis, I chuckled internally.

I raced over to him, and he picked me up, kissed me, then swirled me around, put me down, and pointed at the car.

"How do you like it?"

"I love it. A convertible!" I had never ridden in a convertible. It even had leather seats.

"We're driving to the mountains in style," he said. "Speaking of cars, I ordered my Z3 from the BMW factory. I will have the opportunity to see it being built at the plant in South Carolina while I'm here."

"Holy cow," I admired him. I had never heard of someone ordering a car from the factory. I didn't know that was an option. It sounded expensive, surely there wasn't much room for negotiations on price. "The Z3 suits you." I said. It was one of the hottest cars for Europeans back then. The Z3 was polished, sleek, and compact. *Just like Rikkard's penis,* I thought.

"I can't wait," he grinned. "I have always loved convertibles."

After a long night of catching up, we set off the next day for an overnight trip to the mountains. The weather was beautiful; perfect for driving with the top down. Rikkard had brought a Eurythmics CD, and we were singing along as best we could.

We returned from the mountains the next day, slightly sunburnt but happy and relaxed. While I rummaged through my closet, trying to decide what to pack for our trip to Florida, he remained on the bed.

"Show me that dress," he said.

I turned around, presenting the twiggy dress on the hanger.

"Now, I notice that you seem to have a lot of business casual clothes," he began.

"Of course, I work in an office... as you know," I replied.

"Hear me out," he said. "And you have a lot of jeans, t-shirts, and tank tops."

I nodded, unsure of where this was going.

"But, other than the long, green evening gown, you really don't own any sexy clothes."

I nodded again, "Why would I?"

"Why wouldn't you?" he asked. "You have a great little body. I think it's sexy. You should show it off more instead of hiding it underneath jeans and t-shirts." He paused. "Do you mind if I take you shopping right now? I think we need to get you some sexy clothes for our vacation. I want my woman to match my style. It'll be my treat."

I didn't know how to respond, but I wasn't opposed to him wanting to expand my wardrobe.

A short while later, we were in an upscale department store. Rikkard was perusing the women's evening gowns and cocktail dresses. He handed me a little black dress, "Put it on."

I changed in the dressing room. The dress had a low square neckline and showed too much cleavage. The bottom of the dress flared out in a sexy curve, barely covering my butt cheeks. I stepped out of the dressing room feeling a bit too exposed, knowing that Rikkard wanted to see me in his top choice.

"Wow," he said. "That is hot. What do you think?"

"I don't know," I said hesitantly. "It's way to open for me at the top." I looked down at my cleavage.

"You just need the right push-up bra," Rikkard said. "It's a great teaser. I love it. And just look at your legs. They look incredible. With some black high heels, they will look even longer. We're buying this dress. And then, we'll have to get you some accessories, like a matching purse, shoes, and some jewelry."

This was a first for me. I had never had a man dress me, especially a straight one. I didn't know if I should be thankful, in a Pretty-Woman kind of a way, or if I should feel insulted that Rikkard thought that I was a less than stellar dresser. I decided on the former.

With the sensual additions to my otherwise boring wardrobe packed into my suitcase, we headed to the Regent City airport the next day, where we would exchange the rental car for the trip to Florida. It was my financial contribution to the trip, which would be paid for otherwise by Rikkard.

We drove to Ringling, Florida in a small Kia Sephia without cruise control, which made the ten-hour drive seem even longer. Kia had entered the U.S. auto market only a few years ago and had quickly established a reputation for bad quality and lack of service. However, Rikkard knew how important it was for me to be able to pay for something. It was all I could afford. He never said a word about the car, but I'm sure he was glad that he was in another country and safe from being recognized.

When we finally arrived in Ringling, we settled into our downstairs unit in the same rental complex where my parents were staying. Their unit was on the second floor. Fortunately, their rooms were nowhere near above ours, and we were glad for the privacy. The walls were relatively thin, and we would have hated for my parents to be privy to our sexual activities. (It's true that the Swiss are, and always have been, very inventive.)

My parents were impressed and surprised by my choice of companion. Rikkard was well-groomed, his designer clothes neatly ironed to a crisp, and he spoke in a way that left no room to doubt his intelligence. He was very sure of himself with a hint of arrogance about him. My parents did not mind his pride in his appearance.

"Now there's a sharp looking young man with excellent manners," Mom approvingly nodded in the direction where Dad and Rikkard had headed. They were in charge of getting the drinks.

Petra Weiser

"He always dresses well," I agreed. "He even wants me to wear dresses every time we go out. Not to mention matching accessories, like jewelry, shoes, and purses. And he would love for me to wear make-up. You know how I feel about that."

We giggled in unison. Mom knew all too well that I had always been a tomboy. While I gave into Rikkard's requests to dress up when we went out occasionally, I had made it clear to him that make-up was off-limits. "I would feel like a geisha with her pronounced white face if I were to wear make-up. It's not ever going to happen," I had told him after he had suggested it during our recent shopping spree as we had passed the many make-up counters. Smearing make-up on my face just wasn't for me. I had nothing to hide.

"Looks are very important to Rikkard," I continued.

"I can see that," Mom said. "He's put together nicely."

"No, you don't understand," I lowered my voice. "He has very strong opinions about how things should look. Like… he will never wear shorts because he thinks men have ugly legs."

"That's just silly. What does he wear to go swimming?"

"That's different," I said. "He has swim trunks, the long kind that go down to his knees. And I'm thankful that he doesn't wear Speedos like most Europeans. Americans laugh at Speedos. Rikkard, even on the hottest summer day, will never wear anything other than long pants. I don't think he even owns a pair of shorts."

"It must feel awfully hot in long pants on a day like today," Mom suggested.

"I'm sure he's not comfortable," I answered. "But it won't change the fact that he thinks his legs are ugly. And I'm not going to tell him that they are a bit on the scrawny side. Still, he's the one with the problem; I could live with ugly legs packed into some tight shorts."

We were still giggling when our men returned with our drinks.

Two days later, we decided to visit Busch Gardens in Tampa, about one hour away from Ringling. Dad and Rikkard were huge roller coaster fans, and they had their hearts set on riding the Montu, which had opened earlier in 1996. At that time, it was the tallest and fastest inverted roller coaster in the world.

It was a typical September day, hot and humid. I was glad to be wearing shorts and a tank top. It seemed that Rikkard was the only person in the entire amusement park who was hiding his skinny legs in jeans.

We were standing near the entrance to the Montu ride, and there were a lot of people in line already. The line kept moving swiftly though each time the roller coaster stopped to take-on the next load of thrill seekers.

"Okay, you two wait here while we enjoy this beast," Rikkard handed me his wallet and sunglasses. "We won't be long."

Mom and I watched our men head toward Montu's entrance until they disappeared from sight. The lines looked longer now, and there was quite a crowd around this new attraction. We moved to the side, away from the entrance, to a spot where we could see the coaster come out of a tunnel and up into a loop. We hoped to be able to catch a glimpse of them as they went by.

"I don't know how they can do this," Mom said, shaking her head.

I nodded in agreement. I was afraid of heights and the violent twists and turns, not to mention the loops that would transform anyone's senses into mush. Not knowing whether one was up or down wasn't my idea of fun. I loved having my feet planted on solid ground.

An hour and a half later, we were worried. We had watched rounds of people going in and coming out of the Montu. Yet, our guys had not returned, and we were getting hot just standing around waiting. Mom and I were stuck in our spots, having been left in charge of my dad's bulky VHS[27] analog video camera.

It wasn't until we spotted Rikkard and Dad sitting in the front row of the next ride, when we understood why we had to wait that long.

"They wanted to be in that first row of seats," I said to Mom.

"That's pretty rude," Mom's tone mimicked mine. We were not happy in our now sweat-soaked clothes.

We did not get much sympathy from our men. They were grinning from ear to ear when they returned, looking more like overly excited teenagers.

"When riding something as famous as the Montu, it's got to be up front," they tried to defend themselves. "They had a separate line just for the front, we couldn't have known it was that bad."

While we saw the reasoning behind that argument, the men had not made their intentions clear to us before they proceeded to the Montu. And Rikkard's "We won't be long", had been a deceitful statement to make.

"Now we are going on a ride that *we* like," Mom declared, her blue-gray eyes determined.

"No problem. We did what we came to do," Dad said victoriously.

"Wasting our time," I muttered underneath my breath. *How inconsiderate of them.*

During our torturous wait, Mom and I had seen a water ride in the distance that looked more like our cup of tea: slow, at ground level, and safe. Riders were seated in large round floats, ten at a time, and sent down a man-made river. Along the way, other park visitors had the option to shoot water cannons at the river travelers. On such a hot day, it seemed like the smart thing to do.

The four of us got seated in a yellow float, alongside other hot patrons, until it was full. Traveling down the cool river, we could feel a slight drop in temperature. It was a nice, relaxing ride. People along the shoreline tried their luck with the water cannons, but somehow, we remained dry. From time to time, we encountered a make-shift water feature that would pour refreshing wetness onto an unsuspecting rider who just happened to have his or her seat rotated underneath the downpour at that very moment.

As we got closer to the end of the ride, the four of us were still surprisingly dry while most of our co-riders had not been as lucky. When we entered the last tunnel, we heard continuous gushing of water. It did not sound like any of the previous water features, which had been small enough to only impact one or two of the float's inhabitants. This angry, thunderous noise of whatever was coming up next filled the tunnel completely. We looked at each other, two in terror, two in joy. With a swift turn to the right, we approached the exit and with it, the five-foot width of torrential liquid. The float rotated one final time, giving us four the full brunt of pure refreshment from above. We were soaked.

Mom and I were laughing so hard, our ribs started hurting. Dad and Rikkard looked miserable. We exited the ride, dripping from head to toe, Mom and I still trying to contain our laughter. The men did not make it easy on us. Dad frantically checked his precious video camera for water damage while attempting to prevent further drippage from his body to reach the device. It was fortunate that one of the park's employees had insistently handed him a plastic bag for the camera, "Just in case," as we boarded the float. With the camera protected, a crisis was averted.

Rikkard was a mess. His crisp, white shirt and jeans had been soaked, and they clung to his body, giving him that disheveled and displaced appearance. His black hair, which he had taken great measures to style that morning, hung lifeless into his face, still dripping. Rikkard looked like an unhappy, wet cat.

Mom and I had not fared much better, but we thought it was hilarious that we had gone almost the entire length of the ride unscathed, just to be hosed down to our underwear in the last five yards.

"I'll need to change into some dry clothes," Rikkard said as he tried to smooth his limp hair back into place. It was useless; the bulk of it remained glued to his wet, furrowed forehead.

"You're gonna buy some shorts?" I asked, wide-eyed.

"No, of course not. My shirt is ruined, and it will go all wrinkly when it dries. I need to buy a t-shirt."

"Ah, okay," I said disappointed. I thought for sure he was going to change his pants and not his shirt, seeing that it would take the jeans much longer to dry.

Fortunately, there was no shortage of t-shirt vendors, and before long, Rikkard seemed content in his white Busch Gardens shirt showcasing the Montu in bright colors.

The rest of us did not care about our wet clothes.

Our shorts and tops were made of lightweight material. They would dry quickly in the heat of the sun. Until they did, we would enjoy the coolness of our damp clothes.

Mom and I kept smiling at each other. Payback was a bitch.

I enjoyed being with Rikkard for the limited amount of time that we had together. Yet, shortly after our joint vacation, we lost touch. We would have never worked long-term. He was too much about the look. For himself and me. While I enjoyed dressing up occasionally (and I had no problem getting sexied up for Tadger), I quickly disliked the fact that Rikkard expected me to every time we went out. It wasn't a choice anymore, and it was time-consuming. Not to mention stressful. In the looks department, I had always been a WYSIWYG[28] personality. I hated putting outfits together, disliked the complication that matching accessories brought to the entire process. It was a waste of my time as I had no vision or ambition for a personal brand.

Dressing up with Tadger was different. It was more like role play with him where I slipped into a different life, became a different person. In addition, Tadger did not care if I showed up in jeans, shorts, t-shirt, or tank tops. If he did, he never said a word about it.

Maybe Rikkard was over-compensating with his outward appearance, trying to cover-up another physical shortcoming. We never talked about it, and it wasn't a problem during our time together. As mentioned earlier, he was very creative in the bedroom, and I never thought he was less than adequate. In his way, he introduced me to a safe sexual environment where I could let go of my inhibitions and discover my sensuality. I am thankful for that experience.

Rikkard was truly respectful, compassionate, and even nurturing. While I disliked the expectation of having to look my best all the time, I also enjoyed being admired by him. He made me his center of attention, giving me a boost in the confidence department. He was perfect for me during a time period where I was still struggling to find the true me.

♀

THE GUARDIAN

"Ich will AJ zum grossen Apfel bringen."

Ricardo's German had gotten so much better over the past year. We met in 1996 when I was twenty-four. I had volunteered to be an assistant German teacher to some of my coworkers at the Swiss company. Employees from an Austrian corporation, which my company had partnered with on their apprenticeship program, were also invited to attend. Ricardo was the Marketing Manager for the Austrian company, and he was one of the more advanced students in the class, having had some basic knowledge of conversational German.

Ricardo, at forty, was easy to talk to, and he was very outgoing with a relaxed demeanor. He smiled a lot and had a great attitude about learning German.

When the program neared its end after only two months, he approached me.

"It's a shame this is our last class," he said as everyone was leaving the training room where we held the event.

"You learned so much. That's impressive," I said. "Most of the other students weren't really that interested in learning German." Ricardo's determination and active participation had been remarkable.

"Oh, I'm very serious about it. It helps with the Austrians when making an effort to speak their language. Well, not exactly their dialect[29], but the German goes a long way in trying to establish better cooperation with them."

"Totally," I agreed. Since most Americans did not learn a second language in school, the struggle to study the gutturally challenging German privately was a definite smart step toward improving intercompany relations.

"I would hate to lose what I've learned. If I don't practice or keep going, then I'll forget everything," he complained.

"Yes, that would be unfortunate. I guess nobody else is interested in keeping this class going. And I can understand it to some degree. It's after work, and our companies are just too far apart to make commuting to the class easier."

Classes were held weekly, switching from my company's facility one week to the Austrian's the next. With the distance between the two over half an hour away, it could make for some long days waiting for all students to arrive, and then for the class to finish.

"Where do you live again?" Ricardo asked.

"Lowing," I answered.

"Oh, I don't live that far from there, only ten minutes north. Would you be interested in teaching me German going forward?"

I looked at Ricardo, unsure. At just a few inches taller than my 5'3", and with his small to medium frame, he did not look dangerous or threatening. He was dressed well in his khaki pants and polo shirt, which had his company's logo embroidered on it. We had made small talk during previous classes, and I knew that he was happily married without kids, his wife's name was AJ, and he had an old Ford Galaxy in his garage which he was trying to restore.

"Now, I wasn't assuming that you would teach me for free," his kind brown eyes looked at me. "I could pay for German lessons. You could choose the location."

I could always use extra money.

"Can I think about it? Maybe give me your phone number, and I will call you to let you know?"

Two weeks later, we had our first German lesson at Iris's house.

"No, it's not *Abfall*, that would be trash in German. You are trying to say *APFEL*, there's a *p* not a *b* in the word," I tried to explain the proper pronunciation.

"Who would have thought an apple could be so difficult to say in German? And then to make such a pretty fruit trashy when incorrectly pronounced, that's even worse," Ricardo groaned while smiling at the same time. "Do Germans have to make everything so complicated?"

"Yup," I simply said. "It's more fun that way."

Ricardo's stomach growled. He looked at me as if to apologize.

"Sorry, I had an early lunch. AJ and I typically have dinner around this time since I don't want to eat too late. I was already hungry during my forty-five-minute commute here. I almost stopped at Mandarin to pick up something, but then I would have been late."

"Ohh, I love Mandarin. It's by far the best Chinese food around," I said, my mouth watering at the thought of their Sa-Cha Chicken.

"Yes, they're the best."

"I'm hungry now."

"Well, how about next week, I'll pick up dinner and bring it with me?" he asked.

"That would be great," I replied.

For the next weeks, we enjoyed our Chinese meals while trying to make sense of the German language. Before long, I traded Chinese food in exchange for the lesson. It didn't seem fair for Ricardo to pay for dinner and the lesson. I didn't really care about the money and neither did he. We had quickly become good friends. Within a year, we started to meet at Ricardo's house.

"Ich will AJ zum grossen Apfel bringen," Ricardo said again. "Fuer ihren vierzigsten." He used his eye movement to point in the direction of his wife, who was preparing dinner in the kitchen. I had to smile when I saw AJ completely immersed in cutting celery into thin slices. *That Ricardo is a smart guy,* I thought, *he gets his wife to cook dinner for me, and he gets free lessons in return.* I did not consider that the scene, which was playing out in the kitchen, could be a daily occurrence. I felt as if they were giving me the royal treatment.

I looked back at Ricardo and nodded to let him know that I had understood. He had just told me in German that he wanted to take AJ to the Big Apple[30] for her fortieth birthday.

As he continued to discuss the surprise birthday present in fragmented German, I couldn't help but admire them.

Their cozy brick ranch house had tons of character. Ricardo and AJ had put a lot of work into their home. The kitchen cabinets were gray, my favorite color for kitchens at the time, with warm lighting, double sinks, and gray tile floors. A small dining room was adjacent to the open kitchen, which was next to the living room with its comfortable furniture in earthy colors. A large modern horse portrait hung above the wood-burning fireplace. I loved horses and had just started taking horseback riding lessons.

AJ was a bit taller than Ricardo, skinny with short red hair. Americans seemed obsessed with long hair, and it was refreshing to see another woman with a spunky haircut. Her voice was soft and her eyes a gentle blue.

I felt at peace at their house.

"Ready for dinner?" AJ asked from the kitchen.

"YES," Ricardo and I replied.

AJ was an excellent cook. I had to control myself not to wolf down the food as soon as she put it on the table; it was the best meal I would have all week. This was my indulgence. That and getting to spend time with both of them.

"What are you doing this weekend?" AJ asked.

"Nothing," I was fully focused on the meatloaf in front of me. It was made-from-scratch, as were the mashed potatoes. A green salad with tomatoes, radishes, and celery accompanied the meal in a separate bowl. There would be Swiss chocolates for dessert or another chocolatey delight. They both knew of my love for good European chocolate.

AJ and Ricardo exchanged glances.

"Do you want to go on a hike with us?" Ricardo asked. "We have an Austrian intern who we want to entertain this weekend. And we could always use another German speaking friend, seeing that I am still struggling with my conversational skills. And it gets you out of the house. What do you say?"

"Sure."

It was just one of many examples of how Ricardo looked after me, pretending I was doing him a favor when it was really the other way around. He invited me to many events, ensuring that I would have some chaperoned fun at no cost to me.

Ricardo had a vital part in my realization that I could do anything I set my mind to.

"Why not apply?" he challenged me one day.

I had seen a job for an Office Manager in the paper.

"I'm an Executive Secretary."

"And?"

"This is an Office Manager position. I've never managed before. I just do administrative tasks."

"Humbug," Ricardo said. "What are you doing now?"

"I take shorthand, write letters, make presentations, set-up meetings, arrange travel…" I said.

"Okay, let me ask you differently," he interrupted. "Do you work in an office?

"Of course."

"Are there more people than just yourself in the office?"

"Of course."

"Do you order office supplies for everyone?"

"Yes."

"Do you have a water cooler?"

"Yes."

"Did you set that up with the vendor?"

"Yes."

"Are you talking to customers about your company's products and services?"

"Yes."

"Great, then you have managed an office before."

"Oh," I said flabbergasted. "I haven't thought about it in those terms. I thought it was more complicated from reading the job posting."

"That's your biggest flaw. You get stuck in your daily to-do list. You have to look at the bigger picture of what you do and for what purpose. Upsell your skills. Don't undervalue what you bring to the table by fragmenting out your responsibilities into mundane pieces. Job postings always sound bigger than what the actual jobs are. Heck, most people's résumés are fluffed up to make them look better than what they are. You're very intelligent, and anything that you don't know, you can figure out. Now, go get that job."

Turned out that he was right.

To this day, Ricardo and I exchange thoughts and ideas about many things. And while I have learned and accomplished a lot, I still look up to him.

Ricardo, being the open-minded, non-judgmental, and outgoing person that he is, was one of the blessings in my life. He met me at a time, when I was still naïve and unwise in some of my decision-making, and he unknowingly (or maybe knowingly) gave me direction and encouragement that I needed.

It would be fair to say that Ricardo and AJ were my "adopted" parents in the first years of us meeting. Sitting around their dinner table, or the simple act of being around them, made me feel like part of their family. They also showed in actions and words that a marriage could work. They trusted each other, yet still had independence to pursue their dreams individually. Watching them gave me hope that I, too, could find true love eventually.

Ricardo remains an inspiration to me. Late in his stable career, he quit his corporate job and started his own business to pursue his passion in woodworking. It takes guts to leave a safe routine for the financially unknown. But he showed that with some preparation, any goal can be accomplished, no matter the age.

As an avid musician and entrepreneur, he's always on the go. Living life with passion, he's never afraid to try something new.

"Gotta get it all in before it's over," he recently said to me.

Ricardo was and still is the smartest person I know.

♀

THE BOYS

"Pinkie, you need to kick him if you want him to move."

Ricco called every student Pinkie; he couldn't help it. I felt silly sitting atop Dancer, a lazy Quarter horse, being called that, knowing that 99% of Ricco's students were children. I was twenty-four.

It was a hot July evening.

Why did I have to start taking horseback riding lessons in the middle of summer?

Sweat from beneath my helmet was running down my red face, my short hair was clinging to my skull, and my legs didn't want to move anymore. I was exhausted.

"Let him know you mean business," Ricco instructed.

I thought that was all I had been doing for the last twenty minutes, which already felt like an eternity.

It was only my third lesson. Riding a horse had looked so much easier from a distance. There were too many things to worry about, the biggest one how to stay on the horse while trying to relax every muscle in my body. My butt, thighs, and knees naturally wanted to clinch in order to remain in the saddle.

"Why don't I put Dancer on the lunge line for a bit, so you don't have to work so hard?"

God, thank you. "Sounds good," I groaned between gritted teeth.

Ricco attached a lunge line to the horse's bit and then encouraged him to move on by waving a large whip near the horse's hindquarters. Dancer, now more motivated than before, started to trot immediately. I started to bounce; my senses jarred. I had not yet mastered the art of the rising trot, nor the seated one, and I felt like a helpless ping-pong ball between two expert players. My groin area had unpleasantly rubbed along seams and fabric, and I knew urination would not be fun after conclusion of the lesson. I struggled to lift my butt out of the saddle. If one of my attempts was successful, I hoped to find the correct rhythm that would propel me upward automatically with the horse's tempo and give me relief from the rubbing pains.

"You're starting to get the hang of it Pinkie," Ricco praised. "Looking good. But don't forget to breathe."

I let out the breath I hadn't realized I was holding.

With focus on my breathing, trotting soon became easier to figure out. The burning between my legs subsided to a warm simmer.

"When you forget to breathe, it makes your muscles tense up," Ricco explained. "Feel the difference?"

I simply nodded. It was all I could master. Talking would only confuse my breathing efforts.

"I think we can end on this very good note."

As we walked back to the barn, the horse between us, I glanced at Ricco. He was in his forties and his face showed kindness with his attentive blue eyes and tender smile. He wore a baseball cap, which covered his graying hair while protecting his skin from the sun. I had noticed that he laughed a lot, a nice open roar that showed truth in the expression. The exposure to the elements and laughter explained his slightly weathered face. His frame was small, even wiry, and his voice was soft. When Ricco spoke, it was in encouraging, positive words. I could see how kids were drawn to this gentle teacher. I knew I was the instant I had met him.

"I teach around forty-plus kids each week," he had said to me during my first lesson.

At the barn, he helped untack Dancer, who was napping in the crossties.

"Hey, hun," a voice said.

I looked up, having ensured that there were no rocks in Dancer's smelly, right front hoof, to see a handsome man walk up to Ricco. I guessed him to be older than me, maybe thirty. He looked a lot like Liev Schreiber. *Cute*, I thought.

The handsome stranger kissed Ricco on the mouth.

"How was your day?" he asked.

"Great," Ricco replied. "Meet Petra, she's a new student, and I got to torture her today with Dancer, who was feeling very mellow. You know, his usual self. Petra, this is Richy, my better half."

"Hi," I waved at Richy, not wanting to extend my grubby hand to him. I was tickled that Ricco had remembered my name. But I guess I kind of stood out from forty kids.

Ricco continued, "Petra took Keira's job. And she recently moved in with Iris. Remember Iris, the German lady that would sometimes come watch Keira ride your crazy horse?"

"Of course, I do," Richy said with a charming smile. "It's hard to forget an independent German woman. And on a similar subject, looks like we got a small package from Keira in the mail. I put it in the house already. Maybe she sent us some more Swiss goodies, but surely in this hot weather, she wouldn't..."

Keira was the woman whom I had replaced at the Swiss company. Due to an expiring work visa, she had to return to Switzerland, and that is how I had ended up with her job. I knew that she would come back to the States eventually. Her American fiancé had gone with her to Switzerland, where they would get married so that she could apply for a green card. The company had ensured me during the hiring process that I would not lose my job once that happened.

Keira was a close friend of the gay couple, and during her stay in the U.S., she had had the pick of the litter when it came to choosing a horse to ride. She was an excellent equestrian. Keira naturally also knew Iris, and Iris went to visit the barn on a few occasions. It was Iris who had told me about the cool duo with the horse farm.

It wasn't long before Ricco and Richy included me in their inner circle of friends. I felt honored and lucky since it seemed that everyone wanted to be their "best" friends.

As my horseback riding skills improved, I purchased a horse and boarded it at their farm. I marveled at how perfect "life on the ranch" was: the ease of being around friends and strangers, the open-minded community, the non-judgmental acceptance of adults and children from many different backgrounds. The environment was inviting; everyone was welcome.

I continued to take lessons. I did not mind that I was one of the older riders. There were plenty of adults to talk to, and since most of them were forward-thinking and unbiased, it was refreshing to have conversations that weren't necessarily mainstream. A rarity at the time in a state that seemed to have a church on every street corner.

"Can I bring you some coffee?" I asked Richy. "I'm about to head up to get some."

We were sitting in the small outbuilding next to the riding rink. We called it the "show office", and it was used to house the sound system and the office officials during the horse shows that Ricco would put on during the warmer months. It was October, and today's horse show would include the infamous Halloween class with horses and riders in costumes.

"Black with some cream, please," Richy said. "I'll stay in here to help with the registration process until you get back."

Page | 183

I loved hanging out with Richy. He worked for a furniture designer, and due to his schedule and long commute, I didn't get to see him a lot at the ranch when I was there. I was instantly drawn to him, not just because of his outer cuteness. He was beautiful inside and out. He was attentive and empathetic, as well as sympathetic. Anyone could be immersed in a discussion with Richy within minutes, the subject matter as varied as the weather to Einstein's theory of relativity. Richy had the natural gift of adapting to each person's needs, always saying what they needed to hear. No one was more important to Richy when he was in conversation with them.

There were many tasks that I could have done outside of the office. I always chose to help with horse/rider registration and class selection, which placed me with Richy. Time spent there with him was a special treat. Everyone wanted to be around him, and in that office, I had him all to myself – for the most part.

The outbuilding facing the arena had one large window through which Richy and I could observe the riders on their horses. Protected from the sun and dust, it was a premium spot for watching the competition.

The other side of the show office had two large window-sized cut-outs covered with wooden boards, which were raised during the show. The participants would congregate there to take care of class registration. Most of the time, it was the moms who showed up while their kids were excitedly running around to get themselves and their horses ready.

"Test, test, one, two, three," I heard Richy through the speaker as I headed back from the house with our coffees. He was in charge of the microphone, announcing classes and winners. He was a natural horse show announcer with his calming voice.

"Thanks, love," Richy said as I handed him his cup.

It was early still, and we had not seen many people register for classes yet. There would be a mad dash of frantic mothers and children minutes before the show was due to start.

"So, how's Tadger?"

"He's good. He sends his greetings," I replied.

"Yeah, he's good," Richy laughed, "that new saddle he bought you sure is nice."

"It is super comfortable."

"So are the riding pants he gave me," Richy said with a wink. "I never owned such fancy riding pants. They are a little big, but not too bad. Guess it's a good thing for me that he no longer rides horses. Thanks, Petra."

"What for?"

"For having a Tadger."

"You're welcome."

"What are you two talking about?" Ricco jumped into the office, a glass of sweet tea in his hand.

"We are talking about us being the thankful recipients of riding pants and a new saddle," I said.

"Must be nice to have a Tadger. I'm just sorry that I don't fit into those fabulous riding pants," Ricco said.

"We could fit five of you in those pants," I said, and we laughed.

A little girl, maybe around seven, walked up behind Ricco. She wore khaki riding breeches and an equestrian-themed polo shirt. Her blonde hair was put up in a low ponytail. Her helmet was a size too large, and she was constantly pushing it up on her forehead. She tugged on Ricco's shirt to get noticed.

"They won't let me get Torba," she pouted, tears rolling down her face. "I'm riding her in the first class, and they won't let me practice."

"Awh, Pinkie, I'm sorry," Ricco turned and knelt down to be at face-level with her. "Why don't we go up to the barn and find Torba? You know that the other girls get to ride her as well in the show today? We have to make sure that Torba doesn't get too tired."

The girl nodded, "I'll be careful with Torba, I promise."

"I know you will Pinkie," Ricco said. "Now, let's go up to the barn. I'm sure we will find Torba there. And we need to find you another helmet. This one is a little bit too big for your tiny head, isn't it?"

The little girl nodded again. She had stopped crying. As she dashed out of the office, she yelled, "C'mon Ricco, let's find Torba."

Ricco called out to her, "Hold up, Pinkie. And NO running around the horses, remember?"

Then he let out his famous laugh, and he was gone, leaving me and Richy to our coffees.

Decades went by, and our friendship solidified, like a sapling that grew into a beautiful tree with roots grounded deeply into the earth. I became part of the eclectic "Gang of 8", consisting of eight like-minded but very unique individuals, who all had close ties to the boys. There was Keira and her husband, Axle, who had returned from Switzerland. There was me and my new husband, Kindred, and the two sisters, Phryne and Fiona. All of us drawn in by Ricco and Richy, horses, and fate. Our age differences spanned twenty-one years, but it never mattered; the group was the better for it. The love of horses had been the magnet, the love for "us" was the glue that held us together.

Even after Ricco and Richy sold the farm.

The farm had been for sale for a while. It was hard to imagine that Ricco would give up teaching riding lessons or living on the ranch. Yet in his early years, Ricco had had a much different life. He had been a model, an actor, and a singer. He had traveled around the world, and he was cultured. A fact that most people were unaware of and which he constantly understated by being silly.

While he was humble and unassuming most of the time, he could be boisterously loud when talking about his wild, modeling years. His stories, slightly exaggerated when told, would change to be even more extravagant as they were repeated throughout the years.

It was during a late summer evening at the ranch around 2014, when the boys shared that the farm had finally found a buyer.

"I guess that's good news," Keira said, "but, I'm having a hard time envisioning you two living anywhere but here."

The rest of us nodded in agreement.

Our group gathered at least every other month. Ricco and Richy had voiced their desire to move to Camel City, and they had been looking at houses in that area. It was an hour away, which would make scheduling of our get-togethers more complicated going forward.

We were sitting around a fire, courtesy of Axle, who was our designated fire maker. We had just finished an incredible meal prepared by Richy, and our full bellies pressed us heavily into our camping chairs.

"Which brings us to the reason, why we have asked you here tonight," Richy continued. He grabbed Ricco's hand, who was intently staring into the flames. "We wanted to enjoy one final wonderful evening with our closest friends at this very special place. We've had some great times here."

"We sure have, remember Richy's fortieth birthday party?" I chimed in. "Square dancing in the indoor arena, all of us in country-western outfits, the food, all your family, friends. It was epic. We could never forget."

"Yeah, and how about all the drunken, midnight horseback rides we did in the pitch-black, not seeing which end was front or back on the horse?" Keira laughed.

"The horse shows…" Phryne said. "Especially on Halloween. Those kids made some amazing outfits for the horses and themselves. Remember Betty and the John Deere tractor? I still can't see how she got her horse to wear that huge yellow-green frame on its back without freaking out."

"Or any of the other horses," Axle added.

Then, as we were lost in our own thoughts of the good times, Richy continued, "While we had wonderful times at the ranch, and as hard as it was to sell it, the reason was not just financial."

Nobody spoke, waiting for Richy to go on. We could tell whatever he was about to say next was not going to be easy.

"We wanted to sell it for a while, and we wanted to be able to have a smaller house and yard because Ricco and I would not be able to take care of this place eventually. Well, you see," his voice broke a little, "Ricco has been HIV positive for over thirty years." He paused.

We sat in silence. While the words hit me like a sledgehammer, I could not deny that I had not thought about it at some point throughout the years. Ricco had always been extremely skinny, and no matter how much he ate—and he could eat an awful lot—he never seemed to gain any weight. I also knew that his former lover had died of AIDS and that Ricco had taken care of him until his death.

It was true that Ricco had looked more tired recently, and he hadn't seemed his chipper self the last few times we had gotten together.

"Some years ago, HIV turned into AIDS. We've been able to fight off the disease well throughout the years. Ricco has excellent doctors. And we will continue to fight. But this place takes a lot of work and energy. We want to spend more time together, in a smaller house, and enjoy the time we have left."

It seemed that we all got out of our chairs at the same time. We walked over to the two men, who were beacons in our lives.

"We are so sorry to hear."

"We're here for you."

"Whatever you need."

We hugged Ricco and Richy, all of us crying, then laughing for crying. It was one of the saddest but also best group hugs of my life.

Two years later in September, Ricco died.

While I knew the inevitability of the situation, it was hard to accept when it finally happened. I had lost a best friend, a mentor, a storyteller, a teacher. The world had lost a person who had brought so much light and love to anyone he met.

The ranch and the boys had offered a safe haven for many wounded and insecure souls, including mine. It had been a paradise in an otherwise cruel world, a place where everyone was accepted for who he/she was or for what he/she could become.

While Ricco was the ringleader on the farm, Richy had been the herald who had taken love, equality, and compassion out into the world beyond the ranch's reach. The boys complemented each other perfectly, and I could not imagine how life could go on after them as a unit.

Throughout Ricco's struggle, I was in awe at Richy's strength and courage. To watch your loved one die, a tiny piece at a time with each happy year spent together, is a burden beyond my comprehension. I wish they would have not spared me from the news for as long as they did. I could have been there more, and I could have done more. Yet, I understand Ricco's need to want to be treated like everyone else. Not to be pitied or fussed over something that could not be tamed forever.

Ricco and Richy taught me about true friendship, about caring for others, and how to embrace unconditional love.

Their legacy will live on in the many lives that they touched and through the actions of those they knew and loved.

Including me.

♀

THE SOULMATE

I n October of 1998, I started a new job as an Office Manager for an American manufacturer in Lowing. I was to support a Group Vice President and three Vice Presidents, who oversaw capital expenditures, intellectual property, and research and development. While German was not a requirement, it turned out to be a bonus since some of their suppliers were located in Germany.

At twenty-six, it was the first position I had ever held with the word "Manager" in it. I was very proud that I would be in charge of something, even if it was only an office. Along with the fancy title came more money, and the icing on the cake was a ten-minute commute.

My desk was in an alcove framed by a row of offices to my left and right. The Group VP, Fred, had his corner office to my left, with the remaining three VPs situated in both directions. The offices and my nook outlined a large open area on the second floor, which housed the research laboratory; all part of a newly constructed "Technology Wing". From my seat, I had a great view of all the activities in the lab. There were multiple pieces of interesting testing equipment in use at any given time, and several lab technicians ensured a lively scene.

Fred lived over four hours away from Lowing, and combined with his busy travel schedule, he did not spend a lot of time in his office. It was rare to have all four bosses in the building at the same time.

Two weeks after I started my position, Fred announced that there would be a grand opening for the new technology wing. It would be that coming Friday afternoon. All employees were asked to partake in the festivities alongside the press and other dignitaries. The place was buzzing in preparation for the big day. Since I was still unfamiliar with my surroundings, I was not heavily involved in coordinating this important event. I was stuck at my desk, sorting through capital expenditure requests while trying to figure out how to obtain a travel visa for Fred's upcoming South America trip.

"I'll be wearing my black jeans for this special occasion," I heard a voice say from across the aisle that separated my work area from the benches where the lab technicians worked on their computers.

It was Kindred who had spoken to one of his colleagues.

"You're going to wear what?" I asked loud enough to be heard from ten feet away. It wasn't unusual for me to converse with everyone in the lab since I had to coordinate reports, presentations, and schedules for the entire department.

"They asked us to dress up," Kindred replied. "Which means I will be wearing my black jeans instead of my blue ones." He laughed.

Was this guy serious? I could not tell by the expression on his face. He didn't look like he was kidding.

I had met Kindred on my first day. Unsure of where to go once I had reached the second floor from the lobby, I had waited near two large locked doors. There had been a coffee maker, and I had been pouring a cup when he had appeared.

"You're new?" he had asked.

"Yes, I'm Petra," I had replied.

"I'm Kindred, nice to meet you. I'm one of the research technicians, and I work in the lab, which is straight through those doors. Fred mentioned last Friday that you would start today. He's not going to be here until this afternoon. He typically commutes on Monday mornings."

Thankful for the attention, I had said, "I didn't know where to go. There's nobody in these offices along the hallway, and these two doors were locked."

"This whole building is new to everyone," he had said. "I don't think they know yet who will end up where. We just moved into the lab last week. You will need to get your electronic key card from HR today, so you can enter this area on your own. I can let you in, *this* time," he had smiled. "I'm pretty sure I know where your desk is. It's right across from mine. C'mon, I'll show you, and I can introduce you to everyone in the lab."

Other than on the first day, I had not had many conversations with Kindred, who, by now, had turned his attention back to his composition book. As the keeper of the technicians' notebooks, which served as back-up documentation for patents, I knew that he was a meticulous note taker. There wasn't a smudge or crease to be found in any of his books, and each word was clearly stated in a uniform, neat look. My eyes traveled from his hand up to the dragon tattoo on his arm. *Redneck*, I thought instantly, memories of my ex floating through my brain, *only a poor redneck would make a comment about black jeans being dressy.*

It seemed very disrespectful to the company. In my previous jobs, most employees had worn suits or business casual attire for official functions.

I continued my evaluation. Kindred's arms looked strong, despite his smaller frame. I knew he was around 5'11", and I could tell that he was in good shape from the way he walked. He had great upper body positioning supported by a strong, yet relaxed stride. It looked purposeful and gave his buttocks a good, shapely appearance with each step.

His brown eyes were accentuated by slightly curved eyebrows. His lips were framed by a moustache and a soul patch. His ears were almost elf-like, very angular, complementing a defined jawline.

Kindred's best feature though was his hair, the envy of many men. He had a full set of luscious, black hair with the slightest natural wave. It seemed impossible that his tresses could be that perfect, not a single strand out of place. I would later learn that a strict twice-daily brushing routine ensured hair shape retention and that he did not have to use any hair products.

He reminded me of a knight; valiant, strong, statuesque, and handsome.

"I'm sure I will find something appropriate," he said reassuringly as he looked back across the aisle with a wink. "After all, my black jeans are in pristine condition."

The day of the grand opening ceremony, I was relieved when Kindred showed up in khaki pants and a corporate polo shirt.

"You didn't really think I was serious about the jeans?" he asked.

I shook my head, "Of course not."

Later that afternoon, the event had come to an end. The offices, lab, restrooms, and common areas had looked clean and organized, which was not difficult since the building was very new. Nonetheless, all guests had seemed impressed, and my bosses were pleased when they left. As I walked by the conference room on my way to get my purse from my desk, I noticed that all the furniture had been pushed to the walls to accommodate the many visitors during the presentations. There was no way that I could move all the pieces back by myself. Not wanting to leave the room in disarray, I went to the lab hoping to find some volunteers. Fortunately, Kindred and Jack, another lab technician, were still there, shutting down their computers for the weekend.

"Would you guys mind helping me?"

"What do you need?" Kindred asked.

"The furniture in the conference room needs to be put back in place."

"I think we can help, what do you think Jack?"

Jack nodded, "Sure."

With the conference room back to normal, I realized that both had stayed past 5 P.M.

"Can I buy you lunch next week to thank you for your help today? And for staying late?" I asked.

"I won't say no to a free meal," Jack said.

"Me either," Kindred agreed.

The following week, we decided to go to lunch at Mandarin, the Chinese restaurant in town. As I grabbed my purse and walked across the aisle toward Kindred and Jack, Jack turned in his chair and said, "You two go ahead without me. I just got this project to complete, and I don't have enough time to go out for lunch."

"We can go another day," I offered.

"Nawh, you had your mind made up for today. I'd appreciate if you can bring me back a Sa-Cha Chicken though? I'm hungry and did not bring a lunch, obviously." He pointed at his watch, then his stomach, "You better get going so I won't starve to death. Go on you two, run along."

I was worried about having lunch with just Kindred. I wasn't sure that I would know what to talk about.

It turned out to be an unwarranted worry. Kindred was easy to talk to, and before long, we were chatting about the more personal things in life.

"I'm divorced too," I said after Kindred mentioned his ex-wife.

"Aren't you a bit young to be divorced already?"

"A woman never tells her age," I said. "But I can say this much... I was once *very* young and *very* stupid. And my ex was an alcoholic."

"Mine too," he said.

We looked at each other, both of our faces showing surprise. Then we smiled.

"Well, how about that," I said. "We're both divorced, our exes were drunks, and we don't have any family nearby. What's wrong with us?"

"We are like two lonely peas in a pod," Kindred nodded. "So, you say you were married for five years. What was the final thing that made you say 'Enough, I'm leaving'? Or is it rude of me to ask?"

"It's okay, I don't mind. It took way too long before I realized how bad my marriage was," I said. "In the end, a book pushed me in the right direction. As silly as that may sound. Well, the book made me more aware of my situation and how powerless I was. It helped me to let go. And of course, when my ex started to wave a gun in my face, I knew it was time to file for divorce."

"Whoa," Kindred said, "that sounds serious."

"It's a story for another day," I said.

"Completely understand. Can I ask what book?"

"Sure, it's called *Codependent…*" I started.

"*…no more*," he finished. "I got the same book."

"Stop it, you're freaking me out," I laughed.

When the waiter came to put the check on our table, Kindred said, "I let you pay for lunch if you let me pay for dinner?"

I didn't hesitate, "Okay."

"I don't know what's wrong with my bladder," I cursed as I flushed. This had been the fifth bathroom visit waiting on Kindred to pick me up. I was nervous, my hands were clammy, and at the same time, I couldn't wait for the date to start.

He had told me to pick the restaurant, and I had asked Ricardo, my "Guardian", if he could suggest a nice place.

"Villa Sofia," he had said. "It's this cute little place with tons of character. The food is excellent. For dessert, there's this guy pushing a cart around with all the goodies displayed on it. There's a horn on the cart, and it makes this clownish honking sound. Sure, it's a bit pricy and far to go, but you will love it. This way you can test him, see if he can afford to take you there and if he's willing to drive forty minutes one-way."

"That sounds like a plan," I had said.

"If it makes you feel better," Ricardo had said, "we can be there on the same night. You know, incognito. AJ and I won't mind going to Villa Sofia, believe you me! That way we can keep an eye on you, evaluate if your new beau is a psycho or not. And if you need to abandon ship, we can take you back home."

"Kindred is not a psycho, and he's not my beau," I had laughed. "But it would be fun to have you there."

A knock on the door finally announced Kindred's arrival. We made easy conversation until we got to Villa Sofia's. Ricardo had been right, the place had a great atmosphere with warm, subtle lighting, red seating, white table linens, candles on the tables, and servers dressed in black suits. Despite the formal look, the waiters turned out to have wonderful personalities, which helped make dinner more relaxed. From our small booth, I could see Ricardo and AJ seated a few tables away. They both nodded in approval and showed two thumbs up.

"You know, I turned forty last June," Kindred said.

"NO!" I said in disbelief, because he did not look his age. I had guessed him to be about seven years older than me, not fourteen. "Prove it!"

He reached for his wallet and pulled out his driver's license.

It was true.

"I would have never guessed that," I proclaimed. "You do not look forty."

"I showed you mine, now show me yours," he said with a grin as he put his license back into his wallet.

"You just want to see how old I am," I protested.

"What better way to find out?" he laughed.

By Thanksgiving, we were exclusive, and I moved in with Kindred. Our relationship had evolved quickly, yet it felt natural, the way it should be, starting with the first kiss that night after our date had ended.

My parents, on the other hand, were less than excited about him when I announced that he would accompany me to Germany in February for Mom's 50th birthday celebration.

"I don't know why he needs to come with you. It's too early in your relationship. You've just been dating a few months," she tried to argue.

"He's coming with me. We are serious, and I love him," I announced.

"Love! Don't be ridiculous. Dad won't allow it. Another older man..." Mom sighed through the phone.

My parents had known about Tadger, and they had disapproved of him at twenty-two years my senior. That Tadger had been married was a fact that I had not shared with them. I had seen no reason to add lighter fluid to an already fiercely enflamed subject matter.

They could not understand my infatuation with older men, and they were certain that it would not last (again).

"We're both coming," I insisted.

"You can stay with us, but Kindred... your father says he's not welcome in our house," she said. "And I agree, it's too soon."

"If he's not allowed in your house, then we will both stay at a hotel," I said determined. "You cannot forbid us to come."

It took several more arguments before they gave in.

Mom said when they finally conceded, "It's a good thing you're as stubborn as your father."

Once we arrived in Germany, it did not take long for my parents to fall in love with Kindred. He won them over by simply being himself. He was quiet, calm, yet funny and ready to participate in any silly activity. We spent many evenings around my parent's kitchen table, drinking and laughing.

My parents quickly saw how considerate he was toward me and them. He was confident in a quiet, assuring way, and they could see that he loved me deeply. They saw that he was good for me.

"If I was ten years younger," Mom kidded while waving a finger at my face. She was happy for me. She continued, "I feel better now about you going back to the States. I know you are in good hands; you have found a wonderful man. You are happy, and you are safe. Now I don't have to cry all the way home from the airport anymore."

While in Germany, Kindred and I got engaged. We got married seven months later in September of 1999.

It is hard to explain why I knew we would work out. I just did.

There is peace when I'm with Kindred.

He's the positive to my negative.

He grounds me.

And lifts me up.

He doesn't try to change me.

He lets me be me.

He supports me in everything.

He believes in me.

I am a better person with him.

And that's why I will love him forever.

♀

THE OFFICE HUSBAND

I n early 2001, Kindred and I heard a rumor that our company would soon file for bankruptcy protection. With two incomes at stake, Kindred and I decided that I should try to find another job. Lowing was growing exponentially as a Regent City suburb, and we figured that my chances were better since office skills were always needed in many markets. Kindred had been with our current company for over twenty years, and despite the rapid development in the area, there weren't many new or old research jobs to be had in his industry.

I learned about an Office Manager position for a German start-up from the owner, whose son I had started to teach English a few months earlier for extra income. I submitted my résumé, and shortly thereafter, I had an interview with the General Manager.

The company's facility was not impressive. They rented a small space in an unassuming one-story building in a business park. As soon as I entered, a tall man walked out from a large office at the front of the suite.

"Hello, I'm Richard, you must be Petra," he said.

I accepted his handshake, which was firm, "Yes, nice to meet you Richard."

He was easily over 6' tall and trim with blonde hair. He looked Nordic. His aura was soft and relaxed, putting me at ease within the first few seconds of our meeting.

"Step inside my office," he said.

We sat in his office for over an hour talking, our conversation much broader than just shop talk. He had been born and raised in Germany, and just like me, he had married an American and immigrated years ago. If I wouldn't have known it, I would have assumed that he was American. I had developed quite an ear for European dialects over the years, and I was impressed that his was undetectable to me.

As the General Manager, he had set up the company's first presence in Regent City in 1998. From there, he had steered the business north to Lowing and to their current location. He stated that they had outgrown the facility already and that they were looking forward to establishing a serious and presentable operation for their customers. They had plans to purchase property to have a manufacturing plant completed by the fall the following year.

The company provided goods to automotive OEM[31] suppliers along with small equipment to further process such goods into the customers' own product line. Richard explained that the product components could be tracked for the car's lifetime in case of defects or warranty concerns. As part of the automotive supply chain, it was the company's goal to become ISO[32] certified in the new facility as soon as possible. ISO accreditation was a must in order to do business with automotive suppliers.

My tasks would be diverse: from answering the phones, to bookkeeping, quoting proposals, issuing production jobs, arranging shipments, and everything in between.

I was fascinated with the job. I had never been involved in production, nor a start-up. It was an opportunity for me to learn and grow with a young company.

"So, do you own a passport?" Richard asked at the end of the interview after we had concluded the tour of the warehouse.

"Yes," I replied.

"Would you have a problem spending six weeks in Germany for training?"

My eyes must have bulged out of my head because he quickly added, "Well you see, it is not as easy as it may appear. In order to quote something, you need to have detailed knowledge about our processes, equipment, and materials, not to mention understand the complicated automotive requirements. We have thousands of different materials we can offer depending on the customer's requests. And, most importantly, we need someone who can manage the entire inside sales and customer service process on their own. It is not something we want to rush through. It is a major commitment to the new hire since training for that long is not cheap… but a worthwhile investment, we believe." He smiled. "We want employees who want to stay with us long-term."

Shortly thereafter, the company offered me the position. Since I wouldn't be able to accomplish much at their facility in the U.S. without training, I started my first day as an official employee at their German headquarters in the middle of July 2001.

My first two weeks were spent in production, learning how the various products were made on multiple machines using different technologies. I enjoyed my time in production a lot, especially since there was a tangible finished product at the end of the day. I realized that office work did not give the same instant gratification, and I envied the operators who saw their daily accomplishments as they went home. Naturally, production also had some added pressures: there was little hiding in the output, and management could also give instant feedback on an operator's performance.

The remaining four weeks involved materials and quality management training, as well as spending time with inside sales. Everyone was forthcoming and engaging, thanks to the company's excellent training program and relaxed environment. Besides quoting, making production orders, and trying to make sense of an antiquated German software system, I also studied hundreds of pages of automotive customer requirements in the form of thick supplier manuals. They outlined detailed expectations of processes, timelines, deliveries, and quality. Every customer wanted the best product with zero defects in the shortest timeframe at the best possible price. If a defect was found to be the supplier's fault, the supplier had to rectify all claims including monetary compensation. A defect causing an OEM's production line to shut down could result in penalties as much as $20,000 per minute. It seemed very much like a one-way street, and I wondered why any company would want to do business with a customer who only had demands, posed a high risk in case of warranted claims, and who offered little in return to their vendors when it came to commitment or pricing.

However, I wasn't too concerned. The company had been in business for many decades, and they were thriving.

After each week of training, my head full of new knowledge, I looked forward to my weekend visits at my parents. I did not mind the four-hour drive, and I was thankful that the company had given me a rental car.

Instead of flying home after the conclusion of my six-week training, Richard had offered me another week with my parents as a thank-you for not requesting a flight back home to see my husband during our long separation.

Back in the States in September, I was ready to start my official first day of work in Lowing. I had returned on a Saturday but did not report to work until Tuesday since Kindred and I had spent so many weeks apart. Additionally, Kindred was scheduled to fly out to Oregon to visit his parents that Monday, and so we only had one full day together before our next goodbye.

On Tuesday morning, I eagerly left my empty house. I was anxious to put my new skills to use at the U.S. location. Richard took the time to introduce me to my coworkers, which did not take long since there were only three. I knew there was an additional salesperson in the field, whom I would meet later.

I got settled at my desk and turned on my computer when I heard Richard say, "Someone flew a plane into one of the Twin Towers."

Unsure that I had heard correctly, I got up from my chair to walk out into the hallway from my office, where he was standing with a horrid look on his face.

"What?" I asked, skeptical.

"They just said on the radio that someone flew a plane into one of the Twin Towers," he repeated. "But they didn't give more details."

Immediately, an image of a small plane, like a Cessna, appeared in my head. I couldn't imagine that a small plane could cause much damage to such an impressive structure, and I wondered why Richard seemed so concerned.

He looked at me when his phone started ringing in his office.

"Would you mind going next door?" he asked. "I know they have a TV. Maybe they're watching the news? I would go, but I have to take this weekly call from Germany."

"Sure," I replied. I still did not see what the big deal was, but I didn't mind going next door.

This quickly changed as I stepped into our neighbor's lobby, where a group of people was standing in front of a TV.

"Excuse, me," I shyly said. "I work in the suite next to yours, and we were hoping to find out what's going on."

"A second plane just hit the other tower," someone said from within the group.

My eyes were drawn to the TV. The screen showed a large gaping hole in one of the towers, clearly outlining the shape of a large airliner as it had flown into the building head-on.

I stood in shock. Such a thing had been unfathomable for my mind's imagination. *How does an airplane fly into a building... by accident?* I thought. *And then a second?*

A chill went through me.

I returned to the office and told Richard.

"Everyone, go home," he said with urgency in his trembling voice. "Something's happening in our country. You should be with your families. Everyone, go home *now*!"

It was very lonely at home without Kindred. Even more so after having watched the events unfold on TV for the remainder of the day. The entire country was in panic and in mourning.

I tried to call Kindred several times, but phone lines were jammed. Everyone was calling everyone or trying to.

It was most likely the one day in American history where its entire population said "I love you" or expressed unabashed feelings to someone in some form.

All planes were grounded indefinitely. It was surreal.

When I finally reached Kindred later that day, neither of us said a lot. We could not put our thoughts into words, had never experienced such horror. Even from afar, it had hit home.

"Do you think you'll be able to fly home next Tuesday?" I asked.

"Who knows," he answered. "Hopefully by then, they have an idea who did this and how." He paused. "It's not like I want to fly right now."

I agreed.

From that day forward, air travel changed. Only ticketed travelers were allowed past the security checkpoints, and there were many new restrictions for carry-on luggage. But the impact was much larger.

Just like so many others, I haven't been able to get on a plane after 9/11 without thinking about all the lives lost that September day.

The seed of fear had been planted, and the whole world fell victim to it, including me.

Once life normalized, I settled into my role as Office Manager. We moved into the new building in the summer of 2002. It was a wonderful environment. The furniture, the carpet, the offices, and the kitchen were funky modern and full of color. Walking through the front door, there was a large open work area with four workstations to the right. Down the hallway were three offices, each in a different color scheme: grey, red, and yellow. The colors were representative of the German flag: black, red, and gold. Granted, the first office should have been black, but it is safe to say that it would not have been a conducive place to work in if that would have been the case. As for the yellow, its paint was more available and cheaper than the gold's.

To the left of the entrance were a visitor's bathroom, a yellow kitchen, a large lilac conference room, and then warehouse space that extended from one corner of the building to the other.

Both areas were adjacent to the large production hall that housed our production equipment, raw materials storage, two production offices, and shipping & receiving. The very back of the building was part of the warehouse which held the inventory.

It was a large place for six total employees and a dog.

The dog's name was KC, and she belonged to Richard. She was a beautiful Labrador Retriever and very gentle and calm.

"She was part of the deal," he once said to me. "I would have never taken the job otherwise."

At first, I could not imagine anyone turning down a high-paying executive job because of an animal. It took a while before I realized that he had his priorities in order.

And that there was more room to negotiate at the top.

The grand opening was held in the fall of 2002. My parents had flown to the States the night before, and they stopped in Regent City to spend a few nights at my house before starting a 50-day RV adventure.

When Richard heard about their visit, he invited them to the event. I was proud to show my parents the new building.

As we walked through the front door, Richard was there to greet us.

"It is so nice to meet you," he said in German. "Petra is my right hand and sometimes my left hand too. I rely on her for so many things. She's invaluable to me." He laughed. "Thank you for letting her ship out to the United States."

"It wasn't exactly our choice," Dad replied.

"So I hear," Richard said. "But it seems to have worked out for the best. At the very least for me." He paused for a moment, then continued, "So… where does she get that stubborn streak from?"

And with that, my parents were smitten with him.

It was one of the best compliments I had ever gotten from a boss.

From the first day, when he had sent us home on 9/11, I had known that Richard was a very compassionate man. He was kind and attentive, and he balanced work and private life well for himself and his employees. I valued his honesty the most. He was never harsh with his criticism, but he made sure that I understood my mistakes, at the same time offering suggestions and feedback.

"Now, did you save the email first and then look at it later again before sending it to the customer?" he asked one afternoon.

"No," I said, wondering why I would want to wait to send an email. "The customer accused us of making a mistake, and we didn't. I did not want to delay our reply because their supplier manual states that an initial response is required within twenty-four hours. You know how they want an answer right away."

"I know," he said. "But tomorrow morning would have still been within that timeframe, and we should not rush an answer just to please them. We must do our due diligence. How do you know we did not make a mistake?"

"I asked Joe in production."

"And?"

"He said there's no way that we would have made a mistake."

"How can he be certain?" he challenged.

"He watches every production run carefully. And he says that our supplier did not have any markings on the raw material to indicate any issues on their end. Typically, they set flags so that we can see if there are potential mistakes."

"I know that," Richard nodded. "But it's a long machine, and Joe is just one person. We don't have a camera for visual inspection. How can we be sure that he did not miss a flag?"

"If he missed it, we should have caught it on the finishing machine. The strobe light makes it easy to detect. And, I'm sure we would have seen it at the shipping station," I rebutted.

He nodded again, "But you being sure is not a confirmation of our process. It's only a guess unless you can prove it with documentation. Think of verifiable controls that give absolute certainty in our process. And think about the processes we don't control. What if the supplier did not use a flag this one time? Did we verify during the receiving process if there were any issues indicated on the comment section of the certificate of compliance?"

I was quiet. I cleared my throat, "I hadn't thought of that."

"It is our job to consider everything. We do make mistakes, so do our suppliers, which we may or may not catch. And it's okay if we can learn from them and prevent them from re-occurring. Don't get me wrong, I like your confidence in our team, and I appreciate how you want to defend them. But sometimes, waiting is the better option."

"I shouldn't have sent that email," I admitted. "I feel stupid now… Especially, if they send back the goods and it does show an issue."

"Now, don't beat yourself up," Richard said. "Ultimately, if we did screw up, then it's important that we react and communicate in a professional and objective way. That's the goal in being ISO certified: to make things better all the time," he paused. "For me… I have learned that if I have an emotional reaction to a customer's email, or any person for that matter, I type my response, and then I save it. When I open it a few hours later, I can edit out all the personal feelings and base my response on facts and objectivity. Also, a few hours on the back burner may ensure that you will have more information to include in the email. Trust me, I had to learn this the hard way myself."

"From now on, I will do the same," I assured him.

And I have.

Richard was an incredible mentor. He made a point of including me in many meetings, and he shared a lot of information on anything. Information that, at my level, probably should not have been shared, but he knew he could trust my confidentiality. Over time, he sought my input on many decisions, never afraid to hear criticism or a completely different viewpoint. He would never dismiss my opinion. "I'm not always going to be the smartest guy in the room or have the best idea. That's why I surround myself with great people," he would often say.

He never made me feel that we were operating on different levels.

Years went by.

"How would you like to do PPAPs[33] going forward?" he asked one day when I passed his office on my way to the production floor.

I stopped and paused, leaning on the doorframe.

"You're just trying to get out of them. You hate doing them," I said.

"Of course, I do," he replied. "It's tedious work, and it's boring."

I had seen the documentation for PPAP submissions. It was part of the quality management system that I worked with daily. As an expert in requirements, drawings, and internal processes, I was aware that I could easily handle them. Yet, just like Richard, I was not a fan of tedious, repetitive paperwork.

"It would make sense for you to take them off my hands," he tried to convince me. "You know what the requirements are, and you are familiar with the customers. Any other questions, I can easily explain. It would free me up to focus on sales. The owner wants me to spend more time on the road."

I laughed, "Well, if I must…only because you asked so nicely."

"Step into my office," he said, "and let the torture begin."

Richard took me under his wings for eight years. He never showed any disappointment or disrespect if I did not have enough knowledge in a certain area. He eased me into the heavier topics, such as finance and general management. I learned from him that employee involvement and empowerment are the most important factors in running a successful operation. There could be no progress with micro-management.

He taught me that bosses who don't share or empower, end up doing more work because they don't have trust. A good boss will aim to make his or her employees better, cultivating their strengths.

A great boss does not get intimated or threatened by someone with more skills or know-how.

While Richard took pride in his work and his employees, he often made the point that there was more to life by saying, "In the grand scheme of things, work does not define you as a person or your life. More the other way around. Just remember, the world will not stop spinning because you may have made a mistake at work. So, stop worrying about what you don't have any control over and move on."

He quit at the end of 2008 to establish his own company. His entrepreneurial spirit had been itching, and he was tired of working for other people. In his new endeavor, Richard became one of my suppliers.

All along, he had groomed me to step into his large footsteps after his resignation.

He saw my potential before I ever did.

I try to honor him by keeping fairness and decency at the core of every decision I make that impacts others.

Richard remains my friend and mentor to this day.

He taught me about compassion. Observing him in his kindness, understanding, and sympathy toward others made me a more considerate person. While I had empathy for others, I wasn't necessarily truly aware. I had heard people's words, but I hadn't listened. I had seen their reactions, but they did not register in my brain. I had made a lot of assumptions about people and situations. I had judged quickly.

Richard gave everyone the same chance—to be good—and even when someone wasn't, his niceness never faltered. He had the gift of observation and patience. He didn't rush to quick judgments. He evaluated the person in front of him based on facts. He made sure he listened to the words so that he could understand the actual meaning. He observed facial expression and body language to gauge someone's feelings and then adjusted his response to build common ground. His adjustment may have been so slight, it may have been below the consciousness of his opponent.

He was fair in his criticism. He procrastinated at times about making certain decisions, knowing the impact they could have on others.

He wasn't afraid to be vulnerable. When he liked/loved someone, they would know it through his entire being: his words, his hug, his laughter, his honesty, his sensitivity, and his friendship.

It is one that will last a lifetime.

♀

THE BRAGGING WIMP

I n early 2007, the company hired Pecker as a Sales Representative in Michigan. There was a large automotive manufacturing market that we hadn't been able to tap into from our location in North Carolina. And while most of the actual vehicle manufacturing was done south of the border in Mexico, a lot of OEMs had their R&D facilities in Michigan, alongside many sub-supplies. Pecker had previously worked for a German competitor in this region. Our company had high hopes that he would be able to win some of the northern accounts, or at least, that he would convince some of his old customers to purchase our superior products.

It didn't take long for me to refer to Pecker as the stand-by-dude because he tended to end the majority of his emails with the words "standing by for more information". He was supposed to be in sales getting information, not waiting on it, so it made little sense to me.

By summer, Pecker had scheduled a meeting in Mexico to visit one of our existing key accounts. The date was set for the end of October, and I would join him at the airport in Houston, where we would board our final flight to Chucotown, Texas.

Throughout the years, I had visited this customer with Richard. It was one of my most guarded house accounts, and I had worked hard on building a rapport to expand our business with them. I was not pleased that a newbie would now be the main contact, which could jeopardize the relationship with the customer. Pecker, sensing my uneasiness, assured me that he was familiar with the account. He told me that he had been to that location many times and that he had taken care of all the arrangements for the upcoming meeting. All I had to do, was book my flight to ensure that we would connect in Houston.

I was already at the gate when he showed up.

"How was your flight?" he asked, faintly smelling of cigarettes.

He was about 5'5" with brown hair and a freckly face.

"Fine, how about yours?"

"Good. When does our next flight leave?"

"Actually, there's a delay," I said. "They made an announcement five minutes ago. They did not know how long though and said to stay near the gate."

He smiled, "That means I can go smoke a cigarette... if I can find a place in this airport that allows it."

"I wouldn't if I were you," I said. "The flight was originally supposed to leave in twenty minutes."

"Yeah, but that's before the delay," he argued. "Could be twenty minutes, could be eighty."

I shrugged, "I wouldn't risk it."

"I'll be back shortly."

And with that, he was gone.

Fifteen minutes later, the announcement came that our flight was back on. We would board within minutes.

I looked around. No Pecker. I searched for my cell phone in the bottom of my backpack and then tried to call him. There was no answer.

When I boarded the plane, I feared that Pecker wasn't going to make it. Minutes passed, and the plane was filling up. Finally, I saw him sit down two rows in front of me, his face flushed from running.

"They didn't have any smoking areas in the concourse, and I had to go all the way outside of the airport to smoke," I heard him complain to his seat companion. "And then I had to go all the way back through security and run to make this flight."

Dickhead, I thought.

But I was glad that he had made it. Our meeting was to be in Paso del Norte, Mexico, the next day. It was not a safe city for women traveling by themselves. Additionally, I had no Spanish skills, which already left me feeling vulnerable before getting there. Pecker was supposed to be my translator and protector. Also, since I had not made the meeting arrangements, I did not have the customer invitation letters on me. Paso del Norte was in a designated international trade zone, and business travelers could not visit companies without a business visa. We could only obtain a visa if we had an invitation from the customer in Mexico to present at the border station. I assumed that Pecker had the letters in his possession.

"No dude, *I* speak Spanish. My wife is Mexican. Our kids speak Spanish. My Spanish is *excelente*."

I rolled my eyes hearing Pecker's words drift down to my seat. I was thankful that he wasn't sitting next to me with his smoky breath and inflated ego. Despite the engine's noise, I was unable to ignore the sounds of self-validation worming their way down the aisle for the remainder of the flight.

Once settled in the nicest hotel in Chucotown, which we often referred to as the dust bowl of the Chihuahuan Desert because of its frequent sandstorms, we convened at the bar.

I loved the hotel. It was old and a bit dark, but it had character, and it was very clean. Thanks to the recent smoking ban, it smelled a lot better than during my previous stays. The bar was large with comfortable leather seating throughout, and impressive glass chandeliers enamored the multi-tiered ceiling with its baroque style crown molding. The bar counter was shaped in a wooden half circle, and the liquor bottles were beautifully displayed in a staggered formation behind it.

We sat down on bar stools and ordered two beers while looking at the extensive tequila menu.

"I think I'm going to order this one," Pecker finally concluded, pointing at his selection.

"Holy smokes, that's a twenty-dollar shot," I said.

"Right on," he replied. "This tequila is known for its smoky flavor. I deserve it after my stressful day today." He looked around and frowned when he saw the no-smoking signs.

"Seriously? I can't smoke in here anymore?"

The bartender shook his head, "No smoking in public spaces since September. It's a new law."

"But it's a bar," Pecker protested.

"Si," the bartender responded. "But we are not a private club, so no smoking allowed." With that, he put down our beers.

I took a sip while Pecker took several gulps.

"I knew we should have come here in August if it weren't so damn hot then. What's the world coming to? They're taking away all the fun. I guess, even more reason to order this tequila. It's smoky enough to make up for a cigarette," he snickered.

He ordered the tequila and turned to look at me, "Please don't snitch to Richard."

Dickhead, I thought. *What a waste of tequila.*

When we met for breakfast the next morning, Pecker announced, "I received an email from Carlos asking us to push out the meeting by two hours. It's not until 3 P.M."

"That's kinda late," I said, concerned.

He shrugged his shoulders.

We took our time comparing notes on the customer. Pecker claimed that he knew every one of my contacts and that we would walk away with more business that afternoon than what we currently had.

With hours to kill after breakfast, we decided to go for a walk.

"I don't feel safe," Pecker said, nervously glancing around as we stopped to look at a merchant's window display.

Chucotown was one of the safest cities in the U.S. and very clean, which was quite a contradiction to its attached sister city in Mexico.

The sidewalks were busy with people, mostly Latinos, but considering our location, it wasn't a cause for alarm.

"I think we should return to the hotel," he said, chewing his bottom lip.

Dickhead, I thought, surprised that the same word kept creeping into my subconscious. But I knew that something was irking me about Pecker.

"This is one of the safest cities in America," I pointed out. Internally, I thought, *What will he be like when we actually walk across the border into cartel territory?* I was aware of the violence and the kidnappings that happened daily in Paso del Norte. Despite the danger, I had traveled there before and had always felt relatively safe since the trade zone was in a patrolled area. Shoot-outs and kidnappings did not typically occur near the international companies where police and private security presence prevailed. We should be okay as long as we wouldn't do any sightseeing detours.

At that moment, I missed Richard terribly. He had never panicked, and we had once driven through the desert for hours to visit a customer who had been off the beaten path. I had always felt safe traveling with him.

"Let's head back to the safety of our hotel," Pecker insisted.

When it got time to leave the hotel at the agreed time, he ordered a taxi to take us across the border and to the customer. As we drove past the border station, I realized that we weren't going to stop. Surprised, I asked from the backseat, "Aren't we stopping to get our visas?"

He answered from the front seat, "No, we'll go in as tourists. It's easier. We won't need visas that way."

"I have *never* gone in as a tourist," I said firmly. "We have always gotten an invitation from the customer, then we filled out our paperwork at the border, and then we got our visas to go visit them. I know they are strict with the rules in Paso del Norte since it's an international trade zone. It's not like the other places you can visit without a visa in Mexico for business."

"Trust me," he said dismissively, keeping his eyes on the road. "I've done this before. I've been here without a visa."

We arrived at the customer's gate, where the guard promptly asked to see our visas. He did not care that we had a scheduled appointment and refused entry into the complex. Pecker had to call Carlos, the meeting organizer on the customer's side, for help.

Fifteen minutes later, Carlos appeared outside the gates. Pecker and I were still sitting in the taxi with the windows down. I tried to get out of the car to greet Carlos, but he waved me off, "I can't believe you would show up without a visa. Petra, you know about the visa; we cannot let visitors in without it."

I barely dared to look at Carlos' face. I was pissed at Pecker, and I was pissed that I had let him take the lead.

Carlos shoved an invitation letter into my hands.

"Go back to the border station, get your visas, and return," he said. He was furious.

"And by the way," he continued, "do you even realize that you are an hour late? Our appointment was originally for 11 A.M. and we moved it out to 1 P.M. last night, which Pecker confirmed. It is now after 2 P.M. Not to mention the time we are wasting with THIS. You couldn't even call to say that you were going to be late?" He stomped off.

I was mortified. I looked at Pecker. "You said 3 P.M.!"

"I don't know how that's possible," he tried to defend himself. "It must be some kind of misunderstanding."

Dickhead, dickhead, dickhead, I kept repeating in my head.

Forty minutes later, with the visas in our hands, the guard opened the gate. Fortunately, the customer was still willing to meet with us, and Pecker and I were asked to wait in the conference room while Carlos attempted to round up the remaining participants.

Our seats looked out into the hallway, and we could see the first person walking up. It was David, whom I talked to occasionally about engineering changes. We had developed a friendly, yet professional relationship over the phone, and we had met during my previous visits. As I pushed my chair back to get up so that I could greet him, I heard Pecker do the same. I quickly realized that Pecker's intention was to beat me to David. While I thought it silly to be racing around a large conference table to be first at shaking someone's hand, I also saw, out of the corner of my eye, that David's ring finger on his right hand was in a small metal brace.

The next moments proceeded in slow motion.

I raised both arms in an effort to get Pecker's attention who was rounding the final corner, almost tripping over his feet in his mad dash. I turned toward David and wanted to shout a warning, but it was too late. *NOOOOOOOOOOO*, my inner voice was screaming, its cadence slowed down in a long drawl as I helplessly watched the scene unfold: Pecker reached both hands out to David, and he proceeded to vigorously shake

David's right hand in a tight double-layered squeeze. David's face contorted. His knees buckled under the intensity of the handshake and the ensuing pain, and he went to the ground, trying to escape the two claws encapsulating his right hand.

"David, are you okay?" I called out, horrified at Pecker's behavior.

What was that Dickhead thinking latching on to someone's hand like that? Was he blind?

"I will be, eventually," David groaned as he pulled himself back upright.

"I'm soooo sorry," Pecker tried to apologize while clumsily half-hugging David from behind in an offering of support.

I was ready to go home. Dickhead had become my new mantra, and I was unsure that once I opened my mouth again, I would be able to say anything else.

We got settled around the table and tried to cover the awkwardness with small talk until the rest of the participants arrived. The meeting commenced, and the customer asked me a few questions about an ongoing PPAP. We quickly came to a resolution and then proceeded to talk about the delivery timeline once they would approve the paperwork. Pecker sat next to me, impatiently waiting for his opportunity.

"What else can you give me?"

I did a doubletake. It was Pecker who had blurted out the words. *Surely, this is not the way he is asking for more business?* I thought.

"What else can you give me?" he asked again, desperation in his voice.

The room had turned very quiet.

The customers' faces confirmed that they had never experienced anything similar.

"I know there's more to be had," he continued. "I used to work for the competition. *I* know."

Suddenly, a cartel attack didn't seem that bad. Anything to end our suffering. If we had been on life support at the beginning of the meeting, Pecker had just pulled the plug.

"There is no more for now," Carlos confirmed. "And we have to conclude this meeting. It is 5 P.M., and it's time to go home. Thank you for your visit."

"Can we invite you to dinner?" I tried.

"I have plans already," Carlos gave me a repulsed look.

Our meeting was over.

Carlos was kind enough to drive us to the bank, where we paid the fee for our business visas. The receipt would be kept at the border as proof of our visit and confirmation of us exiting the country. After the bank, Carlos dropped us off at the nearest border crossing. None of us made an attempt at conversation, and Carlos simply drove off without a word once we had stepped out of his car.

As Pecker and I walked across the bridge back toward the United States, he said, "You can't tell Richard."

I looked at him in disbelief.

"We just had the worst meeting of my life, and you don't want me to tell Richard about it?" I asked.

"Please don't," he repeated.

Richard was my first call when we arrived back at the hotel.

"You won't believe this Dickhead," is how I started my report.

Back at the hotel bar that evening, we realized that Pecker's Outlook calendar had saved the meeting time without considering the time zone difference from Michigan to Mexico. Paso del Norte was two hours behind Eastern Standard Time. Fortunately, Paso del Norte changed its Daylight Savings Time a week before the United States that year, and we had unknowingly "gained" an hour since we had not fallen back yet. Instead of two hours late, we were "only" one hour late.

But we definitely had fallen out of graces with the customer, and it would take several years to repair the damage done that one afternoon by one major dickhead.

It probably is of no surprise that Pecker's career with us did not last long.

♀

THE DOWNER

"**H**e's an idiot," Dickwad spat out the words, speckles of foamy spit exploding all around me and Richard.

We had come together in the hallway by pure coincidence.

Richard had just hung up the phone in his office, where he had talked to an irate customer with a stopped production line. The customer had complained that our equipment was not working properly and that he had been trying to get a hold of Dickwad unsuccessfully.

Dickwad, a German, had been hired around the same time as me. We were both training in Germany when I first met him. While my focus was on commodities, he was part of the in-house machine division, reporting to Richard. As an Applications Specialist, he would be quoting, installing, and servicing the company's equipment in the U.S. upon completion of his training and approval of his work visa.

As the call concluded, Dickwad happened to pass by Richard's office, and Richard stepped out into the hallway to confront him.

Returning from the bathroom, I had been walking down the hall when I encountered the face-off. I heard Richard mention the name of the customer, whom I had been trying to help and calm down earlier, and so I stopped to see how we could resolve this unpleasant situation.

"It doesn't matter if he's an idiot or not," Richard replied sternly. "He's the customer, and you can't ignore him."

"I spoke to him over a hundred times this past month," Dickwad argued. "You can't teach stupid."

"Not returning a customer call is unacceptable. He said he's been trying to reach you for days. He's livid. His line is down," Richard said.

"I told him over and over what he needs to do in order to keep his equipment running. He doesn't listen. It's not the machine anyways. It's the crappy goods he buys from the competition. There's nothing I can do. I told him that many times. He's plain stupid." Dickwad's hands were trembling, and he balled them into fists to make the trembling disappear.

Richard took a deep breath before replying, "We can't help the fact that he doesn't buy our commodities. And we all know how easy it is to get the blame for machine non-performance when what they are running on the equipment is the real problem. The product guy says it's the equipment, and the equipment guy says it's the product. The customer ends up getting stuck in the middle without a resolution. No matter what, we have to make an effort to help him. Take this as an opportunity to sell him our complete solution. Make it a win-win."

Dickwad just stood there glowering.

I felt invisible between them, but I was enjoying the scenery.

"Why didn't you tell me that you have a difficult customer?"

"Why should I? I can manage," Dickwad said.

"Ignoring is not managing. If Petra wouldn't have given me a heads-up, I would have been completely blind-sided and unprepared for the call," Richard paused. "You also cannot expect your team members to pick up your slack or make excuses for you. I will not have them lie because you chose to hide from a customer."

Dickwad conceded with a smirk, "Fine, if you insist; I guess I can call him when I get back to my office."

"We're going to do better than that. I already told him that we will head up there within the hour. It's a good thing they're only forty-five minutes up the road," Richard said.

"It's a waste of time. It won't do any good," Dickwad tried to argue. "He's stupid."

"I will have no more of this, Dickwad. We'll be leaving in ten minutes, so grab your tool bag, and meet me out front. We are done here," Richard said before turning around to conclude the meeting.

It wasn't just customers who were stupid.

"Ignorant Americans," Dickwad said one morning as he walked into the front office.

I didn't want to hear what he had to say, but he stopped near my desk and continued his rant.

"They just can't drive. I mean there's no traffic on the interstate, and I have to get stuck behind two slow mothers in their minivans driving their kids to school. Putzing along, completely oblivious that I'm behind them with my lights flashing. Don't they know what that means? It means MOVE OVER." He sighed loudly, "I miss German drivers. Americans don't know how to drive. How could they? Nobody's ever taught them properly. They basically hand you a driver's license for twenty bucks. I'm so annoyed."

Tired of his repeated insults about Americans, I asked, "If you hate it so much over here, why don't you go back to Germany?"

He ignored my comment, turned around, proceeded down the hallway to his office, and slammed the door behind him.

He wasn't much more pleasant when he made mistakes.

"It wasn't me," he protested. "*They* screwed up."

"I know it wasn't you, per se," I said. "But it was your job to ensure with Germany that they would verify the goods before they shipped them to us. Unfortunately, the customer found issues and some of our product sets are not working properly. Which means they can't tell which widget belongs to their respective product lines. It's a fair assumption that Germany did not verify some or all of the product sets during production. My question to you was if you made sure that Germany verified the order before we shipped it to our customer from here?"

"Germany knows about the verification," Dickwad snarled dismissively. "I have no control over their production. I couldn't have known they skipped verification on this order because they ran out of time."

"You did not answer my question if *you* ensured that the goods were verified. Forget about their production and ask yourself if we could have avoided this on our end. Couldn't we have caught their mistake if we would have asked them about the verification logs?" I asked. "Seeing that the verification documents were not included with the shipment, why wouldn't you ask them?"

"You know that they don't send them every time," he tried to argue. "Sometimes they only send the electronic verification files. And sometimes I don't get those until days later."

"I understand," I said calmly. "However, knowing how important this new customer is and the fact that we guaranteed verification to ensure they could identify their widgets with our product set, why would you not pro-actively ask about the logs? It's one simple phone call to Germany."

Dickwad countered, "The order was urgent. We had to ship it out as soon as it came in from Germany to make the deadline."

I was tired of playing the blame game with Dickwad. I thought, *Why can't he just do his job? Now the rest of us have to suffer the consequences of his laziness.* I wanted him to know that he had failed, "Yes, it was urgent. Too urgent for Germany to verify, and too urgent for you to double-check when you did not get any verification documentation. And thanks to rushing and assuming, we now have this huge quality complaint on our hands with our product not working in the field."

"It's not my job to run their production processes over there. I told them. I shouldn't have to do more," he defended himself.

"All I'm saying is that we could have avoided this crisis, if you would have just asked one simple question," I rebutted, my voice raised to show my annoyance.

"I can't help that they are fucking idiots," he replied and then stormed off.

It took a week before Germany was able to send verified replacement product. The customer agreed that the rework could be done by our company. Sometimes, the customer would use their own resources or hire contactors for quality inspection or rework, which could get quite expensive. Five of our employees spent the next three days at the customer's facility, sorting through 20,000 customer widgets. Each widget had two different sets of our goods, and we had to ensure that each set was the correct one for the customer's particular widget.

Our team was comprised of Richard, Dickwad, two people from production, and me. None of us wanted to be there, especially Dickwad, whose mood was miserable the entire time. We soldiered through a newly constructed expansive distribution center in our hard hats and steel-toe shoes in the middle of summer without air conditioning. We had more people in the field than at our plant during that time. The work was tedious, and it was difficult to keep our eyes straight. If one of our product sets was found to be incorrect, it was replaced by hand.

We were relieved, sore, and tired upon completion of the rework.

About two weeks later, Richard summoned me and Dickwad to his office.

"I just got a call from the customer," he started. "We have to go back."

"Why?" Dickwad and I called out simultaneously.

"Seems that there is a very specific location for each set on the widget, and there's not a huge tolerance in either direction. And from what the customer said, when we replaced some of the sets, we did not put them in the exact same spot. Now the scanners can't identify the individual widgets. And those then get rejected in the line."

We sat in silence. Richard looked at Dickwad.

"Anything you want to say about that, Dickwad?" he finally asked.

"Like what?" he responded.

"Well, like… how come you did not know about the specific placement of the product sets?" Richard said.

"I know about the location. I'm pretty sure we put the sets close to the old spots. Why wouldn't we? It was only logical."

"Are you kidding me?" Richard tried to keep his cool. "*You* quoted the equipment. *You* had all the details about where to place our product sets on their part. Why did you not share this information with the rest of the team while we were trying to fix Germany's screw-up? You were with us. You didn't say one word about product placement or accuracy. Now we look like complete idiots. We'll have to go back to replace the ones we just replaced that don't work in their process."

"It can't be that bad," Dickwad said. "The tolerance was like five millimeters. That's huge."

Richard looked at him in disbelief, "Five is a lot for machine placement. But for hand placement, especially on such a large area that has no indication of where the set should go, it's nothing. You, of all people, should know this."

Dickwad just shrugged his shoulders, "Shit happens."

"Shit like this shouldn't," Richard shook his head in frustration. His face was contorted with disgust.

During our second trip, the customer was kind enough to provide us with small templates that outlined the area for accurate placement. It was a support tool that they themselves had been using on rare occasions.

Always great to find out about such things after the fact.

Dickwad's general attitude was: SSSD or SSDD (same shit, same day or same shit, different day).

Everyone was stupid, all things sucked, the glass was always half empty, nothing good was ever going to happen, life sucked, and then you died.

He was the cancer who tried to fester and infect others with his malignancy.

The biggest mistake our company made was not firing him sooner. The rotten apple clung on for nine years before it was finally plucked, thanks to me.

And the positive transformation within the team was amazing from that point forward.

♀

THE ACTIVIST

After Richard left my company, I started moving into operational management. Shortly thereafter, in July 2009, Germany announced that they would be sending over the Global Production Manager, Rikert. The visit was planned for September, and while the main purpose was for him to show me how to complete the U.S. portion of the German consolidated report as it related to production, it was also a sign of appreciation of Rikert's progressive work in Germany. Under his leadership, production efficiencies had increased, waste decreased, and he was liked by most of his employees because of his no-bullshit approach.

I had met him in Germany, and we had hit it off instantly. He was loud and in-your-face, but in a good, energetic way. He laughed a lot, and his eyes twinkled when he spoke. He meant what he said, and I appreciated his bluntness. Everyone knew where they stood when it came to Rikert within a short timeframe.

The energy in the building shifted the instant he set foot in it. He was hard to ignore with his firm voice and lively laugh. I could hear him from my new office overlooking the production floor through closed doors. My eyes were focused on a quality report on my computer screen when I finally saw him approach with a cup of coffee in his hand.

"Do you have some time for me tomorrow?" he asked, grimacing when he took a sip of his drink. "You Americans call this coffee?"

"Slow your insults there, Mister," I laughed. "Why don't I show you how to work the fancy De'Longhi coffee maker tomorrow? It's probably just a training issue, nobody else ever complains about the coffee."

He winked at me, "Just trying to get your attention. You seem lost in your mountains of paperwork."

I followed his eyes to the multiple stacks of papers on my desk.

"You're gonna need a bigger desk soon," he said. "And a bigger office."

"I know, I have a hard time throwing things out. It's a habit I learned from the automotive industry," I said facetiously.

"I'm going to help you to let go. Clear your schedule for tomorrow morning. In fact," he looked around one more time, "plan for the whole day."

The next morning, he pulled up a chair to my desk.

"Today I will show you how to get organized. And I will teach you how to avoid this... accumulation of a mess," he pointed toward an especially tall and seemingly top-heavy stack of paperwork consisting of magazines, catalogs, multi-colored papers, and other unidentifiable objects.

He grabbed the first item, "So what do we have here?"

I peeked at the document and responded, "It's a PPAP approval from a customer."

"Is this where this should be filed?" he asked.

I cringed and tried not blush, knowing very well that my desk was not the proper filing location, "It will be filed in the PPAP binder."

"When?"

"Now?" I answered; my voice barely audible.

"Exactly, no time like the present seeing that we are trying to clean up your desk," he laughed, then continued. "I'm not saying that you should always do all your filing right away. It's okay to print what needs to be filed and then save it for the next morning, especially if you are working on a bigger task. But then, if you are working on a bigger task, why would you open an email anyways? Try not to get distracted by that little icon that tells you that an email has arrived. You may want to disable that option. Be committed to your task, don't interrupt it with benign little things that take your attention, 'cause then it takes you ten minutes to get back on track."

While he shared his valuable insights with me, I had pulled the PPAP binder from the cabinet, filed the approval, and left the binder out. I was certain we would find more of these somewhere on the remaining paper mountain ranges.

Rikert asked, "So, why do you print these out? Aren't these approvals saved electronically?"

"Yes, they are saved. But since these approvals are so critical, it is important that we can show the physical document at any given time. When our network goes down, then we would not have access to the electronic files. This would be crucial if we were to have an audit, and we would be unable to locate a requested document that certifies compliance."

"Very well, I can understand the reasoning," he agreed. "We do the same in Germany for PPAP approvals. I just wanted to see if you could determine if this was a good piece of paper or not." He winked at me, "Now, on to the next."

He took a trade magazine that was getting ready to slide off the first stack that we had tackled.

"Do you read these type magazines?"

"I would like to," I said.

"That's not what I asked," he pointed out.

I squirmed at his correct realization of my attempted diversion, and then admitted the truth, "I should, but… no, I don't read them."

"Then, throw it out. Be honest about it," he looked at me. "If you are interested, set a time window to read it and do it, but if you really don't care or don't ever have the time, then call these magazine people up and tell them to take you off the subscription list. It's too wasteful to get these sent in the mail just to throw them out."

"Honestly, I never read any of them," I said.

He tore the cover page with the address label from the magazine, placed it in a daily planner under tomorrow's date, then threw the magazine into the recycling bin.

"Tomorrow morning, you will call them to cancel your subscription," Rikert instructed. "You'll probably have a few more of these once we get done here."

"How'd you know?"

"I know everything," he laughed confidently. "I'm Santa Claus."

I cringed at his words, fighting off the St. Nick memory from my childhood.

We continued, and it did not take long for me to easily differentiate between keeping valuable records and hoarding unnecessary crap. It simply came down to asking "why" over and over. Almost 90% of what I had been saving for the last five years was useless. Especially since most physical paper had an electronic back-up somewhere else. Or it was catalogs I would never peruse, seminars I would never attend, or emails I would never file because we didn't have physical binders on every customer in the first place.

I soon started to realize that sometimes, it was okay to let go. I had felt committed to having to look at everything more deeply that hit my inbox or was put down on my desk. My fault had been that I wanted to give everything my attention… even if it was to be eventually. I had attached importance to everything. All I had to do, was to be honest and quick about what to do next or decide if there even would be a next step. A leader can delegate, a leader must decide what to focus on, and at the same time, a leader must discard the distractions.

We filled two large industrial garbage bags with recyclable papers and had a stash to shred for the sensitive matters.

"Don't you feel better now?" he asked when we were done.

"I do," I said amazed.

"The lesson is: there's no time like the present. If you have small things that can be taken care of within minutes, focus on those first thing in the morning. Then address the larger tasks later, and make sure you have a dedicated block of time without interruptions. You will be more productive once you have taken care of all the little and annoying things first."

I nodded in agreement. This made sense.

"Let's walk out on the production floor," he said.

Once there, he turned in a circle.

"See your employees?" he asked.

"Of course," I answered, unsure of where he was going with this.

"They *always* come first," he announced. "No matter what you work on, if they need something, you make the time. You have to take care of your employees. Especially in production. You must give them the time, the tools, and the resources to be successful. If you don't, then nobody will succeed. Lost time in production is deadly, as is down-time. So, if any one of these fine people ever ask for something, make sure to listen. And if you promise to do something, just do it. Don't put it off, especially if there is no reason to delay. You will earn their respect, and they will be loyal because they will know that you got their backs."

The look on his face confirmed how important he felt his words were. I held his stare, not wanting to break eye contact.

"It is your job to keep production running; that's your responsibility to the company. The only way to do that is to ensure that your employees have everything they need to make that happen for you... within reason... naturally."

"Naturally," I repeated obligatory. Yet, on the inside, I was totally confused.

It was a whole new concept for me to be a support person to production, seeing that I was the boss. I thought my job was to tell everyone what to do. Rikert's words had hit my ears in the wrong way initially. I had worked long and hard to be in top management, I had always followed orders as an employee, and I had thought that once I got to be management, my employees had to follow my orders.

It took some time for me to understand that management truly was about taking care of employees, which meant that I had to be present and approachable when they needed help; not to mention responsive to their needs. A company or a boss can only expect a successful result if everyone is supported to perform at their best. Oddly enough, it was the easiest (not to mention the only) way to ensure that everyone could come together as a team, as a unit, because they were supported by the company from the bottom up.

Input equals output.

Rikert simply was a doer. He encouraged to act in the now, knowing that people would procrastinate and make excuses otherwise. He loved to question "Why not now?"

Sure, he pissed some people off by being direct and making them squirm because of their own insecurities.

He was driven to make everything better, not resting until he was satisfied. He couldn't be bothered with office politics; considered them a waste of time. "You can't get anything done that way," he would say.

I liked that he made me uncomfortable and that he questioned everything routine. This made me realize that being out of my comfort zone was healthy and that without discomfort, there would be no growth.

He demanded better from everyone. Yet while he demanded, he always put his people first. He kept his promises, and he made time whenever I needed him.

When Rikert quit, I missed his effervescent presence that could propel me forward and lift me out of any slump. Even though we did not communicate frequently while he was working for the company, the loss of him left a huge crater in my morale in the sense that I felt unsupported by who was left. The assurance alone that Rikert would be there if I needed him, had been enough for me to know that I was taken care of by him.

I also realized that this wasn't the first time that one of my great mentors had left me behind. Comprehending that certain good people did not stick around, made me try to think of the reasons why they quit. It's a point in my career where I started paying more attention to a company's core and how owners treated the ones in their direct line of reporting.

Rikert and I have stayed in touch, and I am thankful to get to hear his empowering voice on special occasions. He truly is a person that radiates positive energy and change. I want to be surrounded by people who push me to do better. I miss not having him around, nor anyone quite like him. Diamonds like him are a rare find.

He can still make me feel guilty when I go through a lazy streak (or when I start building paper stacks on my desk).

For him, there simply was no excuse not to get done what someone was capable of doing – and more.

We all have purpose.

♀

THE NARCISSISTIC BULLY

"**W**hat do you think of him?" the owner asked.

The last interview candidate had just left. His name was Prick, he was in his early fifties, around 6' tall, with wavy brown hair, and piercing blue eyes. He had come on strong, boasting his past accomplishments and name-dropping previous Fortune 500 companies.

"He seems very arrogant," I said. "But… it may be what we need for the position. We need someone ambitious."

We were looking for a VP of Sales & Marketing.

"Yes, he definitely has the confidence," the owner said.

"Yup, no lack thereof," I agreed. "I don't particularly like his pushiness, but on the other hand, I think I could appreciate someone who can counter me. Someone with a different point of view who challenges me."

It was July 2010, and I had been in charge of the company's operations since January 2009, after Richard left. While Richard had managed the sales force, the owner had decided to take it on himself at that point, seeing that I did not have any outside sales or marketing experience. However, it did not take long for him to realize that he was just too busy traveling between the three locations (Europe, North America, Asia), to be able to properly lead our sales team of two.

The company, and the country, was just coming out of the recession, and the owner was looking for strong sales after the last struggling years.

"I think he can make sales happen," the owner said.

"Still weird that he has been unemployed for that long if he's as good as he says," I objected.

"Lots of good people became unemployed in 2008 and have struggled to find new jobs since then," the owner said. "Let's give him a try."

Prick started in August 2010. It did not take long for me and him to butt heads.

One morning, with my coffee in hand, I went to his office.

"Got a minute?" I asked.

"Sure, come on in," he offered.

Closing the door behind me, I sat down in one of the chairs facing him.

"Uh oh, am I in trouble?" he kidded from behind the desk, seated in a large executive chair that we had to special order for him since the existing one did not suit his needs.

"Well," I started. "Not really, but I just wanted to bring something to your attention."

"Shoot," he said.

"You've been here six months now, and while you have travelled some, you spend most of your time in the office," I said.

"I do," he agreed. "I manage the sales team. I do not need to be out on the road in order to do that."

"I understand that it's at your discretion," I replied, recognizing that I had just hit a sensitive spot as indicated by his raised eyebrows and disappearing smile.

He looked directly at me, having caught on to the insinuation that I did not care for someone in his position to be office-bound. Personally, I did not think that he would be able to pursue customer sales as effectively than if he was out in the field with his team. With only two external salesmen trying to cover the Southeastern United States, we had hoped for Prick to focus on winning some of the large, strategic accounts located throughout the entire country.

I continued, "I noticed that when you do work from the office, you tend to arrive around nine or ten o'clock, and sometimes not until lunch."

"And?" He crossed his arms and leaned back in his chair with a sour look on his face.

"As a leader to my team, I have always felt it important to set a good example," I explained. "I try to be here when or before they get in, and I don't like to leave the building until all of them have gone home themselves. I think it's the right thing to do to be present and to show that I am no different when it comes to our policy on work hours in the office and on the production floor."

"Well, that's your problem," he said curtly.

"I disagree," I replied with a smirk. I had not expected his indifferent response and was surprised at his dismissive and loud tone, which made me feel uneasy and unsure of my next move.

Hoping to bring my point across more clearly, I went on, "We have set working hours, we have a handbook that outlines the rules and policies on attendance, and we all have to comply, otherwise it's not fair to everyone." *Surely, he could understand my reasoning when considering company policy?* I thought when I had finished.

"I'm in sales," he said sternly, his cheeks flushing with color, his voice raised. "When I travel, nobody cares that I am traveling on the weekends, or at night, or outside of the normal working hours. I also work from home, at night, and during my weekends. Our employees don't see that, I understand. But that does not mean that I'm slacking or being lazy."

My intention had been to raise his awareness of how his regular absence affected the team in the hopes that he could make a few adjustments. Unfortunately, I could tell that Prick felt that I was personally attacking his character instead.

Internally, I could instantly deflate his arguments. I had not seen emails from him arrive during the night nor had he traveled any weekends that could confirm his statement.

I was conflicted to either drop the discussion for the sake of peace or press forward in order to take a stand to clear up his misconception about his after-work activities. I felt it was my duty to press forward and knew that my next words had to be chosen carefully as not to escalate the situation to a point where it could not be recovered.

I took a deep breath to calm my brain and my next words, knowing that he would not receive them well, "I would not have brought it up if you were traveling a lot. But you are not. You have travelled less than 10% since you started, all during the week. So, if you are not traveling at all in a given week, then you should adhere to our handbook and be present just like all our employees. You don't have a home office; you have an *office* office."

By the time I ended, Prick's entire face was radiating crimson anger. Coincidentally, it was the same color as the office's major accent wall - seeing that this was the middle office of the black, red, and yellow German flag configuration.

He moved his crossed elbows from his chest to the middle of the desk and placed his fists close the edge of the table where I was seated. He pushed his upper body forward closing the distance between us, "I make my own schedule and decide where or when I will work. You. Can't. Tell. Me. What. To. Do."

I could feel his hot breath on my face.

I had never been confronted by anyone quite like him before. In words or in physicality. It felt uncomfortable, and I didn't want to be in the same room as him anymore. Every one of his replies had been loud and firm, in a way that a bully would do when going on the offensive or defensive. Prick was also escalating his physical appearance, trying to get me to retreat with his overpowering presence to end my attempted attack on his character.

Yet I knew that I had to remain. I was not going to allow myself to be silenced by intimidation.

I reminded myself that I had deliberately sought Prick out about his attendance issues:

For one, it was obvious that he was ignoring the company's policies and he needed to be reminded that there were no exceptions when working in an office as opposed to traveling during the week. The other, was the fact that I wanted him to be aware that I wasn't afraid to challenge him when I saw an issue arise. He was not immune to oversight and justification, and the sooner he realized it, the less he would get out of hand in the long run.

But most importantly, I had hoped this meeting would give me a good insight into his character, mindset, and hierarchical communication style, which would help me adjust my tactic when dealing with him and my own emotions going forward.

I had not expected him to be so confrontational and rude right off the bat.

Thanks to the quality principles instilled in me over the years, my approach to conflict was less reactive and more observant before addressing any problem at the root. Dealing with irate customers, uncooperative vendors, and variables beyond my control, I had learned to base my opinions and reactions not on perceptions, but on first-hand observations and interactions as well as facts before deciding on a response.

Yet Prick's reaction to my facts and what I had thought to be a normal tone of voice, showed that he perceived me as the enemy.

I decided to go for instant emotional suppression. I had to ignore my feelings which instructed me to retaliate in the heat of this argument, and at the same time, told me to run and hide from this man.

I took another calming breath, without altering my body position or facial expression, before responding, "All I wanted to say is to please keep in mind that we have employees on site that see you come in late every day, take long lunches when you go out, and then sometimes leave early." I continued, "It's not good for morale, and I don't see why you can't be here for forty hours a week if you have no appointments scheduled."

I smiled in an effort to soften the mood.

I was also certain that Prick would hate it. I couldn't help myself. There had to be some reward for suppressing my feelings while letting him know subconsciously that I considered him to be a dick.

His still angry, red face and clenched fists remained unchanged as he bellowed out his next words, "I don't care what you or they think. I paid my dues, I'm not like everyone else. I don't have to justify my presence or absence. I'm a Vice President, not a line worker; I don't clock in or out and never will."

"Prick, please, that's not the point…" I tried to calm him down. My words were interrupted almost immediately.

"Don't patronize me. I don't owe anyone an explanation. And now, if you'll excuse me, I have other topics to attend to. I wouldn't want to be accused of holding a coffee klatch in my office when I should be working."

And with that, he rolled his fancy chair to his left, toward the open laptop on the side table.

I got up and left, realizing that it was the smartest decision given the circumstance.

The argument had taught me that Prick's instinct was to go on the bullying offensive when he was trying to defend himself.

And that he considered himself to be superior to everyone else at work.

With his attitude of self-importance, the rest of the employees also had a hard time knowing how to interact with him. The team operated with a "one for all, and all for one" mentality. Prick's shortened slogan of "all for one", was not easily accepted by all.

"She should work for me," he said to me one Friday afternoon in the yellow kitchen.

She was Lana, my direct report in charge of preparing quotes, production orders, and purchase orders. Prick wanted Lana to report to him. While she worked for him in a support role, he could not order her around unchecked, and she often cleared his requests through me before tending to them… or not.

"Nope, it's not going to happen, Prick," I told him firmly. "While inside sales is part of the front office, we cannot define her position as solely sales. She doesn't even do any inside sales, it's more of a customer service job. Then there's purchasing, production, and quality. She interacts with and works in all departments. It would not make sense to shift the reporting to you. And our company is way too small for multiple Chiefs and only one Indian."

"She fights me on everything," he complained. "I can't get anywhere because she's so set against me. She makes life hard on me and my sales team on purpose. I need control over her job in order to do *my* job."

"Now hold on," I said, annoyed that he had spoken his words so blatantly in the kitchen, where other people could easily overhear us. "There's always two sides to everything. She has told me on multiple occasions that your sales team doesn't provide her with complete information so that she can't do *her* job. And she should not have to run after your sales guys because they are too lazy to ask their customers. We can't just wing it considering that we are in a compliance business. We need supplier manuals, drawings, and specifications before we can quote anything. You know the drill."

"We are losing sales because we are too slow," Prick argued.

I lowered my voice, trying to hint that we should keep our conversation more private, "If we are too slow, I suggest your team gets the information together quicker and more complete. We are not selling products made of cheapo materials here." I paused, then continued half-jokingly, "We all make too much money to warrant making cheapo products."

He didn't get the joke.

"I have never worked for an organization that was this difficult to deal with… in all aspects," he spat, his face flushed with anger. "I'm management, I deserve respect."

I ignored his last statement. Respect was earned, not deserved.

He looked at me, wanting some type of acknowledgement.

I resisted my urge to respond with my opinion, fearing we would end up in another yelling match.

I let him stew for another minute, indicating that I wasn't willing to offer any insights on respect. Then, I tried to divert, "Now, remember, you have only worked in retail. That's a completely different animal in its sales cycle. You can't rush automotive. There's a process in verifying requirements, specs, and then there's the PPAP."

"I get that," he conceded calmly.

I knew that I should give him something in return. Dangle a carrot so that we could move on, "I agree that we are too slow in getting feedback from Germany on the material selection when we need their input. How about I'll talk to Hans in the R&D department to see how he can improve that?"

"I appreciate it, but I would also appreciate if you can talk to Lana," Prick turned to get a coffee cup from the cupboard. "While she may not report to me, she still owes me the respect. She works for me in an indirect way, and she must do what I say. Who does she think she is?"

I sighed. It had been a sore subject for a while, and I was tired of his power plays. Prick wanted to control everything. Especially the decisions and people in my domain that impacted his. While I understood his concern, he made no effort to improve his support for the team. Which made it hard for anyone to want to help him.

"I used to run large organizations where I was in charge of everything," he reminded me. "I'm not used to having to wait on anything. I used to snap my fingers, and my team would support me without questions. Here… it's like pulling teeth."

Understanding that he had no concept of a small enterprise, I felt compelled to explain, "I'm sorry it doesn't work like that in a small company. We all do more than just one job and have larger areas of responsibilities. Yes, in a large company you could delegate many things to another person or department. But we don't have people." I went on, "Everyone has to fill a lot of shoes, so it's even more important to have all your ducks in a row when you expect the next person down the line to take the ball and run with it." Internally I was smiling, proud of my use of multiple idioms in one sentence.

Prick shook his head in disagreement, grabbed his coffee from the machine, then left the kitchen without giving me another look.

"Those Germans are going to cost me my last nerve," I heard him mutter as he turned left down the hall toward Dickwad's office.

Exiting the kitchen to my right and continuing through the main office area, I passed Lana's desk.

"Please, don't ever let him be my boss," she begged. "I'll quit if that happens."

"Don't worry," I said. "You work for me and that won't change as long as I'm here."

"He is so spoiled, all he wants is for me to cater everything to him," Lana was clearly frustrated having overheard part of our conversation in the kitchen. "He expects me to complete the forms, run after the customer for missing information, and then he does not even clue me in once the quote has been sent. Why can't he go back to work for one of his big companies if he misses it so much?"

I could understand her sentiment. It was tough to overhear a manager accuse an employee for being difficult, based on personal perception rather than actual work performance and implemented procedures, like Prick had just done.

Prick had worked in high-level positions in larger companies. It was a fact that he would frequently remind us of. He was used to having a large staff and all the privileges that came with working for a fat, multilayered organization.

I wondered about this lingering obsession. Here was a man who once seemed to have everything in life: a big job, a beautiful wife, healthy children, a mansion, and a fancy car. Now, he worked for less than half his salary in a small no-name company, was bitterly divorced, his children caught in the middle, he was renting a small apartment, and he was driving his father's beat-up Buick. Yet he had lost none of the perception of being rich and important.

I *almost* felt sorry for him.

"I know he's not easy to deal with, Lana," I concurred. "However, admit it, you don't have to be so deliberate at times."

"What do you mean?" she asked, visibly upset at my accusation.

Seeing her insulted face glare up at me, I realized that Prick and Lana had one thing in common: both were very emotionally reactive when they felt attacked.

I had noticed before that Lana's interactions with someone were in direct correlation to how she was treated or how intelligent she judged someone to be. If she was treated with respect, she would return the favor. But if she felt attacked or demeaned, then she could not hide her contempt.

Of course, crude bluntness was a German trait and not one that Germans necessarily wanted to relinquish for the sake of amicability. Unlike Southerners, who tended to overlook rudeness and retaliated with overdramatic niceness, Germans kept true to the tit for tat approach. It was a natural cultural behavior, which typically did not pose an issue until removed from its natural environment.

I pushed on. I was not certain that Lana was even aware of her conduct, and I felt it was important that she could take this opportunity to learn something valuable about herself.

"Admit it, you're making it hard on him whenever you can," I challenged.

She continued to give me a dubious stare.

I finally offered, "You're a stickler for detail. You could be moving things along on your own if you wanted to. We all know Prick and his sales team are not into details, he says so himself. Half the time, you have better customer contacts than they do. In a way, you *are* slowing him down."

Lana's gaze lost its strength as she turned her focus inward. I could tell that she was giving my words serious consideration and that she was struggling with the conscious realization of the truth.

She finally exhaled a long breath and conceded, "I don't mean to, really. I'm just trying to make a point. It's the principle. We have rules. I follow the rules, and why shouldn't he? Just because he's a VP? Besides, he never says anything nice, and he treats me like a lower-class citizen, so why should I go out of my way when he never does anything for me?"

She had a point. Prick always looked out for himself first. However, I could not openly admit that I thought Prick to be a selfish prick. He was part of the management team, and I knew that I needed to be supportive of the entire team as not to encourage gossip and backstabbing. Also, I tried hard not to let my personal opinions rule my professionalism, and in all fairness, Prick had moved our company along quite nicely in the revenue department. He couldn't be all bad.

"I appreciate that you follow the rules. Everyone should, including management. All I'm asking is that you consider the tone and your reaction when working with Prick. Don't forget, he may treat you better if you do the same."

Lana sighed, "He just gets under my skin."

"Seems you get under his as well," I said. "You're taking it too seriously, and it's affecting your response. It's just work; don't let it or him get to you. Why would you let him control how you feel?"

She thought about it for a minute.

"You're right, I let him do this to me. I need to figure out how to ignore him."

"Well, I think you need to figure out how to ignore *your* emotions," I said. "You can't ignore him. The only thing you have control over is how you decide to react."

"I wish," Lana sighed, a sad look on her face. But she also looked relieved, "Thanks for letting me vent."

"Anytime," I smiled, "I got your back."

Despite the apparent negatives, there were some upsides to Prick's presence:

While he was not the best communicator when in the office, he was extremely professional and good with customers. He was prepared, had a great sales pitch, and represented our company with passion and conviction. He stood up for the company in the toughest of circumstances as well as during negotiations with his strong presence. And he was able to collaborate with the customer to reach solutions in times of conflict. In that, he was a miracle worker because he was not afraid to tackle any issue while still finding the middle ground for all parties to walk away with a win-win.

Additionally, Prick's arrogance and pushiness turned out to be a blessing for the company regarding sales. Within a few years, he increased our revenue considerably. The largest growth sector was in the machine division. He preferred selling expensive equipment over the struggles of selling commodities that would only bring in a few cents apiece and that needed large volumes to make an impact on revenue growth. Prick was all about instant gratification. With each large equipment sale came a sizable commission check as a reward.

However, the nice thing about automotive goods sales was that once won, it was a gift that would keep on giving for years. Once a product was qualified, the program would run for the life of the vehicle model. And it would most likely to continue with the next version. It was a fact lost on Prick, and it frustrated me to no end that he could sell the equipment, but then failed to sell the corresponding product to run on the equipment. Even though a product may only cost one or two cents, there was value and sustainability in volume. And some products, with extremely difficult requirements, could cost in the dollar range apiece, making even small volumes attractive.

With the increased equipment turnover, the service aspect became very important. Customers requested maintenance contracts, spare parts, and timely support. Prick quickly became irritated with Dickwad's inability and resistance to perform under pressure. When Dickwad joined him on customer visits to discuss new equipment projects, his rude and uninterested behavior toward everyone was completely opposite of Prick's.

Observing the two of them disagree on almost everything, I figured that I could use Prick to tackle the continuing Dickwad conundrum. If I could get Prick on a mission to take over our service department, then there could be an opportunity to purge ourselves from the evil that was Dickwad.

The fact that Prick could not control inside sales (or me), left room for him to want to manage the machine division, and I encouraged him every step of the way. The service group was under Germany's leadership after Richard's departure, and Dickwad had turned even more uncooperative with the lack of local guidance, as was in his nature. He was a huge risk to Prick's sales efforts and corresponding commission payments.

It didn't help that I was constantly feeding the fire. Every quote Dickwad prepared, every communication, every interaction was scrutinized by me. Anytime I saw an issue where Dickwad undermined the integrity of the company, I involved Prick.

Within a year of Prick's hiring, Dickwad was fired. The accumulation of errors and his horrible behavior finally got the better of him.

After years of me complaining to Richard and the owner, all backed by facts, it was amazing that, in the end, all it took to get Dickwad fired, was one egotistical, loud-mouthed male.

And so, I had finally learned that there were other avenues available to me in order to get my agenda accomplished.

Nonetheless, I much rather preferred the direct, logical, calm, and factual approach. I despised having to resort to manipulative detours as they were illogical and undermined my authority as a leader. I wondered, *Why does **my** voice not matter?*

With Dickwad fired, we soon hired a new Applications Specialist from Germany who ended up reporting to Prick.

The overall mood at the company improved considerably, and the team pulled together into a tight-knit smooth-running machine. It was one of the best working atmospheres I ever experienced.

The only ripple in the otherwise smooth waters came from Prick, who continuously rubbed everyone the wrong way by demanding instead of asking.

"He can't tell me what to do." Chad was clearly upset.

I had just walked out on the production floor to go over the week's schedule, confirming a PPAP run for one of our large automotive customers that morning. Chad was the Production Supervisor, who had been working for me for years. He had quickly advanced from an operator to a supervisor, and he had proven himself to be one of the most loyal and trustworthy employees.

"What's going on?" I asked.

"He told me to interrupt the PPAP for some urgent product that he wants to send out for free today," Chad explained. "He wanted me to stop my set-up, and I told him that I couldn't do that."

"I'm sorry about that. Did you tell him about the PPAP?" I asked.

"I did, but he said he didn't care," he replied. Then he sighed heavily, "You know how he can be."

I did, but this was not the place or time to discuss Prick's past behaviors. My job was to keep the peace and to get Chad calmed down and back on track.

I said, "Well, you and I both know that we must run the PPAP today, so that has priority."

Chad nodded, "I know, it's on the schedule. Prick could see that too if he would look at it."

"I wish he would have come to me first," I agreed. "Maybe it's a huge potential customer, and he was just eager to get things started. Do you think you can run the sample after the PPAP… if we have time left?"

Chad nodded again, "It will be tight, but we can definitely try."

"Thanks Chad," I said. "I will take it from here. Where did he go?"

Chad pointed toward the office area, "He went to see Lana about making the production order for the sample."

Having calmed Chad down, I quickly left the production area and proceeded to Lana's desk. I anticipated that I still had some de-escalating to do, which was confirmed when I found Prick towering over Lana's shoulders, both staring at her computer screen.

"I'll find a tool that is close to what the customer needs," Lana promised.

I could hear the slight aggravation in her voice as she continued, "This old German system is just not as easy as you would think, so I have to look through all the tool sizes manually. There is no sorting function."

I knew that she wanted Prick to leave. She was not comfortable with him looming over her like that. Her head reminded me of a turtle trying to retract into the safety of its shell, all scrunched low between her shoulders.

"Did you tell Chad not to run the PPAP?" I asked Prick when I reached the desk.

He turned around to face me. I could see Lana's shoulders visibly drop with his movement, and I had to suppress a giggle.

"I told him to run my sample first, so I did not say *not* to run the PPAP," he smirked at me.

"Let's not split hairs here," I said dismissively. "We cannot run your sample first. We will run the PPAP as scheduled."

"I promised the customer we would send out the samples today," he countered.

"And we may still be able to do that," I said calmly. "But… you cannot promise something if you don't know if we can truly do it. And running to Chad was not the right approach to find out."

"Don't get pissy feeling left out," Prick held out his hands in a defensive move. "You weren't in your office."

"I was gone two minutes," I responded. "And it doesn't justify ignoring our process or schedule."

He was correct to assume that I was pissy. I was extremely annoyed that Prick constantly tried to interfere in the company's operation. He did not see the value in having sales and operations separated when it came to achieving his sales directives. All the sudden, production was his to command in the pursuit of his own agenda.

I announced, "The PPAP is a must for today. Once the products are run, I must take initial measurements to ensure that we are within the tolerance. Any issues, and we must start over. We cannot risk running out of time at the end of the day because of a sample request. The products have to be sent off to the accredited measuring lab today."

Prick frowned; he was not happy.

"Besides, Lana still has to find a matching size, then we have to see if we have the tool in inventory, plus the material, and then we need to make an order. Does the customer exist in our database?"

"No."

"Do you have the sample-request-form completed?"

"No."

"Then I suggest you provide Lana with the needed information first before trying to disrupt Chad in production," I said, having made my point.

Prick understood that he had lost the battle and conceded, "All I'm trying to do is sell products. You always complain that I don't bring enough orders. And when I do, you make this process extremely cumbersome with bureaucracy."

"I get how frustrating it is when it should be so easy. It can be easy if you follow the process," I said reassuringly. "But... keep in mind that we could have avoided this little unpleasantness if you would have waited for me to return to my office instead of running to Chad and then Lana."

I hated to be arguing in front of an employee. It was never a good thing when management wasn't in agreement or not working together. Nonetheless, I felt it important to reprimand him in front of Lana to show her that I could defend the team – with the enemy present.

Prick stood, quietly digesting the scolding.

I didn't wait for his response. Instead, I tried to defuse the negative with a positive, "The good news is that we may be able to get the samples out today as long as there are no issues with the PPAP run."

Prick nodded. He seemed relieved, "Good. Let me get the customer's information from my office, and then I will step out of everyone's way."

As he walked toward his office down the hall, I couldn't help ask one final question.

"What's the potential behind this urgent sample?"

There was no reply.

I started to get a hunch.

"What's the material?" I asked Lana, who had turned around while Prick and I had been arguing.

She couldn't wait to tell me with a broad smile on her face, "Cheapo material."

We simultaneously rolled our eyes and disbanded before sarcastic laughter could overtake us over having wasted everyone's time for nothing.

Even today, I ponder if Prick had been the right fit for our company back then. Sure, he increased revenues, but his refusal to be part of the team and his desire to want to control the team ensured that the team would never accept him into their midst with open arms.

What I do know now, many years later, is that he probably was a good fit for the time that I was there to equalize his behavior.

While it was impossible to integrate Prick (and Dickwad) into the team, I was able to inspire the team despite of them. I focused everyone toward a common cause, and I was able to provide the needed balance by encouraging their strengths and curbing their weaknesses.

At times, it was fascinating to observe Prick when he went to war for himself, fighting for his "rights". He often reminded me of a rooster about to enter a cockfight to establish a pecking order: his head held high, chest pushed forward, and a strutting walk that looked like a stick up his butt was controlling his legs.

Nonetheless, I appreciated that he had a different viewpoint, which helped widen mine. I loved arguing with him as it gave me the chance to learn about my weaknesses and his. Prick felt constantly undermined and underappreciated and viewed everyone as the enemy out to get him. He had no trust.

It saddened me that the owner entrusted Prick with the management of the company shortly after I quit in the fall of 2015.

I knew my dream team would eventually fall apart under his dicktatorship, and it saddened me deeply. The team deserved trust, empowerment, loyalty, and fairness. All attributes not principally found in an untrusting, narcissistic bully.

When the company got sold within a year of my departure, Prick accused me of knowing about the sale and quitting because of it. Which was strange, as we had often talked about the potential of the owner selling the business. He had attempted a sale once before.

By 2015, the company had become very profitable on all represented continents, which was quite a different scenario from when the owner tried to sell it previously. That fact alongside some other recent activities undertaken by the owner had been clear signs that conditions were favorable for another try. Prick had seen the same events unfold, and he could have drawn the same conclusion.

Yet I wondered if he didn't stay on purpose, knowing that he could move into the top spot once I left. Promotion by way of elimination and convenience. It was a familiar concept to the company. I could not fault them for it as it would be hard to argue that their previous decision had not worked out, as it had. Admittedly, it bothered me that Prick became General Manager, a title that had been denied to me and that seemed to be reserved for male employees. Or maybe the owner finally gave in to Prick's demands for the title, knowing that the sale was in its final stage, which meant that he didn't have to care any longer about who was in charge or what the title said.

Last I heard, Prick quit shortly after the company was sold. He took a job working for a cheapo product company.

♀

THE NAPOLEON

W hile I was thankful to Richard for hiring me, ultimately, it had been the owner who had given me the opportunity of employment.

I was first introduced to Dicklet in 2001 through Ricardo, the Guardian. Ricardo had heard about a German entrepreneur looking for an English tutor for his son while getting a massage. The masseuse knew Dicklet, Ricardo knew the masseuse, and the rest is history.

Once we agreed on an hourly rate, I started going to Dicklet's house after work on a weekly basis. Sven, the ten-year old son, was simply adorable. I had been worried about teaching English to a child. My teaching experiences so far had been limited to adults and German. It was an unwarranted worry. Tutoring Sven meant that we would mainly do his homework together. It was easy, and I quickly grew fond of Sven, who, while sweet and well-behaved, had a mischievous side to him. Hilde, Dicklet's wife, was also extremely nice, and she would always find a snack for us to eat when I showed up.

During these occasions, it was rare for Dicklet to be at home since he was traveling a lot for work. I was surprised to see him one evening in the driveway, getting out of his convertible Porsche as I was leaving his house.

It had been a beautiful, warm April day and the Porsche's top was down.

"How's it going with Sven?" he asked in German.

I didn't like to speak German while in the States. In all honesty, I didn't like to speak German anywhere. It was a complicated language, and after so many years of living in the U.S. and becoming a citizen, I detested it when people just assumed that I wanted to speak German because I was born in Germany. Generally, I also considered it rude to be speaking a foreign language in America, especially when being around Americans, and I would make a point of sticking to English when that happened. However, seeing that there were no other Americans around and not wanting to be rude to my elders, I proceeded down the steps and responded in kind, "Great, Sven's a smart kid, his English is very good, and if he stays in this country, he won't even have a German accent."

By then, I had reached him.

Am I taller than him?

The only other time I had seen him was during my first visit; he had been seated in a car, ready to head to the airport. The introduction had been short, and there had been no visual clues that he was too.

I looked down to ensure that we were on even ground. We were. My eyes moved up from his white Adidas to the embroidered designer jeans and Ed Hardy polo shirt. His clothes said young, hip twenty or thirty-something-wannabe rather than mid-forty-something-businessman. I continued the visual journey upward and stopped to meet his blue eyes, which were framed by glasses. I could almost see the top of his head, and his thin, choppy blond hair, which had been styled at some point, was scattered into a raised mess from the drive home in the convertible German racing machine.

His glasses were, without a doubt, of European origin with their slight feminine shape and bold color. Americans at that time had not caught on to the fact that uniqueness could be expressed through spectacles. Unfortunately, Dicklet's choice of fashionable eyewear did nothing to make him more masculine.

On the flip side, his metrosexual appearance, combined with the short height, helped make Dicklet more approachable in a down-to-earth kind of a way.

I also liked Dicklet for the ease of communication as he spoke to me without coming across as arrogant or pejorative. The fact that he was still flaunting his richness, as was easily observed by the McMansion, the Porsche, and the designer clothes, was not a negative to me particularly. I especially got the car part; I would have been right there with a Porsche if I could have afforded to buy and maintain one. I loved performance cars, including American muscle cars, and a '69 Chevy Camaro SS would have been parked right next to my Porsche in my large garage if given the chance and money.

"It looks like we'll be living here for the next two years or so," Dicklet said. "Sven may sound more American than German by the time we go back to Germany."

"Kids have a better chance of losing their accents than adults," I laughed.

"Don't I know it," he agreed.

Dicklet moved past me toward the steps, and as he took the first one, he turned around.

"How's the job situation?" he asked.

"Not sure," I responded. "We heard that they will be filing for bankruptcy protection before long. It's scary to think both of our incomes depend on one company."

"I may have an opening for an Office Manager in a few months if you are interested in applying?" he asked.

"Absolutely," I said, then inquired, "How do you know already that you'll need an Office Manager in a few months?"

He smiled, "I have a German intern who is currently working in the office. She has to go back in September, and we need a local talent to replace her. We probably want to hire someone soon. German is very important, of course. I think you could be a good fit given your background and work experience."

"I'm definitely interested, thank you," I said.

"Well, don't thank me yet. You'll still have to give me your résumé and then interview with Richard, who is my General Manager. And it'll be up to him to make the decision."

I nodded, "No problem. And thanks for the opportunity. I appreciate it."

Thankfully, Richard decided in my favor, and I flew to Germany in July of 2001. By coincidence, the company had scheduled a corporate event the Friday afternoon after my arrival, just three days before my official training was to begin. I was glad that I would have the chance to meet some of my German colleagues in a more casual setting.

Once at the company's facility, I noticed a large tent that had been set up in the parking lot next to the office building. The July afternoon was warm; the weather was perfect for an outdoor event. As I got closer to the tent, I could see and hear Dicklet talk to another man. They were speaking English. Relieved to have found what I assumed to be another "American", I joined them.

"Petra, it's so nice you could make it," Dicklet shook my hand. "Meet Don, we just hired him to be our salesperson in the Southeastern U.S.A."

Don and I shook hands.

"It's nice to meet you, Don," I said. "I'm so glad there's another English-speaking person here."

He looked at me funny.

"Now, same for me, but I don't quite understand why you would be worried about that," he wondered. "Aren't you German?"

I laughed, "Well, technically I'm American, but yes, I was born and raised in Germany. But I don't speak a lot of German in the States. When I talk to my parents, it's never about work. We talk about the weather and other family members. It always takes me several days to get back into the swing of the full German vocabulary, and until that point, I try not to sound like a jabbering idiot. After a few days, I'm fine, but seeing that I just arrived yesterday, I may have to excuse myself as an American abroad who is struggling to master the German language."

Don and Dicklet laughed.

Dicklet looked past my shoulders.

He said, "Don, I see some of your German counterparts have just arrived. I really want you to meet them; come with me."

And without another word, Dicklet ushered Don away.

Standing, somewhat lost, in the parking lot with not many other people around, I was unsure of where to go next.

"Can I show you my company?" I heard a nearby voice call to me. It had a very heavy German accent. When I turned to my left, I immediately thought of the term gentleman. The short man, whom I guessed to be in his late sixties or early seventies, was dressed in a clean-cut, light brown suit. His thinning hair was styled back, and I assumed that he would normally wear a hat with the outfit, as would have been fitting for an earlier era. He had a gentle face with warm eyes, and he exuded quiet confidence.

Considering his words and his height, I knew he had to be Dicklet's father. I walked up to him and introduced myself in German.

We shook hands.

"Please, call me Reinhard." Then he asked again, "So, can I show you my company?"

I replied, "I would love it."

"Wonderful," he smiled. "Follow me."

We proceeded into the building and entered the production area. There weren't many employees around; work had concluded early for the event, and the place seemed quiet. I was amazed how clean and organized the production floor was. The area was relatively small, but with everything in its place and very little clutter, it seemed much larger.

Reinhard smiled at the look on my face, "I know, we make good use of the space."

He was beaming with pride. He pointed toward a wall at the back of the production hall, "On the other side of that wall is my house. It was quite a day for me when we moved into this added building. My wife wasn't too pleased to have everything so close. Maybe in part because we can hear and feel the equipment run from inside our house." He laughed.

We stopped at different machines, where Reinhard explained the function to me in easy terms without making me feel stupid. From production, we continued to the offices located on the second floor.

Every time we came across people, Reinhard would stop and introduce me. And while he was making conversation, he kept his attention on me the entire time.

I was impressed that he knew everyone's name.

"I don't spend much time in these parts," he said as he was overlooking the open concept office area. "The heart of it all is downstairs, that's where the action is." He paused, then sighed, "I retired some years ago. But it still gives me great pleasure to be able to hear that heartbeat from my living room next door."

I didn't know what to say, so I just nodded my head.

Reinhard seemed lost in his memories.

The sound of approaching people snapped him back, "Sorry about that," he smiled apologetically.

I smiled back, "No, that's quite okay. I get it."

It was his turn to nod. I could tell he was pleased with my response.

"Now let's get you back downstairs so that you can spend your time with some younger people."

Back outside, he steered me toward a group of laughing women. Reinhard made the introduction, then he shook my hand, "Now, have a wonderful time in Germany. We are glad to have you." With another nod, he turned and walked away.

I felt honored that the man who had founded the company, and who had therefore made it possible for me to get this job, treated me so kindly. He had instantly taken me under his care when he saw that I had been left unattended, and he did what he had known to be the decent thing to do. He had earned my respect and gratitude in less than twenty minutes.

It is one of the fondest memories I have of the company.

Fast forward to December 2008. When Richard shared the news with me that he was leaving, I became deeply distressed. I could not imagine life at work without him. He was my source for inspiration and learning.

"Don't worry, Petra," he tried to assure me. "It'll work out, you'll see."

"How do you figure that?" I asked, contemplating his statement.

He replied, "Well, I gave a thirty-day notice, and I submitted a contingency plan to Dicklet that should ensure a smooth transition."

Dicklet was residing mostly in Germany and Asia those days.

"A smooth transition to what?" I asked.

"I recommended that you take over for me. My plan calls for me to stay on as a consultant for another six months so that I can show you some of the higher-level tasks. You're more than capable, and you know the entire company inside and out," he said.

Richard often referred to me as the "librarian", as I had acquired a wealth of knowledge throughout our years together, plus I had an excellent memory of events and people. I couldn't take full credit though. Part of my memory was supported by a vast collection of emails and other documents, which I had accumulated over the years for the "what if" scenario. Being in a compliance industry, it was important to be able to provide proof of certain informal communications, timelines, and agreements. The IT[34] department in Germany, on the other hand, did not like the fact that I constantly exceeded my assigned email storage size limit.

"What about my job?"

"You'll have to hire a replacement, which is impossible," he chuckled. "Nobody can replace you."

"Everybody is replaceable," I reminded him.

"True, but your job has a specific skillset and needs a lot of training, not to mention the German requirement... It may take months to find someone to take over for you. The great thing about you replacing me is that you know the company. And the company knows you," he said. "You're dedicated, trustworthy, reliable... shall I go on?"

While I was flattered about his compliments, I couldn't help but feel panic trying to creep into my brain. I shook my head, hoping to distract the fear, then asked, "Where are you going?"

"I'm not going anywhere. As a matter of fact, I'm going to be your vendor, so we'll stay in touch," he said.

"Are you going to work for one of our material suppliers?"

He laughed, "No. I'm doing my own thing. Entrepreneurship runs in my family, and it's time for me to return to those roots. You know, I've been trying to buy into this company, but Dicklet won't let me."

"I had no idea," I said. Richard had never talked about it.

"I had hoped it to be an option at some point," Richard continued. "I mean, I helped create this company, and I gave up my consulting business to take this job. I've always wanted part ownership so that I can take it to the next level. Unfortunately, Dicklet doesn't see it that way. I have decided to create my own business, going into a partnership with the company that made our equipment out there. As you know, they don't have a presence in North America. Well, they didn't until now. We came to an agreement earlier this year, and you are looking at the entire U.S. operations."

"That's good for you," I said. "What happens if Dicklet doesn't agree to your contingency plan?" My heart started racing at the thought that Richard could be gone within weeks.

"I don't see a reason why he shouldn't. It wouldn't make sense to hire another General Manager, who doesn't know anything about us or our customers," he said. "Six months will be plenty of time for you to master sales controlling and some of the other financial reports, plus training your replacement. It's also the cheapest solution, and you know very well that Dicklet is all about saving money when it comes to salaries."

"The timing is really bad," I said.

"Timing is never good when someone's quitting," he agreed.

"I guess…" I sighed. I was hoping to get him to consider staying. "It's just that I'm already stressing over the ISO audit coming up in mid-January. There's no way I can do it without you here."

"It will be fine," he tried to assure me. "I will be here as long as Dicklet doesn't make things too complicated, at which point my official last day will be December 31st."

My stomach knotted at the thought of that possibility. Loosing Richard by the end of the month was something I was not willing to consider. Mostly, I wanted him to retract his notice and continue his work as usual. His resignation had come as such a surprise to me, and I was disappointed that I hadn't noticed anything different in Richard's behavior that would have clued me in.

With the uneasy feeling lingering in my stomach, I hoped for the best.

Unfortunately, things got complicated.

Dicklet was angry that Richard had resigned, especially given the fact that December was a time in Germany where Germans focused on the Holidays, not work. It was common practice for German companies to shut down shortly before Christmas and to stay closed until the second week of January.

Every day after his resignation, Richard would come to the office shaking his head, "I don't know what he wants to do next, but I don't think he wants me to stick around."

I agreed with his observation. From the lack of action and communication, it appeared that Dicklet wanted all-things-Richard to end without any disruptions to the business. Being left in the dark was a place I hated to be put in with all the expectations sitting on my shoulders. The audit was coming up in less than four weeks, and with the holiday schedule, nobody in Germany was available to offer any support or feedback on what was going to happen. Neither Richard nor I had heard from Dicklet, which, under the circumstance, I thought to be astonishing.

Finally, he called the office one morning before Christmas. Frustrated over the fact that I had felt ignored for too long, I made the decision to ask him about the next phase as I saw his number pop up on the switchboard display.

"It's Dicklet, I need to talk to Richard," he said curtly when I answered the phone.

"Richard's on vacation," I answered.

Seeing that the two could not come together on any terms or a path forward, Richard had decided to take his unused vacation days. Combined with the company's holidays, Richard was done unless they could reach an agreement.

"Vacation? How can he take vacation now? He didn't tell me. I already tried to reach him on his mobile phone, but he's not answering," he complained.

I ignored his little rant. "When are you coming over?" I asked instead.

"I'm not," he answered.

I couldn't believe my ears.

"You're not coming over?" I asked again.

"No need to," Dicklet said. "I'm on vacation with my family and out of the country. It's almost Christmas. We made plans, and I'm not cancelling them for Richard."

"Oh," was all I could manage in response.

"We don't need Richard to transition anything. We are not paying a consulting fee just so that he can make some extra money while he's starting up his own company. How can he give such a short notice and be so greedy? And then take vacation without caring about his responsibilities at work?"

I rolled my eyes at the phone. Not just because he had called Richard greedy, but also for complaining about the terms. A thirty-day-notice was quite generous without having a work contract in place. Dicklet knew that the standard for the U.S. was two weeks. He was lucky that Richard had given four. In Germany, most employees had work contracts which outlined the resignation terms. It wasn't uncommon for top management to have to observe a six-months' notice.

"None of us have contracts that would dictate longer resignation terms," I reminded him.

"It's not common practice, you know that," Dicklet said.

And it's common practice to give a two-weeks' notice without that, I thought.

He continued, "I expected more from Richard as the General Manager. He's putting us in quite an awkward position, now that he has decided to take vacation until the end of the month."

Look who's talking, I thought.

"It's vacation that is owed to him according to our employee handbook," I said, defending Richard. "But what really worries me is our upcoming ISO audit."

"What about it?"

He had no clue what was involved on a deeper level. He never liked to be present during audits. It was too upsetting for him, and he objected to outsiders telling him how to run his business. He viewed any audit as a bureaucratic assault on his dignity, resources, and, most importantly, money.

"I don't know anything about the management review, which is Richard's part of the audit," I said, panicking at the realization that I would be facing the auditor by myself.

"Haven't you sat in during the past management reviews?" Dicklet asked.

"I have, but I have never prepared the report or have worked with any of the data throughout the year. It will be hard for me to talk about it without having been involved," I answered.

Dicklet said, "You know, Franz will be coming over a week early to help you prepare."

NO, I don't know. Thanks for sharing the news already, I thought, wondering if he would have even mentioned it on his own.

Franz was the company's Global Quality Manager. He had been hired less than six months ago, but despite his short employment with the company, I had been very impressed by him so far. He was extremely knowledgeable and calm. Plus, he was a great negotiator.

"I hope we can get everything put together within a week. I have no clue what's missing or what documents the auditor will be looking for," I said.

"Franz will be able to figure it out. I'm sure the auditor will understand if you don't know about something or if something is missing."

Boy, he has no concept of auditors or audits, I thought. Lack of documentation or knowledge because an employee quit would fall under even bigger scrutiny. That was the purpose of a quality management system: to ensure contingency no matter what.

Franz turned out to be my savior. He arrived a week before the audit, and we jumped into action. He quickly determined what needed to be done. It was overwhelming given the timeframe. Mostly, because a whole year's worth of data had to be analyzed for the management report. And there were other documents that hadn't been updated in a while. While Franz could not support me with the actual tasks, given that he was not familiar with how we collected the data, he was still invaluable to me. He would stay late, and he came in on the weekend with me to look over my documentation to ensure that I was on track. And ultimately, he forced me to see a broader view of the company, to think about the risks that could impact the business, and to be aware of the potential outcomes of my decisions in the short and long term.

Franz instilled knowledge and confidence in me, and when the day of the audit arrived, I felt prepared. It went on for two days, and Franz was there every step of the way. His calm and confident demeanor kept me calm and confident. He remained in the background, encouraging me to take ownership, and when I stumbled, he was there to prevent me from falling too far – with grace.

He made sure that it was a great learning experience for me.

He had never doubted my success.

When we walked away from the audit with only a few improvement suggestions, it was like flipping Dicklet the finger. *I showed him*, I thought defiantly, convinced that he had expected a bad outcome.

Of course, that was a stupid emotion to have.

He probably didn't care either way, or he had banked on the fact that I always felt committed to get done what needed to get done.

The extreme positive result of the audit ultimately helped convince Dicklet to promote me to Operations Manager. That, and the company couldn't wait any longer to solve the leadership issue. A solution was needed, and as Richard had pointed out, I was the convenient and logical choice. And cheap. I made a whole lot less money than Richard, and while the company would have to give me a raise for the added responsibilities, plus hire my replacement, it would be considerably less in total.

Nonetheless, I was upset at both, Richard and Dicklet, for throwing me into the waters to see if I could swim. There hadn't been any concern, only selfishness, or so it had appeared. Though I knew that Richard had envisioned a different scenario, I couldn't help but feel betrayed by his absence.

My biggest gripe though was with Dicklet, who had not found the situation, Richard, or me, important enough to travel to the States when Richard gave his notice.

His presence would have shown support to me and the rest of the team and signaled that we would get through this together. Instead, we felt that we were a burden by his abandonment of ownership in favor of his vacation.

I fought hard to find my footing for many years. I did not have any direction from Dicklet or Germany, other than to survive from month to month. The recession years had been very hard on the company; unemployed people weren't buying new cars, and since our automotive customers were struggling, so were we.

It wasn't uncommon for me to call Dicklet to ask for another influx of money in order to make payroll. Dicklet would always come through. While things were tight in all countries during the recession, previous growth years in Germany had ensured that money was available for our survival.

It didn't make me feel any better though. I thought I was failing the company and my employees with my leadership, or lack thereof. Fortunately, once I realized that I couldn't help Richard's awful timing in getting me promoted during a crashing economy, I tried to focus on the positives: I had gotten rid of Dickwad, who had been a horrendous influence on the team's morale. I had also hired employees who turned out to be a perfect fit. The team worked well together, and I knew that we had potential for greatness.

One of the smartest hires during that time was a part-time accountant who showed me how to use the financials for operational management. There was much to be read between the lines when looking at financial statements.

Prick's push and subsequent successes with some large equipment sales, alongside a recovering economy, and additional cost savings, slowly started to get us out of the huge hole that we had been digging for a decade.

By 2012, good things were happening, and I could focus on improvements versus survival.

The German software system had been a thorn in my side since the very beginning. It was an antiquated system that wasn't supported by the developer anymore. The size of the database had also grown so large that it caused some difficulties during full back-up sessions. In my opinion, it was a risk to the company's operation. If it failed, we could not continue to create quotes or customer orders, or issue production jobs, which meant everyone could go home. I knew the cost to remedy such a failure would be enormous when compared to pro-active measures. I hoped to discuss a new software system with Dicklet during his next visit to the U.S.

As luck would have it, he had just flown in from Asia and was scheduled to come to the office after lunch.

A puttering engine sound announced his presence. As I walked toward the lobby, I could see Dicklet get off his motorcycle through the large glass windows. I had to smile as I observed the scene: Dicklet, dressed in knee-length khaki shorts and a red-white checkered, short-sleeve dress shirt, was standing next to the retro-looking turquoise Harley. He opened one of the black leather saddle bags and pulled out a satchel—a man purse—and flung it over his head onto his left shoulder. The long black fringes on the saddle bags and black leather seat danced slightly in the breeze. He wore brown loafers with white socks ending just above the ankles. He pulled another item from the saddle bag; a blue designer baseball hat and placed it on his head.

He looks like a schoolboy going on a field trip, I chuckled.

Dicklet entered the building and shook my hand, as he always did. He once told me that he had learned this behavior in a seminar for executives. "Makes your employees feel like they are being acknowledged," he had explained.

"I can't stay long," he announced after we completed our obligatory greetings of doing well.

"And I won't be back in the office after today. I have to fly back to Asia to negotiate on our new building there."

"Can I talk to you about something before you head back out?" I asked.

"Sure," he said, "follow me to my office."

Once seated in the yellow office, I commenced, "I want to talk to you about a new software system."

He crossed his arms on his chest. I had been mentioning the need for a new software system for years, and he was tired of the constant reminder as indicated by his body language.

He said, "We are still evaluating systems in Germany as I told you before. We are looking at developers that can offer a global software for all our locations."

I had expected his response. Germany had been thinking about or looking at different systems for the last ten years. I was tired of hearing the same old excuse. Furthermore, Germany had "upgraded" to a new system around the time when I got hired. Unfortunately, after just a short period of time, the decision was made not to implement the new software in the U.S. because it lacked a lot of global features and would be too expensive to modify to the American market. I understood the impact of this obviously bad previous purchase. And now, Dicklet did not want to spend hundreds of thousands of dollars again unless he was certain that the new system would work for all locations.

"We cannot continue to kick the can down the road. Knowing that you're still evaluating different companies means that we are years from implementing a new system. And then, it would run in Germany first before transitioning it to any of the subsidiaries," I sighed. "We cannot continue to work with our old system over here."

"It's worked this long, I am sure you can get by for another few years," he said.

I sighed again at his logic. I had to be more specific in mine, even though I knew that he was fully aware of the risks, "Yes, we are fortunate that it has been working this long. But the software limits who we can hire for our inside sales positions. We always need to find someone with German, which puts a premium on the salary as we are competing with two hundred other German companies in this area," I said. I hoped mentioning that we could potentially save money would make him more receptive.

I continued, "You've been talking about a new software system since I started working here. Eventually, it will fail, and we have no Plan B."

"It's a major expense," he said with a frown. "A global system for all locations will require many custom developments. We cannot rush into it."

"Definitely not," I agreed, relieved that Dicklet was still listening; in the past, he had always shrugged me off quickly when the subject had come up. This time, I had prepared for this meeting, wanting to try a more pro-active approach. I offered, "I was hoping that we could find an interim solution for us until Germany comes up with a final decision."

"Such as?" he asked cautiously.

"There are many software systems already proven in our industry that can work for us, here in the States, out of the box," I started.

Dicklet's displeasure was clearly displayed on his face. He squinted at me with his frown scrunched up to his nose and took in a breath, "I've told you before that we are not going with an American cookie-cutter software system. And that's a fact."

"I don't understand why you are so set against it?" I asked, frustrated that he was not willing to explain his reasoning. "So many manufacturers already use such software; it links to all our material suppliers, and it can work with our financial software. Plus, it is affordable. We don't have to reinvent the wheel."

"No," he said firmly. "You have absolutely no clue about any of this. We need experts for this."

"The basis of the order flow seems to be the same," I went on. I could tell by his facial expression that he would end our conversation soon. It was now or never. "I have researched the various software modules through a demo version. Even the sales rep confirmed that we don't have to worry about changing our key processes. Their system follows the same principle as our old software."

It got very quiet. I shifted uncomfortably in my seat. I had never made it this far in our debates over a new software system. I saw it as a good sign, but then Dicklet's silence could be the calm before the storm.

"You've talked to them already?" he asked, eyebrows and voice raised.

Guess, it was the calm before the storm, I thought.

"I have," I responded carefully. "I wanted to educate myself. I know I haven't been involved in a full software implementation yet, but I think that I'm fully aware of what's involved at this point. I don't have any misconceptions that it will be easy."

He waved his hand dismissively, "There's no way you alone could ever manage this. It takes a huge team, not to mention large amounts of time. Time that you don't have."

"I'm not alone," I argued. "I have a team that's willing to help. They don't like working with the old system. It slows us down. We could be more productive and faster with a new system. Time is money. And believe me, I will make time for this. I will work evenings and weekends if that's what it takes."

His ensuing laugh was superficial with callous undertones, "There's no way you could do this, just listening to you confirms that you have no clue. Besides, we don't have the money anyways."

I was getting discouraged by his words. While he was correct that I had never implemented a new software system, I was disappointed that he didn't consider my dedication and drive to see it through, no matter what.

I soldiered on, proud that I had made it this far in our conversation, "Our numbers are looking great. Plus, we could lease the software, so there would be no up-front costs. And because we have few people, we don't need many licenses. The monthly cost is at a point where we can easily afford it."

His face had gotten red.

"No," he hissed between clenched teeth. "We're done talking here. I told you before it's none of your business. I don't want you to ever mention it again."

I knew we were done discussing software systems for good.

I left his office deflated and frustrated. He hadn't acknowledged the risk, and he wasn't concerned with picking up the pieces if the system failed. To him, there would always be other people to clean up the mess.

By 2015, business was thriving. We had paid off the company's debt, and there was money in the bank. Something that I had thought impossible for the longest time.

Life at work was easy. I knew the industry inside and out. The last quality complaint happened over three hundred days ago, which was nothing short of a miracle considering our picky customers.

Other than Prick, who did not work for me, I had no other problem areas to fix. I treasured my employees for making it the best environment any of us had ever worked in.

However, I realized that I missed having a challenge; something that would help me grow professionally and personally. Additionally, I wanted acknowledgement from Dicklet for what I had done for the company.

I had proven myself, yet I hadn't gotten a review or a raise in over two years. My pay was over 30% less than Richard's, who had been gone for almost seven years. Even Prick made more money when considering his entire compensation package, and he hadn't been there half as long as me. Granted, he had a degree, and I had only reached the position that I was in due to circumstances. Yet, over the past six years, I had turned a struggling business into a well-oiled, profitable success story. I saw no reason why I shouldn't earn more money and the General Manager title.

I was certain that I could take on Prick and his sales team. Prick would despise me for it and challenge me every step of the way, but I felt ready.

When I traveled to the international group meeting in Germany in the summer of 2015, I asked Dicklet for a one-on-one session.

He made me wait until the very last day of my stay, repeatedly making excuses that he was too busy with other meetings. I wondered if we would get together at all. It was clear that he was avoiding me, which meant that he probably knew what was coming and that his answer was going to be no.

It was on Friday around lunch time when I finally sat down in his office on the second floor. A group photograph was to be taken before everyone left to travel back to their respective countries, and so our time window was limited. I figured Dicklet had purposely planned our meeting that way. When delivering bad news, it wasn't uncommon for management to wait until Friday afternoon. That way the employee could take his or her unhappiness into the weekend versus putting it on display at work for others to notice.

"What's on your mind?" Dicklet asked.

We were seated around a small table, facing each other.

"I wanted to talk to you about my position in your company," I started.

"What about it?" he asked cautiously.

"Well, I think I have proven myself over these past years. Considering our profitability, no quality complaints, audits without any findings, repaying our debts…" I paused before declaring, "I've been doing the same job as Richard, and his title was General Manager. I want to be the General Manager. I've been running the company for seven years now. It's time."

Dicklet was busy examining his fingernails. He seemed more interested in them than me.

He finally looked at me.

"Not exactly the same job as Richard," he stated. "The sales team doesn't report to you."

He was really good at pointing out the deficiencies right out of the gate.

"There's no reason why they can't," I responded.

Dicklet was surprised by my statement, "Prick won't allow it. You know it. He'll never work for you."

I had expected this comment.

"It's not up to Prick to decide. I can deal with him. If you support me, then he'll have to accept it," I said, then added, "You're the owner, it's your company. You tell people what to do." I hoped charming his ego would work in my favor.

It seemed to work. I could see the gears turn in Dicklet's head. At least, he seemed to consider my proposal.

After a long pause and exhale, Dicklet said, "He'll quit, and we can't afford to lose him."

Internally I cringed. He had just declared that Prick had more value to him than me. And he hadn't been worried at all to mention that fact out loud in my presence.

"That doesn't mean it's not the right decision," I went on, needing to show initiative as a leader would. Dicklet had always viewed me as a support person, and I had to change that. "I want a new challenge; I want to take on more. Prick's department is the only one not reporting to me. I'm not talking about telling him how to run his salesforce. But he could need some oversight when it comes to budgeting and overall decisions that impact us as a company. You know how he's always looking out for himself first. He doesn't necessarily have the company's interest as his priority."

Dicklet was silent for a while, pretending to contemplate what I had said.

"You don't have a college degree," he finally said dryly.

I was blindsided by his response. Instead of considering Prick's wasteful ways, he had chosen to direct his focus on my negatives.

"I don't see how that is relevant," I answered, my voice full of discontent. "Look at the numbers. It's thanks to my effort, and thanks to the team that I created, that the U.S. operation is as successful as it is."

"Well, the economy recovered as well," he said. He could always deflate a compliment. "But you are right, we are doing very well in the States, and I can't deny that you contributed to our success."

It was an admission of recognition, and I felt some relief.

He continued, "Well, to be honest, I've been thinking about a person for the States who can take care of the strategic planning. That person would go out into the market to look for new technologies and new developments and then will set the future direction for our company to ensure continuous growth."

It sounded like me and him were on the same page after all.

Happy that he had extended an olive branch to me, I said, "That sounds great. I would like a new challenge. I feel that I have mastered running the operations. I could develop our strategic direction. It would be fun."

Dicklet looked at me, puzzled.

"I was thinking of Mr. Nimrod for this position."

Mr. Nimrod was a former employee who had once managed Germany's sales department. He had not been known internally for moving things along in a progressive manner. But, he had been very complaisant with Dicklet, and Dicklet liked and trusted employees who saw things his way.

I burst out laughing, "Mr. Nimrod? Are you serious?"

My experiences with Mr. Nimrod had left me with the impression that he had been a poor leader with his indecisiveness.

The stern look on Dicklet's face and the seriousness of his next words confirmed my worst fear, "Yes, I am. In fact, I have been in touch with him, and he would not be opposed to moving to the States to take on the General Manager role."

I was in shock. Dicklet had already talked with Mr. Nimrod about the position. I had never had a chance. Decisions had been made, and I had been purposely ignored.

In the given scenario, Dicklet must have known the potential of me quitting if I didn't get what I wanted. He had obviously given this some thought, and he wasn't concerned that I would do something drastic if he shut me down. He may have figured that I would know my place and would remain there once he had made his point.

It would be moot to continue. Nonetheless, I wanted to share my opinion.

"He knows nothing about the American market, nor our customers, nor how we do business," I said. "I would love a shot at running the company strategically."

He shook his head.

"You could never become General Manager. I don't see how without a degree. You know nothing about business economics," he said, each word cutting into me like a knife.

Dicklet was back to examining his fingernails.

He would always look at me as the Office Manager, I realized that instant. Nothing I could say or do would change his view of who he thought I was in his world.

With a heavy heart, I decided to change the topic. If the General Manager spot was out, at least I would try to get something out of this meeting.

"You have said that if the company does well, the employees will too," I started.

Dicklet returned his attention to me.

"Yes?" he answered, articulating the word into a question.

"It is obvious that the company has been doing extremely well for several years. Unfortunately, neither Prick nor myself have gotten any raises in a while," I said.

I hadn't really planned on including Prick in my next undertaking, but seeing that Dicklet placed more importance on him, I figured it was a better approach.

"I know, but both of you get a bonus every year when you meet your operational goals. If the company makes money, so do you."

"Yes, the performance-based bonus is great. Unfortunately, for this past year, you put a cap on how much the bonus paid out. We didn't have a cap the year before. Which means that my reward for exceptional operational performance was the same as it would have been for just simply good performance. It's not very motivating to want to perform above and beyond when there is no reward for it in the end."

Dicklet stared at me. He hated to be confronted about money. At that point, I didn't care anymore.

I was aware that the German management team did not have any limits imposed on their bonus structure. Of course, it was almost impossible for Germany's operational result to have the exponential growth that we had experienced in the States. The European market had been developed for more than forty years. Dicklet would never have to worry about having to pay out large bonuses in Germany. Yet, America still offered the most untapped potential with growth in multiple digits.

A knock on the door interrupted us.

Bernd, the General Manager for the German facility popped his head in, "We're ready for the photo. The entire team, except for you two, is assembled in the parking lot. We've been waiting."

Dicklet stood up, "We're on our way."

Then he looked at me, "I will be in the States in September. We will do a review, and I will see what I can do for you when it comes to more money. Okay?" He stood up from his chair.

"Sh... sure... thank you," I stuttered, getting up to follow him down the stairs to join the group.

Internally, I had a hard time dealing with my emotions. I had reached the end of my ladder, and there was no other opportunity for me to advance. Dicklet had made this very clear. I hated him that very moment. And I was exhausted.

It was ironic that I was placed next to him, up front and center, in the group's photograph. I wish I could have seen it, as I often wondered if my facial expression or body language showed any signs of how I felt, standing shoulder to shoulder with the man who had just told me that I had no future with the company.

As soon as I returned home, I started looking for a new job.

Kindred was supportive in my decision to leave; but then, I never had to worry about him when mulling over my professional career. He let me be me, and he did not try to influence my final decisions when it came to work matters. While he offered feedback, he never pushed his opinion on me; he knew that I would always include "us" in any decision, and that it was important for me to have the freedom of choice.

A month later, I gave my four weeks' notice. I took a week's vacation immediately after calling Dicklet to share the news.

The hardest part about quitting was leaving my dream team behind. I would have stayed for them if it wasn't for the principle that I didn't want to work for someone who continuously ignored my voice and excluded me from the major decisions.

I'm thankful for the opportunities given to me at that company. I loved my job, and it would have been unlikely for me to move into upper management anywhere else without a degree.

It was 99% great. I appreciated that Dicklet was absent most of the time, which gave me a lot of freedom to do my thing.

It's ironic though how that one percent can be annoying enough to make you want to quit.

Respect is a funny thing. With Prick, I stated that respect was earned, not deserved. Yet, with Dicklet, I think my mistake was *not* demanding respect; I truly thought that respect from my superiors would come as a natural consequence of my hard work and success.

It didn't help that every time Dicklet pulled the "owner" card and told me to follow orders, I gave in; as was expected of me.

I lacked self-respect to stand firm in my beliefs.

I extended more respect to him than he had ever given me, which he didn't deserve.

I vowed to be different in my next job.

Truthfully, all I ever wanted was to be part of, what I called, the Dick Club.

I felt excluded at company events when the men got together and expected me to fetch coffee for them while they "prepared for the meeting" or order their drinks at the bar so that they could arrive to an awaiting cocktail "after finishing up the vital stuff".

The importance of inclusion lay in the exclusion of those who weren't invited to the after-meeting meetings or other official functions.

As an example, during the international sales meeting, it was common to gather at the hotel bar before heading to dinner. Wrapping up the second day at the office, Dicklet, Prick, and the General Manager from Asia, a large man named WingWang, decided to have an impromptu discussion about the global economy in Dicklet's office.

"No need for you to be bored. Why don't you go ahead and head back to the hotel?" Dicklet suggested. He had placed his hand on the back of my shoulder and was using it to usher me toward the stairs leading down to the lobby. We passed his office on the way.

"I don't mind," I said, trying to slow our steps, "I would like to stay."

"It's mostly sales stuff. Doesn't concern you," Dicklet insisted.

We had reached the stairs.

"You just go ahead and chill at the hotel. It's been a long day, and you must be tired," he tried to sound sympathetic as he padded me on the forearm. Then he simply turned around, walked back to his office where Prick and WingWang were waiting, and closed the door with a resolute click.

Shortly after I arrived at the hotel, I found myself sitting at the bar with a beer and a shot of whiskey. I was angry to have been brushed off by Dicklet and upset at myself for having let him.

Fortunately, I was soon joined by some of the other salesmen, and they provided the distraction I so desperately needed.

About an hour later, my phone rang. It was WingWang. His voice came through like his physical appearance: huge, loud, and obnoxious.

"Petra, we're just finishing here. Why don't you order me a draft beer? By the time they're done pouring it, we'll be there. Uhm, and why don't you make that two, one for Prick. And go ahead and order some red wine for my wife, who will be joining us. We're all very tired, and this way, we don't have to wait on our orders. You mind?"

I rolled my eyes. *Why did I have to answer my phone?* I thought. But I complied.

When Prick, WingWang, and his wife showed up ten minutes later, the drinks were waiting for them at the bar. Prick sat down next to me without a word and started gulping down the beer.

WingWang remained standing, leaning on the bar before turning to his wife.

He yawned, "What do you say? It's been a long day. Let's just head up to our room." Then he looked at me, "Petra, be a dear and charge that to your room? We are just too tired. I'm sure you understand."

He lifted his chin in my direction before heading to the elevator with his wife.

I wanted to kick myself. Yes, I wanted to be included, but not in continual belittlement. I was a woman in top leadership at my company, constantly undermined and undervalued. The words and actions of my boss and peers continuously showed that in order to be equal, one had to have a dick; it was the only way to join their "members-only" exclusive club.

It seemed unfortunate that a dick wasn't attached to me when I was born so that I could belong.

But after fourteen years of blind loyalty and dedicated servanthood, I finally concluded:

I was done trying to be part of their club anymore.

I wanted to be dickless.

♀

THE PUSILLANIMOUS PLEASER

&

THE DISTRUSTING CEO

My job search commenced the minute I returned from Germany in 2015. Within days, I came across a Production Manager position for a small German start-up. They had a sales office in Regent City and were planning to add an assembly line.

The fact that I knew nothing about the company's product or that I had never set-up an assembly line did not deter me from applying. I had done a bit of research about the company, and from all indicators, they looked to be a prestigious, well-established business. I also liked that they were active in multiple industries, which meant that there was no dependence on one particular market. The icing on the cake was that they had an international presence with three locations, just like my present company.

Having worked my way up in a small manufacturing start-up operation, combined with the German, I thought that I would have a good chance of being contacted. Just like my current employer, this one was family-owned and focused on quality. My skillset and background were a great match - other than the product experience requirement, which I lacked completely.

I also did not mind that this position would be a step down in title from my current position, seeing that the top range of the salary would be a step up. Additionally, with the global company size three times larger than my current employer, I assumed that there would be room for advancement as the company grew in the States.

Within days, the recruiter called me. She was very excited about my cover letter and résumé. The next step was an interview with the company's owner, Wiener, and the Global Production Manager, Karl, which would happen through an online video conference call.

The morning of the interview, I was sitting at my kitchen table with my laptop, waiting for Wiener to initiate the call. I had taken half a day vacation for this purpose. When the call did not come as scheduled, I started to get worried. Germans were known for their punctuality.

Ready to contact the recruiter, I was relieved when a window showing a telephone icon popped up on my laptop while at the same time, the speakers alerted me with a ringing sound.

I answered and the screen automatically expanded, displaying a conference room with two people seated around a table. From my internet research, I knew that the person at the head of the table was Wiener, one of the two brothers who owned the second-generation company. I assumed the person to his left to be Karl, the Global Production Manager, which was confirmed when he started speaking.

"Yes, hello….? This is Karl, are you there?" he asked in heavy-accented English.

"Yes, I'm here," I responded. "I can see both of you. Good morning, or better said, good afternoon."

"We can't see you, can you see us?" Wiener chimed in. He didn't wait for my reply, "We seem to have some technical difficulty. The recruiter was supposed to be on this call as well as Cocktapus, the VP of Sales and Marketing. Cocktapus runs the operation for us in the States."

"Yes, I can see you," I replied when given the chance.

Both were looking intently at Wiener's laptop, and Wiener was moving his index finger over the mousepad. Occasionally, I could hear a mouse click.

"Hello? Can you hear me?" a new, American voice announced. "This is Cocktapus."

"Ahhh, yes, Cocktapus, thank you for making the call," Wiener said. "But I also cannot see you…just like Petra. Hmmm…"

More mouse clicks.

"I can see you just fine," Cocktapus said.

"Hmmm," Wiener kept repeating. "I don't know why this is not working." He looked up into the air and asked, "You're sure both your cameras are on?"

"I am," I said. "The light is on, and I can see myself in a small rectangle at the bottom of the screen. And… hello to Cocktapus, it's nice to meet you. I can see you at the bottom of my screen."

"Same here," Cocktapus replied, "about meeting you and the visual."

More finger movements by Wiener, angry clicks, and *hmmms* followed. Then, awkward silence.

"I think we'll just have to go ahead without seeing you," Wiener concluded. "Is that okay with you?"

"Absolutely," Cocktapus and I confirmed. I noticed that Cocktapus turned off his camera, and so did I. Wiener and Karl remained visible on my screen.

"Seeing that Cocktapus is on the call, we will continue in English," Wiener said. "I don't see the need for the recruiter to be present at this point to proceed."

We exchanged a few more pleasantries before they started interviewing me about my past work experiences. In turn, I also posed several questions, trying to get a feeling for the company's vision and philosophy. I learned that the U.S. operation was currently situated near the south side of Regent City, but that they had just signed a lease on a larger space further north to accommodate the new assembly line.

I was relieved to hear about their plans for the new site. The old location would have added another twenty minutes to the commute that would already be, at best, thirty minutes if traffic was flowing, which never happened.

Regent City was in the throes of building a toll lane heading out north, all the way up to my exit. The current two general purpose lanes were always packed with commuters due to the aggressive growth the city had seen, and the construction only made things worse. These days, nobody wanted to crawl down the interstate at any time of day. I knew that the average commute would take over forty minutes, and it would cost me more than just time. But I was motivated enough to see where this was going first before making a decision. That was, if the job was even offered to me.

"So, are you worried about not knowing anything about our products considering the task at hand?" Karl asked as we were wrapping things up.

I didn't hesitate, "It doesn't scare me. From what I can tell, your company seems to have good processes in place, and you have started multiple lines from the ground up in Asia in recent years. I believe that with expert support from Germany and Asia, I can get it done."

"I agree," Wiener said. "I think the most important part is attitude. You can communicate with the Germans on the technical aspects, and you can speak with our colleagues in Asia about how they did things. A lot of technical knowledge can be taught during the training here in Germany. I appreciate your drive for quality, and you are familiar with ISO processes. I feel that your background would be a good fit for what we are looking for."

After a few rounds of negotiations, we had reached an agreement by the end of July, and I placed my resignation call to Dicklet.

In the fall of 2015, I started working at the company's new location. They had just moved in, and the paint in the newly constructed offices was barely dry. The production area was empty, and I was assigned a desk in one of the front offices with the promise that furniture had been ordered for my area. Without further training, I could not proceed with the creation of the assembly line, and so I tried to occupy my time reading the company's literature in an attempt to understand their products.

After two weeks, my travel arrangements were finalized, and I flew to Germany to start my three-week training. Wiener and Karl wanted me to spend two of the weeks in production, working on the lines, learning the product that would be assembled in the U.S.

I had assumed that my purpose on the line was to understand how the product was put together, to study each component and how it impacted performance, so that I could teach and manage my own assembly worker in the States.

It wasn't until three days into my training that Karl shared with me that I was to be it: Production Manager, Assembly Worker, and Shipping & Receiving Clerk.

I was taken aback by his revelation. The job posting had made no mention of working the line nor had it been brought up during the interview. Managing a production line was the one thing I was extremely comfortable with. Having to worry about cranking out a perfect product to be shipped to an end user was a completely different animal. While the assembly was relatively straight-forward, it was the testing of the component that worried me the most. Each assembly had to be verified with an oscilloscope. I was familiar with an oscilloscope in the sense that I knew that the screen looked similar to a heart rate monitor. And that it was used to measure the output signals of the assembled device. No more, no less.

Germany had computerized test stations that any assembly worker could operate, but I was told that I would not have that luxury in the States, and that I would need to work with the oscilloscope instead. There were so many numbers and squiggly lines displayed on the monitor that my head was spinning just looking at it. Plus, I could not make sense of what the numbers and lines meant, and I could not fathom how I would ever truly know that my assembly was good.

But as usual, I was going to give it my best, and I could learn. Nonetheless, I wondered how everyone had missed to mention this "little" fact to me sooner and then seemed so surprised when I revealed that it was news to me.

Unfortunately, there was one more detail—or lack thereof—that irked me shortly after I had arrived for my training: nobody knew who I was, as was clearly indicated by the blank stares in everyone's faces when I introduced myself. There had been no communication about my position or purpose with the company, and I thought it was very disrespectful to me and the workers, who now had to jeopardize their efficiencies in order to train me.

Working on an assembly line wasn't easy. The day shift started at 7 A.M. and ended around 3 P.M., making for a seven-and-a-half-hour workday with a thirty-minute lunch break. While that sounded nice, my body was not used to standing all day, with only a thirty-minute rest period in between. By the end of my first week, all my joints ached from standing in a fixed position for most of my day, looking over someone else's shoulder. Between that and trying to soak in the knowledge about the components, assembly, and testing, I fell into bed by eight every night, completely wiped out.

I could have never made it without the support of all the women working the assembly lines. The majority of them had come from Eastern European countries, such as Poland, Slovakia, Estonia, Lithuania, etc. in the hope of finding employment in Germany, where they would earn more money than in their own countries. It was a win for the company as well since they could pay these women less than any German would have demanded, therefore ensuring a low labor cost.

I fondly referred to these women as *my girls*, even though it was them who adopted me during my time working their lines.

They were disciplined, thorough, and fast. I admired them. During break time, they were like their own community, sharing meals and stories with each other. I could tell that they enjoyed each other's company, which was incredible considering that they spent all day working the lines together. They never spoke badly about one another.

When they heard that I was manager and worker in one, they did not believe me at first.

"What, you will run your own line by yourself?" they asked with big eyes in their varied accents. "They will not let us work by ourselves until we have trained for six months here in Germany. It is impossible." And they would burst out laughing, until they realized that I had been serious.

Then they would look at me with pity while trying to encourage me, "We train you good. You can do it. You are doing great already. Almost no mistakes."

Once my two weeks were completed in production, I moved up a floor to the offices where a heavy male presence dominated the more technical jobs. While the girls had been lively and communal downstairs, it was like someone had flipped a switch upstairs: the atmosphere reminded me of a funeral home; there wasn't a peep to be heard for cubicles. Everyone looked like they just wanted to blend in. I almost did not want to make eye contact with anyone, fearing that I was breaking some unmentioned rule of "no look, no touch, no speak".

It was quite a shock after the warmth that I had received from the girls. Even the lighting was subdued upstairs, greyish, as to enhance the haggard looks on everyone's faces.

Missing my girls, I couldn't wait for the final week to be over.

It was like life and death, in the same building, but occupying different floors.

I guess it was a good thing that there wasn't a third floor.

Back in the States in October, my head filled with new knowledge, I quickly realized that the office, production, and warehouse design was less than optimum for my purposes.

Walking in through the front door of the long and narrow suite, which was part of many in an old brick, one-story building, there was a tiny lobby area with a couch corner to the left. A small reception desk with a large TV screen behind it was located to the right at the beginning of a hallway. The first office to the right of the hallway was Cocktapus's, and its large size represented the importance of his title and status. There were more offices and bathrooms located on either side of the long hallway before it ended at a door. In front of it, on the left, was a large conference room. Cocktapus called it the training room, but in my three years at the company, I only ever saw it used a handful of times for that purpose. The space could have been reduced in size to add a production office as there were two large windows at the end of the room overlooking the assembly area.

Instead, my workstation was in the L-shaped production room, which lay behind the door at the end of the hallway. To call the production area anything other than a large room would have been a lie. My desk was at the end of the short vertical side, while the line was going to be built on the long horizontal side of the wall.

Two French type wooden doors, in direct line of view from my desk, led out to the warehouse, where the inventory was stored and where deliveries were received and goods shipped.

One morning, as I was contemplating the room layout from the seat behind my new desk, Cocktapus happened to walk through the door on his way to the warehouse.

I called out to him, "Cocktapus, you've been in the industry a while... How did we end up in this old building? You know, this isn't the best environment for what we are trying to accomplish."

He stopped in his tracks and turned to face me. At only thirty years young, I was surprised that he was managing a foreign-owned start-up. Germans did not like the thought of handing over the reins to a non-German when it came to top management. He also lacked experience for the position, but then, he had a college degree, and some owners liked to put their eggs in that basket. Additionally, he had been promoted to his position less than two years ago when the previous General Manager quit. Obviously, I was very familiar with the scenario of convenience.

"What do you mean by 'not the best environment'?" he asked, using his fingers to air quote the last four words.

I could tell by the way that he crossed his arms when he had finished his question that I had put him on the defensive with my comment about the old building. Internally, I conceded that I could have approached the subject differently. However, sometimes it was tough for me to avoid my German bluntness when I was annoyed.

The physical barrier that he had just put up, alongside a tightly closed mouth, were good indicators that he expected more criticism from me.

"This production area is not ideal for an assembly line," I said.

"How so?"

"Well for one, in Germany, nobody could enter production who wasn't supposed to be there. You needed to wear static dissipating shoes and a lab coat, and the doors wouldn't even open without first passing the electric static discharge test," I said.

"I know, I've been there plenty of times," Cocktapus said, reminding me that he had seniority with the company. It was another defensive mechanism.

"And here, anyone can walk in and through production without any protective measures," I pointed out.

Cocktapus paused for a few seconds.

The pause made me wonder if he had ever seriously considered the newly designed layout of production and the warehouse to begin with.

He finally said, "You can just walk in too. It's just the way it is. We couldn't possibly afford a fancy door lift that only lets someone in when they clear the static test." He smiled, "Also, we need to have full access to the exit door in the warehouse for emergencies, seeing that we only have a front door and a secondary egress is needed for evacuation purposes."

I could tell he was proud that he could present me with a factual explanation.

"I understand egress; it's just a shame that the warehouse and production could not have been designed so that there was warehouse access first, with another entrance to production. That could have worked for egress," I rebutted.

He sighed, "We couldn't, it was complicated. You had to be there, I guess."

I shrugged, "I guess."

Cocktapus said, "Considering it's just you in here, I don't think that's a problem. It's not like anyone will walk up to the line and touch a circuit board. There's a pretty straight shot to the warehouse and no need to linger or detour to the work benches."

"Be that as it may," I nodded, "but follow me to the warehouse, will you?"

"Sure, I was on my way there anyways," Cocktapus said, and with that, he proceeded into the warehouse with me on his heels.

It was dark and hot in there. There was no air conditioning, and it was the end of September.

I walked over to the two large overhead doors at the end of the building.

"Look at the open space between the door and the brick wall on both of these," I said.

"What about it?" he asked.

I walked to one of the shelves and ran my finger over the top. I showed it to Cocktapus. My fingertip was black and grimy.

"It's so dusty in here because of these gaps. Dirt gets into this space too easily. And then you have all these outdoor equipment manufacturers around us that test their lawnmowers and leaf blowers all day long. Dirt is thrown at us from all directions."

"And?"

"Well, dirt and dust are not good to have when it comes to manufacturing our products. And then, we have people tracking dirt into production from the warehouse. Let's not forget about heat and humidity. Our production room should be at a constant setting for both. Any time we open these doors, we are going to fight the elements and the dirt," I explained as I pointed toward the overhead and warehouse doors. I was getting upset. Cocktapus was well aware of these facts with his expertise in the industry.

"I showed Germany the plans, and they had no concerns," Cocktapus justified, shrugging his shoulder. "This building was all that we could afford, and this was the best overall option for the budget."

I was surprised at his statement. I couldn't understand why he would accept mediocrity when ultimately, he was in charge of making the U.S. operation a success. He was technical, and he was familiar with the production environment in Germany. Yet he had failed to plan the layout of the new facility in a way that made sense for our assembly. Or he had willingly underrepresented the status quo of the current environment to the owner.

The warehouse should have been accessible without having to walk through production first. I couldn't believe that Germany would have agreed to jeopardize production after all that I had observed there, where static dissipation and cleanliness had been top priorities.

In my opinion, the layout should have been changed, but there was no time or money, as was confirmed by Wiener when I complained. While he agreed that it had been poor planning all the way around, he insisted that I had to make the best of the situation.

Another less-than-optimum circumstance was the fact that the intended line was in use at one of our customer's site in the States under a branding agreement. And had been for the last six years when it had been shipped there after it had been in use in Germany for many years before. For some reason, I had assumed that we would be getting a new assembly line, after all, everyone had called it *new*. Obviously, that had turned out to be another shattered misconception on my part. But then, it would be new to me, so I did not argue with the terminology.

I booked a trip to the customer's facility shortly after my return from Germany. I needed to see the condition of the equipment, even though I wasn't sure if I would be able to tell from one quick overview if the line was operationally sound and could produce a high-quality component.

Once there, I realized that this particular assembly line consisted of several small individual pieces that simply needed to be put onto individual workstations. It wasn't even a "line" as I had worked on and seen in Germany. The component inventory that would accompany the equipment would take up more space. While I was relieved to see that my production room would be adequate, I was pulled into desperation by knowing that this was the oldest existing line in operation, which hadn't been maintained by the company since 2006, when the customer had taken ownership of it.

I struggled with the realization that every piece of machinery was outdated, scratched, and beaten up, and most likely in need of an overhaul. There was no way to know if the line was functional and reliable to the company's standards until I could get it up and running.

Nothing had been ideal so far, and I got the distinct feeling that the company talked a big talk while it lacked the follow-through in the walk.

Yet I wasn't even sure that anyone was truly aware of the challenges which I faced, or even cared. When I submitted a detailed report to Wiener and Karl about my observations, I was told to do the best I could. If I ran into huge issues, they would consider sending over a technical support person to "fix the line into a usable one". Both remained completely uninvolved.

I didn't know how to feel about their trust in my capability to get the line up and running with my lack of technical knowledge. While I generally appreciated a hands-off approach when it came to day-to-day operational tasks, I had expected more support and guidance. I found it hard not to panic; I thought I had bitten off more than I could chew. Defiant to make the best of the situation, I soldiered on. I was stubborn, and I would show everyone that I could succeed even with the odds stacked against me.

The line arrived in December 2015, and by then, Wiener had promoted me to Operations Manager. Cocktapus was simply spread too thin, and he had never managed human resources and finance before. It made sense to hand these areas over to me, seeing that I had extensive experience. Wiener wanted Cocktapus to solely focus on sales.

With the added responsibilities, Wiener understood that I would be too involved in the management of the company to be assembling products on the side. In January 2016, I hired an assembly worker, Paul, who had massive electronics experience—including the dreaded oscilloscope. It was one worry I could scratch off my list.

Together, we resuscitated the old equipment, and before long, we started shipping tested assemblies to our customers.

At the end of 2016, we expanded the line to offer additional products. We also added a second line, which allowed us to create one of the sub-assemblies versus buying it from Germany. It was quite an ambitious move by the company. It was also way too soon, but Cocktapus had convinced Wiener that the extended capabilities would result in more sales.

Instead it would result in more debt with the German headquarters. It was another scenario I was familiar with. The decisions had been made without consideration of the return of investment, and I was frustrated, knowing how difficult it would be to dig out of the hole. It had been a decision purely driven by the sales team; operationally or financially, it had not made sense.

Fortunately, production ran smoothly and without any complaints. At least we could show that the line was successful based on quality if not on revenue.

I was thrilled with my promotion to Operations Manager. Seeing that I had managed a plant before, combined with the fact that Cocktapus was not moving the company along when it came to procedures within the office, Wiener had asked me to step in to streamline all operational processes.

Cocktapus lacked leadership skills: he demanded nothing from his employees, and there was no accountability - not to mention that he did not provide any support to his team when they asked. He was extremely unconfrontational, and when he was in the office, he hid in his large safe room.

Cocktapus not only kept himself isolated physically, but also emotionally, which made it even harder for me to try and mentor him, as Wiener had hoped. At times, it felt like Cocktapus had no feelings or emotions. His demeanor was vanilla in the sense that he tried to keep his voice and face neutral, so it was tough for anyone to know what he was thinking. I didn't think that he was doing that on purpose like some leaders do to confuse others or throw them off their game. It seemed more subconscious with Cocktapus as an introvert, who did not seek out conversations or human contact naturally.

When Cocktapus left the safety of his office, it felt like a wildlife documentary; I'm sure I wasn't the only one with that visual. I could hear the narrator's whisper in my head as he observed Cocktapus waddle down the hallway to the kitchen for another Red Bull, shoulders hunched, head slightly forward and down, eyes vehemently pointing straight ahead, avoiding eye contact with others, ears on attention for any distractions, "…and in the extremely rare event when the animal finally feels secure enough to leave its den, it is typically only to search for food or to relieve bodily functions. At any unusual sound or movement, it will startle and retreat quickly back to its lair."

His team did not respect him because of his abandonment of leadership. Of course, he had been a co-worker just two years ago to most. Earning respect as a leader, when having worked alongside your subordinates without any huge positive impact for that long, could not have been easy to begin with.

Wiener made Cocktapus's isolation even more attainable by constantly asking for more Excel lists or long-winded PowerPoint presentations, helping Cocktapus to stay hidden away.

"What's the matter?" I asked him one day as I entered his office to wait for Wiener's weekly Friday call. He was seated behind his desk, but I could barely see him; two computer monitors provided a barricade for his short and stocky body to hide behind in plain sight.

Wiener's commitment to keeping scheduled appointments resulted in a 50/50 chance that the call would happen. When it did, there was always some type of error on Wiener's side, such as a non-functioning video or the lack of sound. Nothing ever ran smoothly or on time. Additionally, if Wiener made the call, we would spend at least two hours discussing various Excel files concerning sales and marketing before getting to production. As part of the management team, I could not excuse myself; Wiener expected me to remain present. It was a huge waste of time for all involved, and other than additional busy work for Cocktapus, which he would then not delegate, it never resulted in anything positive or conducive.

"I'm not sure that he'll understand the Excel file that I created to report on the distributors' performance," Cocktapus replied. He was nervously twisting the large gold college ring on his right ring finger.

I could never understand why any grown man would want to continue to wear such ugly looking jewelry. In my opinion, the only allowable instance was if that person had won a Superbowl, but none other; especially after having entered the working world. Cocktapus even had his wedding band designed to match his college ring. That and the occasional college polo shirt completed the immature outfit, which made it even harder to respect him.

"I feel for you Cocktapus," I said. "I'm so lucky that he never asks me to compile more reports. How much time do you spend on creating and updating all these files for him?"

"Hours," Cocktapus sighed. "Well, more like days, I think. I can't focus on sales because I'm always redoing files, and then he keeps adding on more and more. I mean, look at this."

He pointed at his sales controlling worksheet. The entire screen was filled with columns and rows of numbers, highlighted in different colors. It almost looked like the Vegas strip, only there were no flashing lights (yet).

"It's ridiculous," he said and sighed again. "And then there's multiple sheets with the same information, just shown in a different format."

"Did you at least get one of your team members to pull the data into this file for you?" I asked.

"No, I did it," he said.

"You know, if you show it to them once, I think they could do this work for you going forward," I suggested.

"It's easier and faster this way," he responded.

I nodded. I had assumed as much. Cocktapus never delegated any work to his team. A team that was willing and able to take on more to free up his time. But Cocktapus hated to ask for help, and he would rather do it himself if it meant avoiding any potential negative feedback from his team.

"Do you think he'll approve?" I asked.

"Nope," he responded. "He emailed me last night at three in the morning German time. Said that I needed to clean it up and to add the commissions to it at the same time. But he did not tell me what exactly he is looking for as the end result, so it's hard to know what to change. I've been working on this all morning."

Wiener was known to email and call Cocktapus at any moment. We weren't sure that man ever slept. When I told Cocktapus to turn off his phone at night or not to answer every single call from Wiener, he simply said, "I can't do that. I should have done it in the beginning, but I was trying to impress him by being reachable, and now I can't go back."

"I'm glad he never calls or emails me," I said.

"Good for you," he sighed again. Then, there was a ringing sound, "Look, who's made the call…" With these words, he clicked the answer button on the screen, and we switched on our smiles as Wiener's face appeared.

Of course, Wiener said that he couldn't see us.

Three hours later, we were exhausted.

Wiener had asked Cocktapus for a new PowerPoint presentation and a new Excel file to clarify the existing sales distribution structure.

While I felt for Cocktapus, I was frustrated that he would not take a stand to protect his time. There was no way he could be productive at selling when he was wasting away creating and re-creating documents.

It was a general problem with Cocktapus though. He couldn't say no to customers or Wiener. No matter the cost.

He was such a pusillanimous pleaser.

Cocktapus wasn't the only person who constantly bent over for the owner. It seemed that everyone at the company always did what Wiener expected and demanded, no matter if the request was within reason or not.

And then they tried to deceive him behind his back.

I refused to bend the knee like that. I had sworn to stand up for my beliefs and principles as I had lacked to do so with Dicklet.

Fortunately, since there were no shortcomings in operations, I stayed under Wiener's radar for a long time.

That's until the fall of 2017, when Wiener announced that the company would hold its first international operational meeting in conjunction with the annual international sales meeting.

I was excited to hear the news. I felt an operational meeting was important. It seemed that the three manufacturing locations operated with different tolerances and procedures in each country. It was time to standardize our processes and methods.

The announcement for adding the operational meeting came only three weeks prior to the scheduled international sales meeting, and I scrambled to find a reasonably priced flight.

The meeting was supposed to start Tuesday after lunch, and I decided to fly over on the previous Friday, which would get me to Germany the next morning, a day later. I would spend the weekend with my parents, and then I would take the train on Monday to meet up with Cocktapus near the airport, where he had rented a car. Together, we would complete our journey to the company's location.

The week before the meeting, my phone rang. I could see that it was Wiener.

"Hi Wiener, how are you doing?" I answered. I wondered what he wanted as he rarely called me.

"I'm fine. How are you?" he asked in return.

"Fine, what can I do for you?"

"When are you arriving next week?" he asked.

I cringed. I had dreaded this question. Wiener had a horrible reputation for micro-managing travel arrangements. In fact, he constantly undermined the leadership team with his hands-on involvement on the least important matters.

Cocktapus often told stories about traveling with Wiener. It involved plane rides spent working on the laptop, arriving at the destination ready for more than a full day's work, heading to the hotel sending emails all night, and getting up early the next morning for a rinse and repeat.

There was a running joke in the company that Wiener held videocalls while flying on airplanes as not to waste any time; only, it wasn't a joke, it was a constant reality. Sometimes, he would sit in economy when he was on a video call (when there were no upgrades or business seats available), next to a poor soul who was trying to catch some sleep, and who would continue to complain about the disruption while being completely ignored by Wiener.

Wiener would hate my flight arrangements. Based on his obsession with efficiencies, arriving into Germany for some private downtime with my family was not his idea of making good use of the company's time or money.

I took a deep breath. I had already made the decision to be honest—unlike most employees—who lied to him about their true travel plans in order to avoid confrontation.

"You will see me on Tuesday late morning," I tried to avoid a direct answer.

"But when are your arriving?" he asked impatiently.

"I'm arriving on Saturday. I'll be spending time with my parents first," I said.

"So why can't you come to work on Monday?" he asked next.

"Because I'll be with my parents all weekend until Monday, when I will travel to meet Cocktapus near the airport. We'll be driving down together in Cocktapus's rental car." Of course, I did not tell him that Cocktapus had made arrangements to fly out the day before me, and that he was taking a few vacation days to explore Germany on his own. He had told Wiener that his flight would arrive on Monday.

"I don't understand," he said. "You should be at work on Monday if you are flying in on the weekend. I don't really get why you are arriving on Saturday. You should be flying in on Monday morning and then come straight to work."

"That doesn't work for me," I said determined.

"What do you mean?"

I could hear his frustration.

"Well, first of all, you don't want me in the office after I have just flown fourteen hours after having been up all day without any sleep," I stated. "I need rest, and I'm not functional without a good eight hours of sleep. Matter of fact, I would be extremely grumpy and unpleasant."

Silence.

I continued, "Second, I'm taking a vacation day that Monday. My parents are very important to me, as is the rest of my family, and I will not miss an opportunity to spend time with them while in Germany."

I hated the fact that I was explaining my actions. I was a grown woman in management and quite capable of making decisions on travel and vacation time. What I really wanted to say was, *If you are worried about your leaders screwing the company out of time and money, then you should not have a company.*

However, I bit my tongue and simply waited. I had dealt him the family-is-important-to-me card, and I knew that I had put him into a spot where he could not argue anymore. Wiener had a wife, who had been very sick once, and he had two beautiful young children. He adored and loved them; his face and voice would always soften when he talked about them.

Family was important to him. I was sure that he could not deny me the same feeling once I had made the statement.

More silence followed, then I heard an exhale.

"Now… if you put it that way," he said, "I can understand your reasoning. Family is very important to me too, so yes, go see them. I understand that it's not easy to be that far away from your parents."

Relieved, I released my shoulders which I had drawn up to my ears in a defensive move. Then I smiled, because I had heard the surprise in his voice. It may have been the first time an employee had said "no".

It was a victory for me and my confidence. Even though it felt stupid to have had that conversation in the first place.

The international operational meeting turned out to be a joke. When I arrived at the hotel, Cocktapus introduced me to the Asian Sales Manager.

"Where is Patel?" I asked him. Patel was my Asian counterpart in operations.

"He could not make it, unfortunately," was his response.

"He couldn't make it?" I asked in disbelief. "Is he coming tomorrow?"

"No, we had to fire our financial manager, and we needed him to stay to run the company," he said.

"Did this just happen in the last few days?" I probed.

"No, this happened over a week ago," he said.

I had figured as much at that point. Meetings of any format were constantly skipped without notice, or the Germans would either call in or show up late. It was such an untypical German behavior and just plain rude. Cocktapus and I spent countless hours waiting on Wiener or other managers from Germany, while they found it extremely acceptable to forego a courtesy call or an email informing us of a delay or cancelation.

I was furious. I could have stayed in the States. The company could have saved on expenses, not to mention that my work would not get done by anyone else during my absence. It was ironic that Wiener complained about his employees wasting time and money, when in the end, he caused much of that by simply not communicating.

There was no point in having an operations meeting between me and just Germany. Asia was supposed to be my back-up. They had struggled through the same issues as me, and they had said that they were being ignored by the headquarters when it came to information or support. If it was just me complaining, then I knew that they would call me bitchy because everyone viewed women as emotional when they were criticizing something or someone; even when presenting facts.

Germany insisted on keeping the operations meeting, which meant that I would sit down with Karl to address any concerns. It came as no surprise when Karl was a no-show the day of the meeting. He had been pulled into a different crisis by Wiener.

While that meeting fell through, I took the occasion to request a sit-down with Wiener. I wanted to discuss a more sensitive subject with him, and I was sure that a face-to-face would be the best approach.

Researching the personnel budget the previous year had opened my eyes to the fact that the treatment of employees at the U.S. facility had not been quite as equal as I had hoped for.

The team was 50% female and 50% male. With the exception of my assembly worker, all the men made more money than the women. Which was not unusual since most men in the office had higher titles and were in sales, which gave them access to commissions and bonuses. However, commissions were handed out very generously, and bonuses were based on easily attainable goals set by Cocktapus and Wiener. Some goals were as simple as sending out a set number of quotes or scheduling customer visits each month. Another was to partake in training. None of these goals were what I would have considered outside of the normal scope of work.

Commissions on sales were one thing, but if the outside sales team had an opportunity to earn more as a reward, then the targets should have been based on extra effort. I felt it was unfair to the rest of the team to be denied the opportunity to earn more money if they exceeded expectations when the sales team was rewarded additionally for simply showing up to work.

With the company struggling financially, it made no sense to pay out bonuses for standard work, especially since the money could have been used to repay the debt to Germany. I was in favor of bonuses, but these seemed like hand-outs to me and were unjustly distributed.

Additionally, Cocktapus had given one of his employees preferential treatment by giving him large annual raises, which had resulted in a considerable pay increase. Not to mention that his bonus was based on training, which already was a benefit, not an accomplishment. While other employees also had the chance to attend training, there were no bonus payments attached if they did. In that scenario, training was considered an expense, not an investment.

While I could understand that some concessions may have been made during the hiring process of Cocktapus's friend, it did not seem fair to the other team members. Especially since that employee was a personal friend of Cocktapus. The entire scenario screamed favoritism.

Of course, Cocktapus had not shared any of this with me when I had taken over the human resource function. It was information that I came across while trying to prepare the personnel budget. Wiener had tasked us with considerable cost savings, and since we were a very lean organization, the only way to reduce costs in a major way was by looking at salaries and benefits.

The overall benefits offered to the team were exceptional. The company covered 90% of the health and dental benefits, including spouses and children. Wiener saw the opportunity to reduce costs by reducing the employer's portion of the premium. By law, the company didn't even have to offer health insurance since it was below the threshold of number of employees. There were a lot of companies that did not offer health insurance or made their employees cover a larger portion. I had never heard of another company that paid for dependent's premiums. I knew that the team had become accustomed to this great benefit. Taking it away would be a major problem as it would result in higher costs to the employees, who would consider this a reduction in pay.

Looking at health insurance options as a small employer can be extremely frustrating. The costs were huge, and it was understandable that it was the first place companies looked to cut when faced with financial struggles. The insurance was also age-banded, which meant that the costs for older employees and females tended to be higher than for males and younger employees.

The top earners of the company, with my exception, were males of younger ages. Considering lowering the company's covered portion of the premium would result in punishing most of the women in the office—and the older line worker—with a much higher cost. These were employees who weren't making a large salary to begin with. Even at the current 90% coverage, they paid a lot more for health insurance than those who made more money.

One of my goals was to fight for equal premiums to avoid the less-earning team members to have to take the larger hit if the company decided to decrease the premium coverage.

Commissions, bonuses, and insurance were the topics that I wanted to discuss with Wiener. And that I had been excluded from the bonus program as part of the management team. I felt this was unfair, especially since my department was producing results.

Wiener had agreed to the meeting and had scheduled it for a late afternoon, after conclusion of the sales agenda. Since I had no other plans, seeing that my meetings had been cancelled, I decided to sit in. I found it interesting to listen to what the other countries had to share and what challenges they faced. It seemed that we were all on the same page with our complaints.

It was the third and final day, and everyone was tired and annoyed. Sales representatives from several countries were frustrated by Germany's refusal to listen to or acknowledge the general consensus that

Germany only thought of themselves. Everyone felt forgotten and disconnected from the mothership, yet the expectations were extremely high from Germany on what they demanded each country to supply. It was a one-way street.

It was a fact lost on the Germans, and their insistence of everyone bowing to their demands had frustrated the outsiders to a point where they all just wanted to go back to their respective countries. Tensions ran high.

During a mid-morning break, I heard two voices in the stairway, located outside of the conference room on the second floor. It was the owners, both brothers, in a heated argument.

While I couldn't make out the words, it was clear that Wiener was very unhappy. He entered the room, ignoring everyone, and sat down at the very front where his laptop was waiting for him on one of the tables, and started typing. You could hear his anger with each keystroke.

The meeting commenced, and so did the wrath of Wiener's displeasure. It seemed that he took any opportunity to interrupt the next speaker with meaningless comments or by undermining the presentation by criticizing the content in a very dismissive way. Wiener was an expert at public-shaming; he loved to point out someone's weaknesses in front of a crowd. Experience had shown me that this wasn't unusual for some company owners. Sometimes they had to tear down others in order to feel better about themselves.

While I felt sorry for the presenter, I was also horrified. Wiener's mood did not seem encouraging for my one-on-one later that afternoon.

My concern turned out to be true.

After the meetings concluded, everyone left to return to the hotel. I stayed, waiting on Wiener, as we had agreed.

I waited for two hours before he showed up without any apology or explanation. He was rushed, flustered, and annoyed.

He shut the door and took a seat next to me.

"What do you want to talk about?" he asked.

"I wanted to address some of my concerns about equal pay and equal treatment of all employees," I started hesitantly. Internally, I wanted to postpone the meeting. Wiener was in a bad mood, which would impact the outcome of our discussion.

"Okay," he said without enthusiasm.

"I had sent you an email outlining the issues in detail," I continued.

He interrupted, "Obviously, I don't have it in front of me. Remind me?"

I knew it would be difficult to relay the points verbally. His mind was clearly somewhere else. I decided to tackle the most serious subject first, knowing that my time and Wiener's patience were limited.

"For one, I am not happy how Cocktapus seems to be favoring one of his employees," I said. "Mac was hired right after Cocktapus was put in charge, and he has given him raises over the past three years that resulted in a considerable increase in Mac's salary. Not to mention the huge bonus pay-outs every January. Bonuses that were based on technical training which are a benefit to the employee. Nobody else at the company has the opportunity to make more money year over year. We can't continue rewarding Mac when he's not really putting in the extra effort. Where and when will it stop? His position shouldn't be exempt. He's a technical support person, and he should be clocking in and out, which would show that he doesn't even spend eight hours in the office every day."

It felt good to share. I couldn't believe that Cocktapus had been getting away with favoritism for that long. And I was mad that Cocktapus, in his role as leader, had not felt that his actions had crossed any ethical boundaries.

Wiener was giving me a blank stare.

"Why are you telling me this?"

I could see he wasn't happy that I was tattling.

I calmly said, "Our mission statement talks about equitable and fair treatment, and this clearly is not fair treatment. There isn't anyone else who has access to these type raises and bonus payments in the U.S. And for what? For attending training which will broaden that person's knowledge, and which will help him advance in his career? If we are offering raises and bonuses to a non-exempt employee, then we need to extend that courtesy to all of the team members."

Wiener paused. It seemed that I had finally gotten his attention when I mentioned the company's core values.

"How can he be getting such huge raises?" he inquired. "Cocktapus submits budgets every year, should he not have mentioned that?"

"Well, the budgets are submitted with only the top layer. So you only see the summarized totals for each category. Cocktapus has never submitted a budget that details each employee's salary and benefits structure," I answered.

"You're right. I don't like how he would just do this without my permission. It must have been agreed upon when Cocktapus hired Mac," he suggested.

"Maybe," I said. "But in light that the company is not making a profit, plus that we want to be fair to all our employees, we need to ensure that, going forward, we put a stop to this. Cocktapus should have known better; he should keep the company's interest at heart, not his friend's."

Wiener nodded, but I could tell he was still annoyed. Yet, he also knew that he could not ignore me, seeing that I had just touched on one of the company's publicly stated core values, "Absolutely, we can't just give money away when we are struggling. When you finalize the budget this year, I want to see the full details, outlining salaries, benefits, commissions, and so on. We will set clear guidelines. Nobody will get a raise or a bonus unless it's approved by me."

"Thank you." I was relieved that Wiener had listened and understood. "Will you mention this to Cocktapus when you see him next time? I want to ensure that he understands that we are done with raises and bonuses unless you approve."

"I will," he confirmed.

I continued, "Speaking of giving money away. Can we talk about the bonuses for the sales team?"

"What about them?" Wiener crossed his arms and leaned back in his chair. Commissions and bonuses for the U.S. sales team were set by him with Cocktapus's help.

I tried a smile, "You agreed to pay out bonuses if the sales guys make twenty visits a month. Or when they submit twenty-five quotes over $4,000 in total."

"Yes," he said.

"Those aren't goals that warrant a bonus," I said. "That's just part of the job. They are in sales, they need to go visit customers, and they need to send out quotes... otherwise, they wouldn't be doing their jobs. They should be getting a bonus for the extraordinary efforts in cheating their way to that goal. They'll list a product with ten different quantity breaks just to get to the 4K in total. Extra goals that warrant bonuses should be hard to achieve. Bonuses are rewards for exceptional successes, not standard tasks. Like winning a national account, or a certain percentage of won customer orders based on quotes. Also, commissions are paid based on order entry. And then another commission is paid out based on invoicing. That's double dipping. Order entry and invoicing have the same basis: one and the same customer order; they just happen on two different dates. Why would you pay out twice for the same thing?"

I had known going in that this was a touchy subject. I was basically telling Wiener that he hadn't thought things through when it came to the sales bonuses and commissions, which he could interpret as an insult.

The look on Wiener's face confirmed that he was appalled that I had attacked him like that.

"Petra, who are you to question my sales strategies? I can't believe you would accuse me of making it too easy on the sales team. You know nothing about sales," he said, his face red.

Here we go again, I thought.

"*I* set those targets; *I* made those decisions. You just have to trust me that I know what I'm doing," he spat. "I know what I'm doing. There's more to these bonuses than you know. Stay out of the sales arena."

I couldn't, "You have tasked me with equality and fairness. It is my job to let you know when that is jeopardized. I'm telling you that we need to fix certain past decisions, and that we can also save money that does not need to be wasted on what is considered to be normal work."

"When it comes to sales, stay out of it." He got up from his chair. "Anything else you want to talk to me about?"

Obviously not, I thought. Wiener had just given the cue that he was done.

"Not at this time," I replied, and Wiener left the room without another word.

While he was a dick during our meeting, I am glad to say that he later agreed to change the health insurance for the following year so that each employee paid the exact same premium, no matter the age or gender. And the bonus program was put on hold, pending corporate profits.

Despite the disappointments at work, I took it all in strides. I had accepted the job in 2015 as a means to save up money for a future sabbatical. While I had joked about writing a book about the Dick Club for years—and I had started to pay off my debt as a first step—I had also hoped that my new job would be satisfying enough in the female-leadership-respect department that I would not have to relive my past and the Dicks in it.

However, the book sabbatical avalanched into action after a few months at my new job, based on several factors:

Cocktapus's inability to lead his team and to fix what was within his authority to be fixed, together with Wiener's failure to assign authority and accountability from any of his leaders, were clear signs that I could do little to improve the company's situation.

The equality and fairness discrepancies were also topics that I could not make peace with. It was systemic through all levels. It was no surprise that there were only two female top leaders within the entire global organization: me and the personnel director in Germany, who was hired around the same time as me and who quit before I did.

Contradictory to my previous encounters with an owner, I was very blunt in sharing the ugly truths with this one. While I appreciated that Wiener always listened to my criticism with open ears, he chose to remain blind to the issues at hand. He had no vision nor the guts to want to make the change from the top down.

Managers in Germany never got reprimanded nor were held accountable because they all pushed responsibilities from one person to the next. It didn't help that Wiener would involve twenty managers to get one objective accomplished, and in the end, everyone ignored him, blaming the next guy or circumstance for their failure to comply.

And so, nothing ever got done.

That's not to say that I did not put in 100% while I was at work. Yet I could only put up with indecision for so long, and Wiener's trust issues contributed to me wanting to break free from the corporate world for a while.

By the end of 2017, I had saved enough money to walk away from the job and to finance my sabbatical for a year. The plan was to give my notice in January with the hope to stay on until the end of August in order to save additional funds. An eight-month resignation notice was more than adequate, but knowing how the company delayed every decision, I knew that it was needed.

I had created a transition plan, offering multiple approaches to choose from to lessen the impact to the operation with my resignation.

In the middle of January, I called Wiener.

"What can I do for you?" he asked.

"I'm sorry to have to tell you this, but I'm resigning from my job," I said.

"What?" he asked.

"I'm giving you my notice, but I was planning on staying on until August so that we can find a suitable replacement," I responded.

"It… it's not a good time," he said. "I have to head into a meeting now. Can I call you later?"

I thought it was funny how all the sudden he had to be on time.

I replied, "Of course. I will send you some documents that outline a couple of scenarios for replacing me. And my official written resignation. We can talk about it when you're ready."

"Okay," he said and hung up.

He called me back a few hours later.

"Thank you for sending the documents," he said. "The transition plan looks to be very comprehensive. You have obviously given this a lot of thought. I will review everything in more detail tonight. I'm really sorry to hear that you want to leave us; can you give me a reason?"

I said, "The commute is killing me."

It wasn't a lie. Even though I started at seven in the morning, it took me fifty minutes to get there. Same in the afternoon. The interstate could have cut that drive down by twenty minutes if it wasn't packed with other frustrated commuters trying to find their way safely through the construction zone that went on for miles.

Since I hated stop-and-go traffic, I made the choice to drive into the city using only country roads. It offered a much nicer scenery, alongside some challenging curves. Which I would have enjoyed more if it wouldn't have been for school buses or distracted drivers in SUVs or minivans dicking around on their cell phones.

I continued, "I also just want to take a break, go on a sabbatical, spend time with my husband and friends."

"Those are tough reasons to beat," Wiener said. "But I will ask either way if there is anything that I can do to make you stay?"

"No," I responded, "As you said, I have given this a lot of thought, and it's something I have to do."

"I understand," he sighed. "Again, I'm sorry you want to leave us. But I want to say that I appreciate you giving such a long resignation term. August gives us some breathing room to make the right decision about what to do next."

I said, "I figured it may take months to find a replacement, depending on which route you want to go. Personally, I think it would make more sense to give Ingrid the operational responsibilities. Now that we have established procedures, it's all about managing them not creating them from scratch. Of course, she would need to get more money, and she may need support eventually on some of the standard accounting tasks, such as entering bills."

Ingrid was the Accounting Manager, who worked for me.

"It would be the easiest but also the cheapest solution," I continued, knowing how much Wiener appreciated a cost savings alternative. "And for production, we can hire a production scheduler to take care of the production processes and shipping."

"I will let you know which way I want to proceed," Wiener said. "For now, I want to keep this a secret. Please do not tell anyone that you are leaving. We have plenty of time."

"I won't," I agreed. "But what about Karl?"

"No, I don't want to tell him yet," he said.

I couldn't understand why, "Karl is my boss. He's the Global Production Manager. This resignation impacts his department directly."

"Petra, we are not sharing this with anyone yet. Not even Karl," he insisted. "He's got enough problems on his hands, and we have time to spring this on him when things calm down a bit. I want to be the one to tell him, so please do not say anything to him."

"Okay," I said resigned.

It wasn't an unusual request by Wiener. Many people had quit in the three years that I worked there. Sometimes I would find out someone had left by trying to call them, and then whoever picked up that person's phone would tell me that the person had been gone for weeks.

Wiener never wanted others to find out when employees quit, especially managers with higher profiles, who would cause some water cooler talk within the company if found out. He deliberately chose not to acknowledge resignations in public, and he forced everyone else into silence by asking managers not to share the news with their team members or discuss it.

I'm sure he took it very personal when people quit. Any company owner should feel some type of discomfort when employees leave. After all, they made a conscious decision to choose another company over theirs.

Wiener was always worried about the company's image to the outside world. He figured he could control that image by trying to isolate the employees from each other and any news concerning them. There were no intercompany communications about new hires or departures, or any other announcements when it came to the employees.

With a continually revolving front door, the company had a hard time finding new workers, but they blamed the extreme low unemployment rate in the area instead.

By the end of March, Wiener still hadn't told anyone about my resignation. I was starting to panic. Sure, five months until August seemed like a long time, but we had already wasted valuable time for two months doing nothing.

It was also killing me inside not to be able to tell anyone. I did not understand what Wiener's hold-up was. There was simply no reason not to share the news with the rest of the team. Every day that had gone by, and would continue to go by, was a day lost that I could have used in training someone else.

Emotionally it was tough as well. It felt like Christmas Eve, when my sister and I would be sent up to our room in the afternoon so that my parents could put up the tree and wrap our presents. The suspense and anticipation were hard to contain. I wanted to be free of keeping a secret that did not need to be kept and which was doing more harm than good that way.

Occasionally, Wiener would call, or we would email, and I would take every opportunity to ask him if he had told Karl. He would always respond, "I will do it next time I see him."

Then, when I spoke with Karl a few days later, I would ask him, "How was your meeting with Wiener?"

And he would say, "Same old, same old. More Excel lists to create and PowerPoints to redo."

Going into early April, I decided that I had had enough of the cat-and-mouse game. It was unfair to exclude Karl; he had every right to know that I was leaving. I was his direct report, and it was disrespectful, to say the least, to keep him in the dark any longer.

During our next conversation, I caved in.

"Karl," I started, "I'm so sorry, but I have to let you know that I gave my notice a while ago."

"You did what?" he asked in disbelief.

"I handed in my resignation in January to Wiener," I said.

"JANUARY? Why didn't you tell me then?"

"Wiener wanted to be the one to tell you," I said. "He told me not to share the news with anyone. And he said that he would tell you, and then he didn't and said he would do it the next time. I just couldn't wait any longer. I've wanted to tell you back in January. I'm very sorry that we haven't told you sooner."

Karl's silence only confirmed that he was very unhappy with the news. He managed to ask for some details before trying to end the call.

"Maybe don't tell him that I told you?" I interjected before he hung up the phone.

Thirty minutes later, Wiener called me.

"You told Karl?" were his first fuming words.

"We were on a call, and I simply asked him if he had talked to you," I answered. "And then he questioned me why I kept asking him about your meetings, and then he asked me if I had quit. I wasn't going to lie to him." It wasn't exactly the truth. But it was a good enough explanation for Wiener.

"I had told you that I wanted to be the one to tell him," he said angrily. "You went behind my back; I don't appreciate it. That was not okay for you to do."

"It just came out," I said, trying to keep my voice strong.

I hated myself for not screaming back at him that it had been a disgrace not to have told Karl for months. But his accusatory tone had brought me right back to the St. Nick event, and with it, my need to feel ashamed about having gone against his orders to be a good girl; as I had promised.

I rummaged around the heap of guilt and tried to find the confident woman in me.

"He needed to know," I finally said, my voice gaining strength.

"It wasn't your place to tell him," he screamed. "He stormed into my office and confronted me. I was not prepared. You made me look like a fool. I do not appreciate what you have just done."

"I'm sorry you feel that way," I said defiantly. I was not going to apologize for the act, but I knew that if he heard the words "I'm sorry" that he may take it as one.

"I have to go now, but again, it wasn't your place. I had explicitly told you not to tell him. I'm not happy about this whole thing," he said.

"Again, I'm sorry you feel that way," I repeated.

He hung up.

A week later, I was given the green light to tell the rest of the team and to start delegating my responsibilities as well as hiring a production planner for the daily production tasks. By the end of June, I felt confident that the chosen transition plan would work.

I was happy that Wiener had worked with me to keep things amicable between us to where we both could walk away from one another in peace.

But… the last two months felt like an eternity. I had disconnected emotionally from the job. I couldn't stand to be in an environment any longer where constant disappointment had a daily presence.

I don't think I'll ever give an eight-month notice again.

On my last day, I left at lunch time.
It was a beautiful sunny August day.

A perfect day to start my journey as an author.

♀

THE DADDY COMPLEX

I can't deny that I have a Daddy Complex.

Neither can my sister. We both married men who resembled my dad: dark hair and a moustache. I did it twice.

It's something that I will most likely never get rid of, and if I'm being honest, it doesn't even bother me that much anymore. Okay, maybe a little more than that.

Important is that I'm aware of it, and I have dealt with the fact that I cannot continue to seek my father's approval through other men.

In my past, and in general, it was futile to think that I could measure up to somebody else's expectations. Or continued trying for decades. I had to own *me* and accept my achievements as personal rewards and recognition.

I firmly believe that my dad is proud of me and my sister. We have had different paths in our lives, and while I have achieved some success climbing the corporate ladder, she has provided for our lineage to continue. Not in name, but in the knowledge that the Weiser bloodline will not completely disappear based on her four sons.

When I became a citizen in 1997, it was important to me to change my name back to the name that I was given at birth: Weiser. I did not want to be reminded of a bad marriage. When I got remarried in 1999, I decided to remain a Weiser. There were four other women who had Kindred's surname: his mom, his ex, his brother's ex, and a cousin. I didn't want to be another one of many. I was unique with my name, and I wanted to keep it to honor my family in Germany. I was the last generation left with the Weiser name. Even though I knew that it would eventually disappear from our family's tree. I did not have children nor wanted any. But as odd as it may sound, I want the name to survive for as long as it can. If I outlive my parents, our Weiser name will die with me.

Kindred also liked his surname, and he declined my offer to become Kindred Weiser. But I figured I would offer, equal rights to all.

Think about it: When it comes down to the meaning of life, that is it in a nutshell. We want to live on, and the only way to achieve this is through others who carry our genes and our names.

And, if not through children, hopefully through the influence we may have on others, who will remember us by our actions and our compassion; or lack thereof. I want to believe that we can touch one person's life and impact changes in behavior and thought that will carry on in their families.

It is true that for me, roots have become more important the older I get. While in Germany in February 2018, my dad—knowing of my interest in our history while writing this book—handed me two "ancestry passports" from his parents; the ones who were expulsed from their home when he was an infant after WWII.

The passports depict an eagle, its talons gripping the Swastika. The first few pages describe the importance of the "German bloodline" and remind the passport holder of the importance of truthful completion. Ancestry down to at least the 1800s was desired.

It also states that Jews could never have true German ethnicity and therefore could never be German citizens.

To the best of my knowledge, this ancestry passport was not mandatory, but strongly encouraged. Even more so in 1933, when the government required that a person had to prove their ancestral lineage, and this was pretty much the only way to do so.

As we looked through my grandfather's parental history, we noticed that the Weiser name had been passed down from a woman, which was highly unusual for the time.

In August 1884, Wilhelmina Weiser gave birth to my grandfather's (illegitimate) father. While the father's name was listed as Josef Weihoenig, there is no marriage date, and then, in my great-grandfather's section, there is no name listed where it says, "Father of". Notable is that the child had his father's first name "Josef", which was carried down to my grandfather, Josef Weiser, and which also is my dad's middle name.

While I hate the idea of a government setting an ethnicity standard and then demanding proof of such "clean" genealogy, I am glad to have an overview of my roots on my paternal side down to the late 1700s.

It makes me wonder though what Wilhelmina endured as a single mother in 1884, and what had happened that she wasn't married. There's a story there.

I would like to think that Wilhelmina and Josef loved each other, given the fact that her child bore the father's first name, and it was important enough to carry it down into two more generations.

My grandmother's passport also showed that she had some Czech ancestry, which was not uncommon with that part of Germany having belonged to the Austrian Empire, then dominated by Germans. After WWI, when Austria-Hungary was dismembered, the Germans in those regions found themselves living in the country of Czechoslovakia. Eventually, these regions were annexed to Germany and then dissolved after WWII with the expulsion of the remaining Germans.

Unfortunately, I don't have that history on my mother's side, and little is known of "her" people preceding my maternal grandparents.

My dad, who I have described as a tyrant in the very first chapter, is still a very important person in my life. Our relationship has evolved greatly over the years, and of course, with me aging. I can see that he just wanted the best for me; he wanted to protect me. He tried to prepare me for life; as he had known that life can be unfair and hurtful.

He once said that he was not a wanted child and that his mother tried to have a miscarriage. Granted, it must have been so difficult for his parents to realize what uncertain future may lie ahead for a newborn in such horrid times, but I cannot fathom why my grandmother would not have kept that a secret.

And so, my father did not grow up with a lot of maternal love, while his older sister was doted on. And maybe that alone explains some of his behavior.

Because he was so tough and said "no" to almost every request, I had to come up with ways to circumvent the "nos". Just like my mom, as the pit-bull, had found ways to make things happen, so did I.

Because of his conviction, I know I can deal with just about anything if my purpose is just. I know that I will always be okay, no matter what. There's a purpose. And there are many ways to solve a problem. And sometimes there is only one.

I do not regret anything in my life.

I know I am where I'm supposed to be.

I hope that my life will continue with the liberties that I have come to love and respect. I was fortunate in all my circumstances out of my control, and I'm thankful for that.

While my strict and *follow-the-leader* upbringing has shaped my entire life with men, I do recognize that my daddy complex has been my biggest handicap in my professional career; chosen, accepted, and relived by me.

Any time a man questioned my values, decisions, words, reasoning, etc., I had a hard time finding me as a female individual who would stand up for herself and her fellow women. It was just so much easier (and expected) to fall back into the *my house, my rules* mentality instilled by my dad.

Knowing my pattern though has helped me to make a change in the way that I react to men who are trying to undervalue me as a human being and equal.

There are lines I will never cross. They all have to do with honesty, decency, integrity, fairness, morals, and ethics. I know that the lines are not gender specific anyways. However, a lot of those lines are shrugged off without much thought by men, merely because that's the way it has always been, and they don't want to be viewed as soft or weak. In their defense, they have been taught by society to be tough, and toughness is often confused with strength. If men were more aware, they could see themselves more clearly. They're stuck in their bubble, and it's easier for them to stay in it because it benefits them.

And in the corporate world, it's all about profits. Profits tend to outweigh the human cost. Greed is one of the biggest Dicks.

It saddens me to consider what societies looked like thousands of years ago. There was a world where life was centered around the mothers and where men had equal rights, despite their lesser importance. There were goddesses, women owned the land and named "their" children.

Matricentry has a huge part in human history, yet most of the world has no clue it existed.

Today, our statues are mostly men, and the history of women has been erased or has become forgotten.

There's power in knowledge. And knowledge is awareness.

I know who I am, thanks to every Rick and Dick I have ever met. I recognize that a Dick can be a Rick, and vice versa. The Dicks in my book are not evil people, and I did not try to depict them as such. I was factual, with some creative freedom, as I surely cannot remember every event and dialogue in detail. I want to be clear that I do not hate the Dicks. I saw each Dick as an opportunity to learn how to adapt and to deal with my emotions when encountering them.

Speaking of emotions, I will not feel guilty about how others feel based on my actions or words in this book, as I am not responsible for their actions and words as they happened in my life.

I have plenty of good memories with most Dicks. I don't believe there was premeditated malice in any of their actions, thoughts, decisions.

The purpose of this book is simply that: AWARENESS of the world around us, our circumstances, who we are dealing with, and how we react and why.

I recognize that I can be a Dick. I don't deny it. Mostly, it's in reaction to another Dick's action.

And I'm sure it's going to happen again as long as there are Dicks in the world.

I will continue to preach awareness to all.

We are the same, but different.
We are different, but the same.

♀ ♀ ♀

THE ACKNOWLEDGMENTS

I would like to thank the real-life members portrayed in this book. I recognize that their memories of the events described in this book may be different than my own. They are each fine, decent, and hard-working people. The book was not intended to hurt anyone. I regret any unintentional harm resulting from the publishing and marketing of Dickotomy: A Dickless Memoir.

I t takes a village.
I love mine.

I struggled, trying to decide who to thank first.

As weird as it may sound, it should probably be the Dicks in my life. For planting the seed, mostly by way of exclusion. For making this book possible.

And while initially I had not thought of including the Ricks, I'm glad I did. The Ricks gave the book the needed balance. I am so thankful for all my Ricks. While it may seem that there are more Dicks in my book than Ricks, the quality of the Ricks totally outweighs the quantity of the Dicks.

Kindred, "Gary", is my soulmate, no doubt. I chose Kindred for him because he is a kind and gentle soul. He has the gift of likability. I am thankful that he tries to tear down the walls that I constantly put up to protect myself; not letting people in. It's tough for me to let my guard down, even with my husband, who has supported me in anything I seek to do. Thanks to him, I can be me, and there's nothing more important in a relationship than that.

Ricardo, "Marte", has been there for me for the longest time. I am thankful to have a friend who lives less than five miles away, making him close in distance to my house and heart. I was in awe of AJ, "MJ or Mary Jo", the minute that I met her. She's so humble, kind, compassionate. Just like Gary. How great to hang out together to enjoy food, beer, or wine, and have great conversations about anything.

With Marte, I could steal horses. Okay, probably need to explain that one. In Germany, when "you can steal horses with someone", it means that you can rely on that person to do something out of the ordinary, mostly something mischievously. Marte always volunteers to partake in anything silly or outrageous. I love how he loves life.

Speaking of friends I could steal horses with, includes the Gang of 8:

The Boys Ricco and Richy, "Sherman and Drew", had a very deep emotional impact on me. I will never be able to put into words what they meant to the world and me - and do them justice. Maybe the best word for them is love; okay, two words: unconditional love.

When I try to think about them, it's not words or actual thoughts that pop up. It's simply one very specific feeling. And it touches me in my core, beyond any wall I could ever build. It encompasses the entire world filled with love and gives me a glance of something familiar, yet unknown.

It's the best I can do to describe the feeling.

I still mourn the loss of Sherman, and my world will never be fully alright without him in it physically. But he resides in my heart - as do all my friends.

I need to thank Drew for giving me the ever so slightest push toward writing. As a child, I wrote short stories, and as an adult, I had forgotten how much I missed it. Then one day, he handed me a book. The book inspired me to write my first short story in thirty years. (The book was *The Eternal Smile* by Pär Lagerkvist). Drew always knows what to do for others.

Besides the Boys and Kindred, I owe my deepest gratitude to the remaining four members of the "Gang of 8". Even though they only had a small appearance in this book, it does not undermine their importance. Without them, there might have never been a completed Dickless memoir.

I owe Phryne, "Nanci", my biggest thanks. As a fellow author, she has donated a huge chunk of her time reading and editing this book. Her input has been invaluable. She's a strong, independent, funny, intelligent woman and mother, who had a professional career, and who remains humble about her accomplishments despite her sense of ownership. Nanci is my champion, supporter, critic, director, and mentor all rolled up into one awesome friend.

Keira, "Coni", is no doubt, my best friend forever. When I first met her, I wasn't sure we would like each other (my perspective). She's very competitive–and can back it up with brain power and physical fitness–and I think I was intimidated by her presence. I am in awe of her resourcefulness, kindness, and selflessness. I love how we refer to each other as "Euro Trash", even though now that I think about it, it does not sound very nice. But it just means that we can lovingly pick on each other without feeling insulted. We can always be honest. Coni immigrated from Switzerland (please don't call it Sweden), and let's face it: Swiss can be a bit arrogant at times because they think they are so smart (which they are). Coni is a doer, speaks multiple languages, she's beautiful, perfect and precise, smart, and independent. Not arrogant at all, maybe even a bit too much on the humble side. We are each other's sounding boards when the Dicks in our lives try to ruin our accomplishments by tearing us down. She is always there for me.

Fiona, "Maggie", gave me my first short story title. I'm thankful for having her in my life. I cannot explain why we jibe; we just do. She's spunky, intelligent, deeply compassionate, and simply a whirlwind. She always encourages me, and she does not believe that there are boundaries, other than the ones we set ourselves.

Axle, "Mark", is Coni's husband. I'm thankful that he can balance the Gang of 8 behind the scenes. That's not an easy job. The Gang can be out of control and very eccentric. Yet somehow, Mark can simply appear, and with his calm Albemarle voice, he irons out the wrinkles in space and time that were about to form. I'm not sure the rest of the group has realized his hidden talent as of yet. Mark, your secret is out. Without you, the Gang wouldn't be the same.

I owe a huge thanks to the Gang for reading my book as it developed over the months and for their feedback and encouragement.

Richard, "Olaf", was my biggest mentor in business. He's the one that set my expectation of all my future bosses very high, and not a single boss after him has ever lived up to that. One could argue that he wasn't the business owner when I worked for him and therefore, he could be more relaxed in his management style. But, I also know him as an entrepreneur, and his values have not changed because of that. He too, is compassionate and kind. And super smart; he will not blindly accept anyone's statement. He keeps his finger on the pulse of society, and he educates himself on what's happening in the world versus only relying on the media or social media for facts. He is a forever friend and a positive influence in the world.

Rikert, "Chris", is a powerhouse. Just thinking about him makes my energy levels spike. He's full of life and passion. He breathes his purpose with each inhale and creates action with each exhale. What must it be like to wake up every day knowing that you *can* change the world? He also is a forever friend and a positive influence in the world.

Another group I owe huge thanks to is my "White Paper Project" Writers' Group. Katherine LE White, foremost, had the biggest impact with her literary insights and grammatical corrections. From the day we met, she has inspired me through her passion for this art, through her excellent writing, and with her compassionate nature. She is the best critic and supporter in one.

Dale "Doc" Borland, Carrie Humphrey, Alana Demaske, and Tom Poole complete the core of my writers' group. I don't just go there for critique; I also go because of friendship that is honest. Writers bear their souls, and it's never easy sharing our most inner thoughts and fears face-to-face with nowhere to hide. My fellow writers are empathetic, sympathetic, authentic, and inspiring. I love them all. We will remain forever friends.

I owe a huge thanks to all my beta readers. Thank you for catching the flaws and for the feedback. Handing my book over to you was scary and exciting. I can't wait to do it again!

I want to thank my parents and my sister.

It must have been a shock to hear that I was going to write a book about all the men in my life who have influenced me. Germans are very private people and not knowing what I was going to say about each man and how it may reflect on them, could not have been easy.

I love my dad, my mom, and my sister to pieces. I see myself in them and I see them in me. And while we may not have communicated well during my childhood, I feel that now I can talk to them about anything. If they ask me to.

We will never be the family that volunteers feelings. We will keep to ourselves our struggles and fears. We will keep up our strength for others and ourselves, and we will not burden others with our problems.

I am thankful that I can sit around my parent's kitchen table with them and be silly for hours. I'm also thankful that my mom hasn't served me any carrot salad during any of my visits.

I love the fact that my parents say "I love you" every time we say goodbye on skype.

I love that my dad gets all mushy when it's time for me to return to the States. I love and appreciate even more so today that my dad's good-bye letter to me—the one with the *Schweinehund* reference—was full of emotions and honesty. I wish I could have understood that sooner.

I love that Mom is a force to be reckoned with. Her life has not been an easy one, taking care of five siblings when she was just a child herself. She has carried a deep sense of responsibility on her shoulders that would crush a normal person.

I looked up to my sister throughout my entire childhood and adolescence. She was very pretty, had a great sense for fashion and make-up, and she was determined. She was also quiet, but when she spoke, her words had meaning. They still do.

Raising four boys was—and is—not for wussies. I don't think I could have done it. I have learned that life should center around the mother. I wish it were so.

I'm thankful that she provided my parents with grandchildren and that they all live close to one another. I love her for that and more.

Thank you to all the unmentioned Ricks. There are far more out there than I have depicted in this book. They all have a special place in my heart, and none will be forgotten, and all will be remembered in my actions.

Thank you to all the unmentioned Dicks. There are far more out there than I have depicted in this book. None will be forgotten, and all will be remembered in my actions.

Thank you to my readers. As any author will tell you, we are worried that you will not like what we write. We try to pretend it does not matter, but it surely does. Our goal is to make you happy, sad, mad, excited, contemplative, empathetic, curious, smart, aware, and so much more.

Your emotional response is our most prized reward.

We try to accept that criticism will make us better, wiser, or hopefully at the least, thicker-skinned. We thrive on praise and encouragement.

And yes, we do write for ourselves; it's our therapy, our passion, our drive, our duty; we cannot stop, we have thoughts to share with the rest of the world.

Words matter; WE matter. As authors and as readers.

One cannot be without the other.
Thank you for being a reader.

♀ ♀ ♀

PETRA'S DICKTIONARY

DICKLESS [**dik**-lis]
Adjective informal
1. without a penis.
2. reference to being born female.

DICKOTOMY [dik-**kot**-uh-mee]
Noun slang
1. a division or contrast in a man that determines if he is either a Rick or a Dick at any given time.

DICKS [**dik**s]
Noun slang
1. a penis
2. a mean, stupid, or annoying man
   In this book, commonly referred to as
   A. Schweinehund
   B. Pee-Wee
   C. Dickie
   D. Wanker
   E. Cazzo
   F. Dickson
   G. Tadger
   H. Pecker
   I. Dickwad
   J. Prick
   K. Dicklet
   L. Nimrod
   M. WingWang
   N. Cocktapus
   O. Wiener

DICKTATORSHIP [dik-**tey**-ter-ship]
Noun slang
1. the office or tenure of a dictator.
2. a state or government under dictatorial rule.
3. absolute or despotic control or power.

ABOUT THE AUTHOR

P etra Weiser was born and raised near Frankfurt am Main, Germany. At the age of 18, she moved to the States where she worked in corporate America for over twenty-five years. In 2018, fed-up with what she called "The Dick Club", she quit her job to write her first book "Dickotomy, A Dickless Memoir" about her life with men.

Petra is very passionate about women's rights, and she is dedicated to raise awareness about women's inequalities throughout both genders.

For more information, visit: www.petraweiser.com

FOOTNOTES

1 *Schweinehund* literally translated means "pig dog". It refers to your inner asshole-self.
2 Saint Nicholas Day is observed on December 6 in Germany. He's the bringer of gifts - as long as you have been nice.
3 *Don't Ask, Don't Tell* was an official U.S. policy regarding homosexuals in the military (1993–2011).
4 A small building with an open area for selling merchandise.
5 Schellekloppe literally translates to "doorbell knocking". It is a prank that children played in my hometown. Since most houses had fenced-in yards, the doorbell was also located in a fence post. A chosen child would have to ring the doorbell multiple times and then run away immediately without being seen. The purpose was not to get caught by the adult, who would hopefully open a window or come to the door to see what the multiple rings were about. Multiple rings represented urgency. It was impolite to ring the doorbell more than twice to announce visitation.
6 The Soviet Union, Britain, and the U.S. met in Potsdam, Germany, in the fall of 1945 to negotiate terms for the end of World War II.
7 NATO = North Atlantic Treaty Organization
8 Since 1955, Germany has had quite a presence of guest workers.
9 Cola-beer is beer mixed with cola.
10 The legal drinking age in Germany is sixteen for wine and beer and eighteen for liquor.
11 A pager was a device that could receive text or voice messages wirelessly (also known as a beeper).
12 PX = Post Exchange; it is the general store on a military base.
13 Morgenschoppen is when you start drinking in the morning.
14 A green card allows a foreign national to live and work in the U.S.
15 MP = Military Police
16 *Douglas* is the name of a famous fragrance store in Germany.
17 Baying = howling
18 Water moccasins = cottonmouths, = aquatic snakes that are active at night.
19 A *jon boat* is a flat-bottomed small boat, perfect for gliding through shallow waters.
20 Codependent No More, by Melody Beattie, published by Hazelden Publishing & Educational Services (first published 1986)
21 *Cazzo* = dick in Italian
22 Dum Dums are small round lollipops.
23 Resp. Profit & Loss, Merger & Acquisition, and sales revenue.
24 Tadger = British slang word for dick.
25 Twiggy was a British icon and teenage model in London in the sixties.
26 Victoria Secret is a fancy lingerie store.
27 *VHS* is a standard for consumer-level analog video recording on tape cassettes.
28 WYSIWYG = "what you see is what you get"
29 Switzerland and Austria have their own spoken dialects, but in writing, German is used.
30 Big Apple = New York City
31 OEM = Original Equipment Manufacturer

[32] ISO = International Standards Organization
[33] PPAP = Production Part Approval Process. It's a way to approve products into OEMs, validating specs and requirements.
[34] IT = Information Technology

www.ingramcontent.com/pod-product-compliance
Lightning Source LLC
Chambersburg PA
CBHW060311030426
42336CB00011B/998